Magda,
In the spirit of
Friendship!
Lydia

Dedicated

to

Life and Human Dignity, Freedom and Truth

Table of Contents

In the Dim of Light this Diary Entry I Make

March 10, 2008

I wake in the darkness of night, startled, uneasy. A dream puts to motion a foreboding feeling. Deep loss waits in the entry, soon to visit my life. Restless night, why do you whisper graveness looming on the horizon?

Yet, you cast light from skyscrapers outside my bedroom windows, beckoning I put pen to paper. To your call, I awaken.

What sense summons to make sense of this financial world I live in, the seeming senselessness of its direction? Who spun the web that will drape our heartland with such debt?

Solemn night, I fear for what lies before us. With hope I wait for the sunrise, from deep slumber us to wake.

Once upon a time, there was a Cinderella of Wall Street with a story to tell. As she swept her way through the Street, she did her best to keep things tidy. It is for the love of her trade and our future this story is told.

The Foreboding Dream

The clock struck twelve with force and might.
Its clang chased magic out the door.
Echoing bongs a menacing prelude made.
I fled the Ball and through misty meadow ran.
A breathless heart and rhythmic rustling formed,
as my splendid gown,
of yellow satin,
swept the low wrung grass.

The full moon swelled through ashen clouds,
unveiling bleakness of a damp cold night.
Its light a carpet laid to the entry,
of a smoldering place.
My once enchanted forest,
took this new form as it beckoned to its gate.
A gate now flanked by twisted trees,
their gangly roots a jagged entrance made.

I wandered in to see,
what foul the hand of darkness came to breed.
What souls it bought its bidding to unleash,
upon a trusting land.
The swarthy trees with crooked arms,
so many came to claim,
with bend and twist as if to say,
"There's time to join us yet."

Yet time's a flowing, as time so does,
for earthly souls,
the day bids near.
For those whose foul made human sorrow grow,
no coffin draped with power, lined with dollar bills,
will shroud the debt,
they have entwined,
whilst they danced the Dance of Death.

In the distance, hunched and ashen soulmates march,
in clanging rusted chains upon the bone.
They come to claim undead friends.
With breath of vapor cold,
gnarly sounds they make,
to drown an anguished cry,
as they reach for souls to enfold,
into River Foul that vanishes into eternity.

Oh dissonant forest symphony, you came to drown,
singing creatures true and small.
An odious breed came to feed,
toxic vapor to create,
sunlight now to dim for years to come.
Clay-like soil,
my gait slowed down.
The path I walked nonetheless.

My eyes
lanced through forest murk.
I sauntered forth with hopes for light,
yet darkness glazed my path.
Once lavish beast,
a massive grizzly sight became.
Upon the forest floor, a sea of carcass drifts.
Oh ebon night, not even you a cloak provide.

Wolves were out in packs,
loping for plumpest of gore.
Forest now bereft of life,
how will they find their meat.
They secured their wanting needs,
with cunning enterprise,
unconstrained, complicit in their hunt,
rapacious appetites to satisfy.

Oh thumping heart, you raise my gait,
this barren land to leave.
Restless night, I walk with such quick stride,
And then I stop,
a wheezing sound to hear.
Horrific sight,
as I come near, death rattle sound now past.
Snaps and snarls reveal the ravage taking place.

Wolves claimed their latest victim,
as moonlight unmasked bloodied fangs.
Lush ruffs of hair mere beauty capes,
disguised the nature of their beast.
With stony paws atop carcass of beguilement,
howls unleashed unto the moon.
Echoes clung to hanging fog of the evening,
branding fear within a human soul.

Oh gluttonous feast,
you a sea of vapor made.
You leave behind,
trillion entrails on a forest floor.
The odious pack disengaged,
to scamper,
so pretend forest floor,
not a graveyard be.

I woke to a magnificent Chicago morning March 2008. The orange sun opened its arms slowly, then burst above Lake Michigan, unfolding like the curtsy that I, as a little girl, practiced years ago. Brilliant light pierced through windows, embracing two grand pianos statuesque against the marble floor of my apartment. With rapture and reverence I welcomed the new day. A crystal clear azure sky framed glistening skyscrapers of a sprawling midwestern metropolis.

I scurried to get ready for work. Not even my lightening speed manner slowed wistful thoughts. They took me to the mood on Wall Street, one of funereal tone. Melancholy wasn't just mine by day; it claimed my nights as an uninvited guest. What guest was this, created by financial winds adrift in ways I've never seen.

Not a single heart will escape the shiver, a shiver unlike other boom-and-busts I lived through in over two decades on Wall Street. What formed this shiver born of mortals straying, then amplifying their creation, a debt funnel for our nation to make; one swirling with toxic debris, sweeping dollar bills to the top, leaving wreckage in its path. Its deafening thunder formed of greed, muffed a human cry.

Lost in fantasy is what so many came to be. Mere mortals enthroned our financial institutions, swathed in millions, some in billions and lifestyles surreal. To the altar of greed they marched, one by one with wreaths of decadent spoils, to worship *Plutus*, the god of wealth. The anointed made profit and investment miracles happen, even if just for awhile.

Commonsensical growth and rewards, the kind that gives thought to restraint and proper engagement, seemed far too outdated for a "what's-in-it-for-me" bunch. Big bank business models flowed like lava, burning anything in their track, scorching lives in the process, only to scorch themselves. Turbo charge and accelerate is what this decade of amplification chanted; the mantra — Grow big, Grow fast, Make the deal, Make more, Make a mess, Get out, Don't look back, On to the next!

Speculative frenzy flourished, fed by trillions of cheap credit and technology-enabled financial engineering. With a wave of the securitization wand, mortals turned pumpkins into coaches, rats into coachmen, as debt of any kind came to be packaged under its spell. Bank capital and investment portfolios vaporized around the world.

Financial warriors, awash in monies, armed with debt and cryptic proprietary trading programs, scavenged the markets. A masquerade of wannabe investment geniuses, vultures underneath; even some fraudsters!

This crisis, with mind of its own, speaks, with a hiss that will not stop until infection festers no longer for symptoms to make. Billions are not miracles. They make a dent. There are two sides to a trade as we are one world.

A billion made or lost in one place, may just come out of another. What's to say of trillions borrowed or printed to stem what's lost? What kind of debt lock-down for our children are we creating to now fix this man-made creation born of debt?

What fantastical investment creations have men

wrought that came to be combined with reckless debt usage of fools that made others look like geniuses, if only for awhile?

The world suffers no fools for too long. Geniuses it discovers. Sooner or later, too many a fool a tremor makes.

Within the tremors of turmoil, don't we all long for the same, safety?

A sentimental moment took me by surprise that morning. Back home, as a child, is where I wanted to be, even though I had grown-up children. The sentiment sparked a yearning for a simpler world and way of living, for back-to-basics to be returned back to this world of ours. Thoughts tickled my mind. What if my mom or dad managed any one of our institutions?

Nothing got past them.

Where did my beautiful childhood world go?

I carried it with me all these years, keeping it lit. My candle flickered within temples of greed, populated with "good old boys," many of whom got lucky along the way.

They introduced a new way of being within our economic system, living in cloistered worlds, surrounded by inner sanctums, seldom a walk amongst us to take. I call it, "capitalism gone awry," one that echoes delusional self-interest. Others call it "crony capitalism." Over the years, habits formed within them. It came to be the new "normal," as they collected tens and hundreds of millions. Rewards born of friends or was it compensation?

Alas, trillions in bailouts and backstops are sure to be thrust on to our lap. We'll soak up entrails left behind; no remorse, no atonement, no giveback, yet many a mop will come our way.

I'd have gotten a spanking or two for a *raucous mess* like that!

Is it all about the money or the vote, for the mighty and powerful within a complicit world, not easily understood by us simple folk, the trusting type?

Throughout the ages, things don't seem to change. They just play out through a different forum. Civilizations lose their edge; even disintegrate into chaos. Systems fail, even self-destruct, as raw human nature takes its hold, where primordial instincts overpower a semblance of common sense.

Mortals, not harnessed, drift. The more from pure intention they stray, the more they liken to rapacious wolves consumed with sight of their meat. What if many stray from pure intention towards fatal flaw, from calm to torment, perverting that which they've been entrusted to protect, even underneath the Masonic all-seeing eye of our everyday dollar bill?

Infection then festers, with slow creep, creeping slowly, as it entwines and makes its presence ever present, as the symptoms of scandal blister.

We all know that children unbridled take on a habit or two, that may die hard as they grow. Could it just possibly be that some never learned playground rules or made their own along the way?

Maybe learned and unlearned with temptation all too near, as harness of any kind sat on dusted shelf.

Do you remember the schoolyard?

"I got the ball, it's mine!"

"Give it to me, I want it!"

"Not now, later!"

"Monkey see, monkey do!"

School bullies bully until conditions change. They produce distress as they cause stress, but they push until something pushes them back. Then, they fold or scamper, pointing the finger at someone else.

Where does it all start?

Chapter One

Childhood, Discovery of the World

Snowflakes

January 10, 2009

I take a long walk in the heart of a snowfall. Beautiful snowflakes, you move in slow motion, falling gently before my eyes, chanting, "see us?"

I surrender to childhood excitement, the first snow of the season. I see windows of my childhood home, framed by snowflakes, each with a unique crystalline formation.

A little girl squishes her nose against the frosted window...looks to find two snowflakes, the same, but can't. Snowflakes come and go, so quickly...each one, each time, is different. A magical blanket of snow snowflakes make.

I discovered beauty in my childhood, the kind that takes us to serenity and carries us through life...one that brings tears of joy to the eyes, one that makes us cry if we let it go...one that lives through music, love and art.

What is beauty?

It's Samuel Barber's "Andante" from his "Concerto for Violin and Orchestra."

It's seeing life with a heart...it's sensitivity, gentleness and sincerity...it's influencing a life through thoughtfulness, and loving, where one finds sacrifice natural.

It's the artistry of a simple flower.

Childhood...what does it mean to us as individuals and parents?

School - 1962

Early memories stay with us. In the hand of destiny, some shine as defining moments that sculpt us.

Second grade, the school bell rings, we take our seats. A tall and robust Mrs. Mayfield, a redhead with a pageboy hairstyle quintessential for 1962, presents me with an opportunity this fateful day. She assembles her reading groups from best to worst. Formal in manner, she runs an orderly classroom.

"Group 1," she announces as black glasses swing from her nose to her chest.

Her delivery of the twelve names that make up Group 1 comes with metronome precision. My name isn't called. She goes on to the next twelve destined for Group 2.

I keep my eyes closed, hands squeezed, with infinite hope that maybe I'd hear my name, as if to say, "please oh please, call on me, I'm not stupid!"

I get fidgety, rearranging myself uneasily on the hard wooden seat of my desk, tapping my feet.

"This isn't looking so good," I weigh in.

By the time she gets to Group 3, I beg the question "could there possibly be a Group 4?"

Do I hide under my desk or sneak out of the classroom?

I feel embarrassed. I'm little, but not petite enough to fit under the desk. Sporting a green plaid uniform and a Dutch-boy haircut, of light brown hair, my mind goes into overdrive looking for an escape hatch. I don't want to be teased by my fellow classmates.

With chin in my hand and fingers thumping up against my face, I contemplate, "hmm...how do I deal with this?"

Well, dead last on the Group 3 list is where I am. Mortified and in typical childlike fashion, I immediately think it's a mistake. All sorts of thoughts run through my head.

What's so special about little Susie that she merits Group 1 status?

She picks her nose.

Is an adult like Mrs. Mayfield actually capable of making mistakes?

She sets her hair the wrong way every night. I can tell from the curler lines on the back of her head. Those rollers don't always go in straight. Her suntan nylons sag around her ankles. But wait, I can't blame her. My mom and dad taught me to respect adults. Mrs. Mayfield is an adult. She sets the guidelines and I need to respect them. I can't possibly point the finger at her.

Maybe my parents made the wrong assumptions about the place, this Catholic grade school. How about if I sneak out of the classroom, make a quick get-away?

Nope, I promised my parents that I'd take care of my younger sister; walk her to my grandmother's after school. I have to keep my word as I mean what I say. Others count on me to follow through.

Quite the tough spot; I don't belong in the bottom group, that Group 3. Things aren't going my way, but it isn't all about me. I feverishly rummage through that little brain of mine, like scouring an attic, to assuage my discomfort.

I sigh, roll my eyes, snap my fingers a few times and then boom! There it is. I'm bilingual, reading in two languages, not just one. That's special! Stitching all this together, with parental lessons about patience and wait your turn, I collect myself. Mrs. Mayfield's grand manner in assigning reading groups isn't going to get me down.

I discover a dogged determination to work through problems, to persevere in the right way. Not to give in, not to give up, but to accomplish goals with others in mind, to have a *heart of a lioness.* Stars in the sky glisten just about every night. I'll stretch to reach them, even on my tippy toes. Focus and hard work will take me there. And, I'll walk my sister to my grandmother's not letting down those who count on me.

Mrs. Mayfield teaches me a lesson, whether intended or not. I adapt, deal with a situation. She hands me an opportunity to choose, doing it right or wrong. The desire to achieve and be the best can't be snuffed, if you believe in yourself, but I have to do it the right way. I place ambition on one of the ledges within my soul, right next to the heart. And so, I accept life in Group 3. I help a few young recruits get organized; encourage them to do their best. I catapult into Group 1 in short order.

My love affair with school begins. It's my organizing principle, as work would someday be. Predictability and daily routine bring comfort.

The structure of the parochial classrooms reflected just that. Wooden desks, nailed to the floor, lined up neatly. The plain large white silver-trimmed clock hung over the door, with wanting eyes wishing the small black handle ticked ever faster towards three o'clock. Alphabet cards trimmed the upper border of the chalkboard. Outside the window, we viewed a tree-lined street, Rectory or Church.

Girls weren't supposed to be super achievers back then. Many were schooled for marriage. It was the times. I just forged ahead to explore the world of knowledge without being aware that a differentiation between boys and girls even existed.

Natural inclinations take us places. Mine steered me towards achievement and doing well in school. I just took to it. Unusual for the time; that unusual, in part, was nurtured by a home where all things were possible; one boy, three girls, the opportunities and expectations were equal. My parents encouraged all four children to excel.

From those early days, I moved in the direction my heart told me to go. I'd come to live in a professional world of men someday. From that world would come my closest friends and confidants.

So, what do you suppose some of my fellow classmates did with my budding competitive spirit?

Aiming to throw me off kilter with hoo-hah and spitballs, the distraction was theirs. I had the eye of an unswerving lynx, known for its focus and sharp eyesight. So much so, that in ancient times the lynx was thought to possess powers to even see through stony walls.

I kept preparation and organization in my toolbox. At the start of each new school year, I rushed to the neighborhood dime store, with school supply list in hand. The proprietor knew us by first name. I loaded up before supplies ran out. Imagine, waiting till the last minute to get ready. Calamity struck for those who saw an empty shelf with a sign serving up the word "out." No, not me; I wouldn't be out of anything as I was in the game.

As each new school year began, I unzipped my pencil case with such resolve, ready to go with pencils sharpened. Selecting the pencil case color was always a dilemma. I wanted them all. With my parents explaining the difference between "wants" and "needs" I chose only one; sometimes a red, the occasional pink and, if the mood struck, I'd go psychedelic.

I organized my notebooks with color-coded tabs. And if there were a way to swing it, why I secured a first row seat of any classroom, not to miss a beat. If I wasn't attentive to detail, I might not get a good report card. I heard my teacher once say, "The devil is in the details." The expression befuddled me. I didn't try to figure it out. I just stayed away from anything with the word "devil" in it. It scared me.

Before the age of the computer, teachers dispensed sticky plastic, meant to protect book covers. Our task was to apply it, an exercise in patience and detail. You should see what went on in our classroom. Contact paper stuck to hands and desks before it even settled on to our books.

I took care to apply the sticky stuff. If one didn't line it up the right way, the whole thing looked crooked. There was a check-like pattern throughout the clear plastic. If not properly applied, the book looked lopsided. So, one could tell who didn't do the job right. A few youngsters in Group 1 rushed right through the process. They didn't even take the right steps. The end result made their books look like a Cubist painting.

Cutting corners showed up during bathroom breaks. As legions of children catapulted out of class into water closets, I put fingers in my ears to muff the sound of the boisterous. Metal bathroom doors slammed amidst the flushing. Water splattered out of the sinks. The cacophony of loud voices reached a high pitch. Toilet paper stuck to *Mary Jane* shoes. A few boys cut corners. They actually came back to class with zippers down or toilet paper hanging outside their pants; even with zippers jammed. I reminded them that underwear goes inside the pants and, only then, to zip up!

My girlfriends and I kept our desks neat, not some of the boys. They'd keep old assignments crinkled up inside, stuffed to the brim. Wooden desktops barely closed. Panic struck when the teacher announced, "desk check." What a kerfuffle it made.

They torpedoed the garbage can to unload unwanted paper in the five minutes the teacher gave us to get things in order. In the rush to cover up and be done, they threw crinkled paperballs at the can, missing it all together. The can overflowed, leaving trails to their desks. They pretended the mess had nothing to do with them, walking away as the teacher requested the mess be cleaned up.

Such helter-skelter could make a *raucous mess* when they grow up. The mess could even look like the one in Dr. Seuss' The Cat in the Hat when mom was away. Sitting at my little desk, I kept fingers crossed that someone was putting control on a handful of the super rambunctious. Otherwise, they'll need teachers and supervision for the rest of their lives.

My classroom was a spice rack, no doubt about it. All sorts of personalities showed up. Some youngsters were the genuinely good salt-of-the-earth types, obeying and respecting the rules. Others thought themselves hot. They belonged sealed tight in paprika bottles with their showboating ways. They'd make fun of the kids with the glasses and pocket protectors. I told the inflicted, eating chives would help with the pain the unruly caused them.

A few shifted in a direction expedient for them as they lived in their *Orwellian* world, oblivious to what was real. I'd put them right with the dill weed, thought in ancient times to have a lulling quality. Lulled into creating their own reality, some twisted the truth to take on a form to their advantage, making you believe it real.

Do you remember those who just went along and accepted whatever came their way?

They didn't take a stand as others made decisions for them. They needed some thyme in their diet to develop some courage. Even the ancient Roman soldiers bathed in it before battle to give them vigor and strength.

Then we come to those who held the universe in their pocket. Do you know the type?

Into the bay leaf bottle they went. Try biting into a bay leaf. No one's world or opinion mattered, but their own, leaving only a sharp bitter taste for those around them. Intoxicated with their own persona, the be-alls and end-alls, oozed with tendrils vast, creeping to the edges of the universe. Those tendrils entwined, in a way so as to dominate everyone's attention.

The self-interested lot, destined perhaps to be future conquerors, like the Romans and Napoleon, didn't fool me. Just think what happened to them and their friends, in the quest to get bigger. They fell apart in the end, leaving devastation in their path.

Out of respect for the refined ancient Greeks, they didn't go into an oregano jar. The Greek word "origanon" means mountain. My previous study of Roman history revealed that empires, thought to be mountains, could crumble; at the hand of even unrefined men like Attila the Hun on a horse and his brood of wild men!

"Goodness gracious!" I'd think.

If I married a conqueror vast, blinded by ambition and power, I'd have to fit into their game plan. Imagine what would happen to my life if things don't go their way, as they grab for themselves. I'd have to ride off into the sunset on a warhorse with a Wildman, like Attila the Hun!

Do you remember the cheaters and deceivers, doing anything to get what they wanted dishonestly?

I knew who they were. They stretched their necks so long, to steal the answers off their neighbor's test. A sprinkle of rosemary might strengthen their memory, to recall answers to tests on their own. I kept my arm folded and hand cupped around my work. They gamed the system to their advantage when the teacher wasn't looking. I would've felt guilty if I'd done that, stealing something from someone else. If they don't change as they grow, so many around them could even get dragged down through their crooked ways.

When the recess bell rang, wily cunning ways blistered. First in line to go out, some just shoved others out of the way when supervision wasn't nearby. Walking a straight line was even a challenge. They made all sorts of promises to others, like they needed to get out there fast to save a spot on the monkey bars for them. They quickly redrew the map, with ambidextrous adroitness, as they bolted onto the playground with their own agenda in mind.

With their eyes on the prize, to be first on the slide, they "threw caution to the wind." Like rapacious wolves eyeing their meat, out of control consumed with the sight. Once they took hold of the slide, they forgot about anyone else, but fun with their friends.

What a ball they had as they hung off the sides of the slide, disregarding the rules, making up their own along the way. They'd make sure that no one else got in on their game, their power to retain. If anyone outside their pack came down the slide, why they'd walk up the slide, keeping their self-interested agendas in mind. What a problem they'd cause. If held to account, they'd point the finger at someone else. Imagine that!

The Family

There's something nice about being a child. It's like participating in a cruise where your schedule is planned for you. Everything is structured from port stops to meals. All you have to do is show up for the cruise, or so I thought.

As we cross that bridge from childhood to adulthood, what helps us move away from those perfectly natural childhood inclinations that childhood affords? What potent influences do we encounter as we're discovering the world?

If a lot of sculpting dust is any indication of parenting work, then our home was powdered with it. My childhood was structured somewhat like a cruise. I showed up, but into my palm went a surprise itinerary, one that made me deliver. Not quite what I liked at first, but spelled out clearly were the words — expectations, responsibility and accountability.

No choice in the matter and not much I could do about it, as this was the family I had. I stayed on that cruise and you know what I learned?

The predictability of it all gave me a basis; a foundation that helps us live our ordinary lives day-by-day accomplishing little tasks greatly for our families and others.

The Home

It's the early 1960s on the South Side of Chicago. Our home is a split-level, occupying the corner of a rather modest Irish Catholic neighborhood. My father's a physician. That's considered well-to-do then. My parents guard us from being spoiled in any manner whatsoever. They emphasize simplicity, a respect for others. They purposely don't want us to live in a fancy neighborhood.

I'm five years old when we move into our home.

The upper half of the house is done in blonde brick while the lower half is of a rust color. My parents landscape the home with meaning. Our physical surroundings whisper messages taught in the home.

Three evergreen trees, representing the three girls, decorate one side of the front lawn. A single lone evergreen tree sits nearby, representing my brother. Every time I water those trees, I'm supposed to love my brother and sisters. We take turns. If I see the ground cracked dry underneath my tree, when it's not my sprinkle week, I submerge into espionage mode to sniff out who isn't loving me!

Birch trees, the signature tree of Lithuania, surround the perimeter of our home on one side, a daily visible reminder of our heritage. My parents fled their native Lithuania, under gunfire, during the Communist invasion of Eastern Europe, to escape the aggressive forces that subverted human rights.

They came to this country for those "inalienable rights" to "life, liberty and the pursuit of happiness." Within our home, I am taught to respect life, and to understand that freedom is not a given, but something to cherish and fight for. Whenever I look at those birch trees, a few more ledges within my soul fill up. I place life and human dignity, freedom and truth one on top of the other and label them, "Cherish and Preserve."

I learn about inner beauty.

"Happiness and beauty flow from within," my parents would say.

And so, I become keenly aware that there are two parts to me. Both need attention.

We sleep on mattresses when we first move in,

until my parents could afford furniture. This house is our home. That's what matters most. With time, my sister and I have our bedroom furnished. My mother takes the care to appoint the room, albeit small and simple, in a way to make us feel special. And for little girls it is. As we are but a year apart, we share our childhood together.

Two twin beds sit on opposite sides of the bedroom. They are appointed with aqua patterned quilted bedspreads, like *Emilio Pucci* with a twist. Two gold leafed crowns, draped with the same fabric, hover above the beds. An off-white embroidered carpet graces the wood floors. White paint covers the walls. Shared dreams, pillow fights and laughter make for a place and point in time captured within the walls of our bedroom, in a home where wholesome innocence is preserved.

Within that split-level, life revolves around our faith and family. I know that in addition to my family, I have a Father and Mother in Heaven, with a guardian angel to watch over me.

My illustrated prayer book sits on my nightstand, as a child's visible reminder of a world invisible to the eye. It's of maroon color with lots of pictures. I spend half an hour before falling asleep at night sitting up in my bed comfy with the pillow behind my back. Like a princess underneath the crown above, I look at all those illustrations, trying to figure out what each represents. As I turn the pages, I try to make sense of it all, flipping them back and forth just to connect everything together.

I reflect, "hmm...what is going on here?"

Someone sits on a throne surrounded by all sorts of people on a set of clouds. A bird hovers above the throne. Underneath those clouds, a child walks along a lit winding path with cracks in it, with little crosses on those cracks. A Man with a Halo prods this child along, ever so gently, up a path connecting to clouds. An angel hovers over a kneeling child in one of the pictures. This, quite frankly, is a lot to put together for a six year old. All this is happening on a set of clouds?

I didn't know that one could actually sit on a cloud. First, I have to figure out who all those people are. It looks like I have a few more Fathers than just one up there. I reread the simple words that explain what this is all about until I get it. It's like being in school and learning.

Those atop the clouds are saints who lived virtuous lives in spite of adversity. The bird is the Holy Spirit who inspires, teaches and guides us, giving us wisdom and conviction to do the right thing. The Man with the Halo gave His life for us, showing us how to live through His example. But it's not always easy. We may falter, but could always get back up and walk the path. He prods us along.

This gives me comfort. I learn what actually goes on in those clouds. No matter where I am, a Man gently prods me along and, just in case, there is an angel hovering over me. So when I look up at the clouds, lots of busy people live and work up there, taking care of us down here.

As I leaf through my prayer book, I stumble across the *Ten Commandments*. Now that sounds tough.

Why ten? At least they're numbered. "Don't steal" and "don't lie." Oh oh! I got into trouble for doing that. I stole, and then lied about my sister's *Kissy* doll.

We had matching *Kissy* dolls with red-checkered dresses. They were two feet tall, and sat right next to our beds. The dolls made a kissing sound, like a "pop," whenever you squeezed their hands together. Curiosity took hold of me one day. I wondered how they made the sound. I embarked to explore. Didn't think at the time that a stretched out paperclip going into my doll's mouth, would make the kiss fade, but it did. I jammed the sound apparatus. She no longer kissed. I found myself at a crossroad as to what to do. Hence, a plan was soon in the making.

With my little pink jumper and white turtleneck, I peek outside the bedroom door to scope out the terrain. I look to the right, then to the left. The clandestine cover-up is about to take place. I tippy toe slowly back into the room, like the *Pink Panther*, towards my sister's doll and swoosh! The surreptitious exchange takes place. Unwittingly, half an hour later, my sister walks into the room to play with her doll; the shout "my doll's broken!" The sneaky sister pretends to have little knowledge.

No doubt, parental intervention surfaces. I confess, but only after repeated denial, interrupted by an excruciating stare down. I'm punished. With pain, I learn that integrity and trust are the basis of any relationship. Dishonesty hurts.

I make my way through my prayer book, night after night. The Man with the Halo talks about loving God above all else, our neighbor too. No doubt, plenty to keep in mind, then to act upon. An important message unfolds. As I grow older, I connect the dots. The family's heartbeat comes from its members. We learn to behave within our homes, no? As we grow we open up like a fan, to form the basis of society, reflected in its institutions and government.

Am I to love kids in my neighborhood who aren't lovable?

Some run after me, launching spit in an unseemly fashion. Others mock us for speaking a funny language at home. Loving them?

I deliberate, "OK, this'll take some work, but I think I can do it."

Courage and standing up is what my parents said one should never lack. I practiced bravery, regardless of the teasing, in speaking Lithuanian with my siblings outside the home.

Weekdays

No bailouts exist in that split-level on the South Side of Chicago. No way my parents could ever be fooled. They hold our "feet to the fire." Education and excelling in school are emphasized. Inscribed on the front door of my mind are the words "Do Your Best and Be True."

Life is simple. I go to school, study, visit with my grandmother and practice piano.

Are you drawn to things that words can't explain?

At age six, I fall in love with a *Cremona* Italian

upright piano. Yes, a piano, can you believe it?

This first guest arrives in our living room, decked in dark polished starburst wood with a brilliant display of keys, fifty-two white and thirty-six black. That first night, while my family sleeps, I sneak into the living room. My little finger presses one of the keys. It casts a spell that lasts a lifetime. Happy, peaceful feelings sprinkle like the glitter from a magical wand. It's beauty! Music joins that little prayer book to form the vessels flowing into my heart.

Someday, I'd have quite a relationship with the piano. You know, the back and forth, the give and take. My piano had character. It would take no less than single-mindedness. I'm to listen as it teaches endurance and self-control, surrender and sacrifice. To my parent's delight, it harnesses my active nature teaching me self-discipline.

My piano craved attention. The keys on the keyboard needed exercise. I spent hours on technique to develop finger strength and dexterity. That's just the cement mixing part, the preparation. A strong, properly executed technique lays the foundation. It is then applied to the practice of a sonata or any other piece. Measure-by-measure one toils until the whole piece comes together to make the ephemeral real. Difficult passages create some lonely moments, but one pierces through them.

There is integrity to the process, a calm that comes with the proper engagement, the patient and deliberate manner; no short cuts, no dodging. The end result doesn't quite come together otherwise, requiring a total unwind of the process to get it right.

The keyboard encapsulates the principles of life. It offers a blueprint even for running a business.

Let's now go back to the 1960s and 1970s.

My parents drop me off on Saturday mornings for lessons at the Chicago Conservatory of Music on Michigan Avenue. As I walk through its door, two souls become one, in a place pulsating with an old-world feeling, bedecked with all the accoutrements of a bygone era. Greeted by clacking elevator grates, I make my way up to the third floor; then disembark.

Dissonant sounds ripple from rooms with wide-open transoms where lessons take place, flowing together as if to create an orchestra tuning before the curtain rises. I meltingly entwine in the mellifluous cacophony. I make my way step by step on a creaky wooden floor down a hallway dimly lit by bowl-like ceiling fixtures.

I arrive early for my lessons to simply listen to the virtuosity of a student years my senior. Her playing is magnificent in emotion and athleticism. The enviable Julliard School would soon be her destination to launch a career in performance. I sit outside that door on a bench, eyes closed, taking in the mystique of her playing.

Like clockwork, the door swings open around 10:00 a.m. I walk into the large studio with the two butterflied grand pianos on a stage, statuesque against a set of four twelve foot high mullioned windows, overlooking Michigan Avenue. My senses pulsate, intoxicated with the beauty of the studio landscape as I walk to take my seat.

My teacher is one of "the" piano teachers in

Chicago at the time. He's in his late fifties with gray thinning hair, not too tall, stocky and impeccably attired. Thick black glasses frame his face. A distinguished presence exudes classiness.

His enigmatic personality intimidates me a bit. An inner strength seeps from his demeanor and persona. He doesn't talk much, keeps to himself, but for the love and rapture reserved for his twin pianos.

I stand in reverence as I watch his hands descend upon the keyboard with the wingspan of a graceful bird. His fingers have the tight grip of its claws. They hit the keyboard in a way so as to replicate the up and down motion of the hammers inside the piano. We connect through pianos as lovers would. With discourse confined to instruction, those lessons are a total immersion into a world for that hour that goes by too quickly.

I leave the studio in a trance-like state, walking slowly, as a sluggish snail, making my way hallway to hallway, just listening to the cacophony of sounds. I don't want to leave a world that transcends beyond the here and now. On the wings of music I fly to a place of grace. Waiting another week seems all too long and so, I become that sluggish snail.

My Conservatory had a soul, where so many before me traveled with their hopes realized or redirected. History was immortalized in this single place. My hopes would be redirected as I felt that something else was in store for me, which would manifest itself. Music became a serious avocation for the rest of my life.

My fingers stayed plenty fit during the week. I practiced an hour or so a day. It grew to several hours daily during high school years. That didn't stop my mother from stuffing her children with all sorts of lessons. She was a wonderful mother as she paid attention to every aspect of our development. There's something about those Eastern European mothers and their love of culture.

Ballet lessons came on Mondays and Thursdays, with none other than a Lithuanian teacher, a ballet master who immigrated to this country, like my parents. We took lessons at The Lithuanian Youth Center on the South Side of Chicago. A yellow brick building housed classrooms, some equipped with ballet bars. I took to yet another love.

As I rekindle the fond memories, precision is what my ballet teacher was all about. He'd smack a long stick on the floor with such swagger, to extract the best out of us. The motion alone agitated his black slicked-back hair, throwing chunks of it out of place.

He'd make us repeat *pliés* to perfection. I obliged, practicing diligently under his instruction and at home. I'd stand still in the fifth ballet position with arms above my head and fingers coming together in perfect symmetry. While lining up the fingers above my head, I was perplexed. How did my teacher become a ballet master missing two middle fingers on one of his hands?

My parents explained the difficult plight of many talented immigrants, who took on tough work to get by, as they came to this country for those "inalienable rights." An accident in a factory claimed his fingers.

At that point, I realized what saints must have been like. They suffered too. It must have hurt him deeply that his life's work was taken away through no fault of his own, as he immigrated to this country. Yet, he taught ballet in his spare time to preserve the human dignity and self-esteem that come with one's work and vocation.

Ballet introduced me to my favorite composer, Sergei Prokofiev, a Russian and pianist as well. I feel his *Romeo and Juliet* ballet score has no rival. Upon passing in 1953, Prokofiev left us the ageless, music of another world, deeply melodious, emotional and textured, with haunting undertones. Each one of his piano and violin concertos is associative with a period of my life.

Don't we all have music that triggers memories in our lives, transports us back in time?

Prokofiev's *Romeo and Juliet* ballet — it's the lynchpin that connects the memories of my life.

𝄞

Friday nights — don't we just love them?

Before I comfortably slid into mine, we shuffled to our Lithuanian lessons after school, to learn about our heritage.

I'm around ten at the time. My Lithuanian teacher's a tad over sixty, with a brunette bun atop her head. She's of average height and weight, but for her amplified chest. An amber necklace, strewn from the folkloric stone so many Lithuanians wear, sits propped up, very much displayed by an amplified chest.

Our teacher lived through the Russian revolution of 1917, so history lessons about Lithuania came first hand, through an animated forum. Instead of teaching only by way of a book, she taught through the vignettes of her life. They created a film in my mind.

Leafing through my Lithuanian history book, I once gasped in horror. Rasputin, with his long black scraggly beard and icy eyes, frightened me. He beguiled the *Czarina* with ambidextrous ways. This monk posed as a holy man, yet was truly corrupt and debauched. He switched back and forth between the two. That could make anybody dizzy.

That Russian revolution taught me a few lessons. People can be deceptive, posing as one, yet entirely different underneath. They may not even mean what they say, like they're wearing a mask. My antennae went up, like the rabbit ear antennae of my grandmother's TV. Imagine how hard it would be to trust and get along with someone like him. One could be fooled. People got on to that Rasputin, but had a hard time getting rid of him.

After Rasputin, we moved on to the savory, pound cake and hot chocolate, displayed in filigree china. While our teacher took care to prepare our weekly treat with such kindness, I snuck into her bathroom, quickly like the *Road Runner.* Curiosity led me on an archaeological dig, to ascertain the contents within bottles sitting on her toilet cabinet. Discovering that she dyed her hair, I quickly reported my archaeological find to my sister in time for the arrival of pound cake and hot chocolate.

𝄞

Do you spend time with your grandparents?

During my early years in grade school, I spent

the time right after school with my maternal grandmother. She lived with her son-in-law and his two children, taking care of them when my mother's sister passed away at a young age. They occupied the second floor of a three flat apartment building in Marquette Park on the South Side of Chicago.

Widowed at the age of forty, her industrious nature could not find a match, nor would want to. My *bobute* (Lithuanian for grandmother) embodied unmistakable Eastern European grandmother flare. She stood at 5' 3", slightly plump. Like Mrs. Mayfield, she wore thick suntan nylons and nun-like laced up black shoes. Wire rim glasses framed her face. A perfectly styled pepper gray bun sat on the back of her head.

She was the type that got a lot done quietly, with telltale efficiency. No detail was unattended. Her cooking, her tortes could have rivaled those in *Fauchon*, a luxury pastry shop in Paris. Had the chance been presented, I'm convinced she could've have built and run a gourmet food emporium.

Right off the kitchen of that Marquette Park three flat, a tiny room was her sewing boutique. For years, she artistically designed our clothes, made sophisticated ensembles for my mother until my parents could afford to buy them in a store. Needling brown paper patterns on to me was a challenge, as she persisted in meticulous measuring. Standing still never made it into my dictionary as the perennial "what's next" tormented me. Yet, her loving patience seamlessly produced the most exquisite and creative clothing designs.

Vivid to this day, are fichus trees that spruced up the living room of her modest apartment, so tall they brushed the ceilings. They sat in simple white plates to contain extra water, as invariably I over-watered them. Upholstered in a maroon fuzzy fabric, the sofa lounged alongside the wall. White lace curtains adorned the windows. They danced in the summertime as the gentle breeze blew through the windows, bringing nature into the home.

The TV, with the rabbit ear antennae, sat in the corner, ready for my grandmother's favorite daytime soap, *Secret Storm*. I'd sit Indian Style, cuddled up right next to her chair in front of the TV for that half hour. This was the only thing she did for herself, devoting her life to others. She told me that I could learn a lot about relationships from this particular soap. I didn't quite get that at age six. Seemed like there was a lot of crying and fighting going on. Someone was always walking out, suggesting perhaps that togetherness was not to be. How could all this make anyone happy?

But, I was happy, being just with her in that cozy apartment.

She continued to teach me about life as she made her own "hooch." Maybe this was the secret of her living close to ninety. I didn't realize that potatoes had so many applications. My parents weren't too happy when I told them that my grandmother gave me a taste. After the first time, it never happened again, a result of parental intervention.

In the arms of my grandmother, I found a way of just being in the moment with her. She passed on her wisdom, the stories about the women in my bloodline as I sat wide-eyed listening attentively.

I'm to remember their strength and resourcefulness; their uncanny ability to adapt to life's unexpected in a productive way. She taught me how having a heart and living ideals in the pursuit of goals is what it's all about. This, the legacy, those within my bloodline passed on to me to uphold.

After my grandmother and mother fled their native Lithuania back in 1944, they lived in the displaced persons camps in Germany. My grandmother made coats out of green army blankets, to sell and survive. Those family stories taught me to respect and appreciate all the opportunities that life presented, that things are not to be taken for granted, nor if you have them that they last.

Living ideals, it's not easy as so many things come along to distract us, but it's the effort that counts. Knowing where I came from, I'd live to honor the women in my life and all those in my lineage. The torch of a brave heart was mine to carry and pass on, so that we all remain strung together one life after the next.

Beautiful memories make our lives rich. They surprise. After my grandmother passed away, she made her presence known. While visiting Buenos Aires, Argentina at age fifty, I stumbled onto a boulevard eerily reminiscent of my walks with her to the local *Tastee-Freeze* for a five-cent ice cream cone.

As I turned the corner onto a boulevard in that romantic city of love and tango, an out-of-the-blue gust of wind suddenly swept the leaves into a swirl, upwards to the heavens. She was with me then. How an ice cream cone and love go together, only those who indulged in both would know.

Weekends

Don't we all love weekends?

Way before the handle on the big silver trimmed clock in grade school hit three o'clock on Fridays; I'd already be planning mine.

On Saturday afternoons, after my piano and French lessons, I'd sometimes accompany my parents to the local Savings and Loan, to deposit a portion of my twenty-five cent weekly allowance; to me, it was a bank. Going out to a place, like a bank meant dressing up, looking nice and neat.

So, on one particular Saturday when I was seven years old, I dressed in yellow. I donned a short yellow plaid A-line skirt, with a white crisp cotton blouse, sleeves to the elbow with ruffled lace. To match the sleeves, I wore white anklets with lace trim together with my black patent *Mary Jane* shoes. My light brown hair was perfectly crimped, a bob with a very short bang.

It was cool outside that day, so I topped off the outfit with a light yellow cardigan, with pearl-like buttons and a set of white gloves. Whenever the yellow cardigan hung in my closet, I moved everything else around it out of the way. It was my only one, a jewel. Like a dame, with a black patent purse slung over my arm to match those *Mary Jane* shoes, I was ready for that bank; all gussied up!

My parents used to say, "don't let money burn a hole in your pocket and always save something when you earn it." Clearly, my parents were teaching us the value of thrift.

I wasn't yet working, but chores around the house generated an allowance. That was like earnings. Twenty-five cents came in every week and that meant "need to budget." Five cents went towards my *Tastee-Freeze* ice cream cone and a nickel was dropped into my piggybank, the emergency slush fund. I pocketed ten cents for my spending money. The last five cents went into my bank account, my long-term savings, locked up, but for a rare occasion.

With aplomb on that one Saturday, dressed in yellow, I shimmy into the back seat of our 1952 family Buick, all white with an azure blue hard top. Our car is unique, quite frankly, in sporting a hole from the rust, in the floor just in front of the back seat. The hole is about three inches in diameter. My parents put a cover of sorts over it, but I know it's there. So as my father focuses on driving, I furtively remove the cover to watch what's going on beneath through the hole, as the car speeds along.

There isn't much to see, but it's something new. I'm tempted, but I don't give into the urge of sticking my foot through the hole. Imagine, if someone discovers this and finds a way to stick a foot right through. Something inside told me to behave.

In short order, we arrive at the bank, and then park. I walk with my parents towards those revolving doors, ones that speak to me. They tantalize me into thinking that I'm in a theme park. Round and round I go before I even make it into the bank. Eventually I do and what a sight it is.

Everest-like ceilings and rose-toned statuary marble floors create the patter of sounds throughout. People frenetically buzz about. One main room houses the tellers to the left, cherrywood desks to the right. I'm not sure I understand what all those important looking people do behind desks, but it has something to do with keeping my money safe. They're probably reporting to someone who is running the bank. I sure hope that the president and whoever is watching over him are doing their job to keep my money protected. That's why I am there with my twenty cents, my savings for the month.

In a swirl of grown-ups, a few feet taller, I make my way confidently towards the teller. I walk up acting like those important people behind desks, lifting my arm above my head to place the coins on a black veined marble. My head barely reaches the counter, but I slip those coins forward, nickels and pennies, followed by handing over my passbook. I push the coins just a bit further on my tippy toes inside those *Mary Jane* shoes, ankle socks graced with white lace. I wait for the teller to mark the deposit into my passbook, checking to make sure it's correct.

Seeing my savings grow mattered to me. Those coins came from my work, my chores, and the conscious decision to sacrifice some of those twenty-five cents for something in the future. So, I put a lot of trust in the people who ran the bank to keep my money safe. That money grew and eventually went to pay for some of my graduate school tuition.

My parents were leery of debt. It had to do with their values, conditions of life as they came to this country with thirty-five dollars in their wallet. They paid for everything in cash, but for the modest mortgage on the home we bought when I was five. They saved and sacrificed, waiting to finally afford a home for us. My parents used a credit card only when we took family trips across the country, like to secure a deposit at a motel. We lived within our means.

"Only buy what you can afford," they'd say.

I learned that "ins" need to equal "outs." That's why I earmarked five cents a week for my piggybank as a backup, just in case my "outs" exceeded my "ins" for any one week.

Once in a rare while, I used some of my long-term savings when we went to *Bargain Toys*, the neighborhood toy store. If I bought something, I really enjoyed it. It meant a lot to me. The wait and sacrifice of saving made it so.

𝄞

On Sundays, I'd wear the same yellow sweater to the Romanesque style Church located on the South Side of Chicago in a predominantly Lithuanian neighborhood. To me, it was a beautiful Church, not so much because of how it looked, but because of the warm feelings it elicited once I stepped through those doors; feelings as lustrous as those little pearls on my yellow sweater.

I'd walk in, hearing the pitter-patter of *Mary Jane* shoes on the white marble floors, as we made our way towards the front pews. Calm filled me up, as a reverence for those sitting on clouds, looking out for us from up above, took hold.

Mass was in our native Lithuanian language, officiated by the priest who presided over the Baptisms, Marriages and Burials of the extended family. He delivered a Homily every Sunday from an imposing marble pulpit, one that came to life as he spoke with such strength and certitude. I knew it had to be important, as the eyes of adults fixated on his emotional delivery. Behind me, some even sobbed.

My eyes moved side-to-side as I sat in the pew adorned with my white gloves and lace mantilla. Instincts told me to behave and listen as I tried to make sense of it all. Time moved at snail's pace in Church. But, you know, I figured that whatever was being said from the pulpit would probably matter someday. I always lit a candle for my family before leaving Church.

Have you ever done that?

Once, the little stick caught such flame that I had a hard time blowing it out.

I thought for a moment, "this isn't looking so good, like what if I put the Church on fire!"

The more I blew, the bigger the flame. I got scared, so I jammed the stick into the sand box, suspended near the candle holder, with such vigor that it broke. I walked away all sweaty from the incident, with my mantilla halfway off my head.

After Mass the extended family convened at my grandmother's to feast and watch my uncles play chess. Every Sunday was an extravaganza. The finest china and crystal graced the white crisply pressed linen, on a table that practically extended into the living room, almost to the fichus trees jammed in the corners.

My grandmother prepared her version of a simple meal, all homemade from scratch — starting with spinach egg drop soup, then sauerkraut and sausages, *kugelis* (Lithuanian for potato pie), pickled beets, an assortment of vegetables, topped off with homemade *Napoleonas*, a staple Lithuanian torte.

The frenetic preparation rush culminated in a serene moment. We'd sit down hand-in-hand in prayer and thanksgiving for being free in this country together. After a solemn moment, on to the phonograph went the Lithuanian folkloric records. The skipping needle interrupted the tug-of-war between the choral voices and record crackle. Occasionally, we'd listen to Mario Lanza, the renowned opera tenor of the time.

Celebratory shots of whiskey would invariably be part of the festivities, as my uncles would make a toast for the "Freedom of Lithuania" with a light hearty *Sveiks*, the Lithuanian "to your health!" My twelve-year-old female cousin stealthily polished off any whiskey the adults left behind as the feast moved on to the living room.

Summer

Who doesn't like playtime? Don't we all wish three month vacations would last forever?

As children, stretching summer days to infinity seems all too familiar to most of us. Who hasn't had those feelings!

Some things were stretched in that split-level home of ours. The deck of one brother and three sisters stacked up slightly in favor of the brother. He had lone boy status and as such, the girls were to keep him company. My sisters and I learned to love hobby shops and war movies, even car and boat shows at McCormick Place, a big convention center in Chicago. For little girls with little footsteps, the parking lot alone felt like an ocean crossing. As an adult, I could never go back to one of those car shows at McCormick Place. Surely, there must have been an easier way to learn about compromise.

My precocious brother introduced me to chess at an early age. He always wanted to win, but I never gave in. I even mastered war games like *Stratego*. If it looked like the win was mine, he just flipped the board and walked away. It nurtured my competitive spirit.

Unforgiving were the softball games my brother orchestrated throughout grade school. If it wasn't the ball hitting one of us in the head, it was the sweltering heat of the Chicago sun, scorching the concrete, and us on the corner intersection where our home was situated.

Let's picture the scene. The sizzling summer softball team had four players. My youngest sister, four at the time, was the shortest in the bunch. Adoring and beholden to my brother's whims, she succumbed to growing red cheeks as the sun torched her face. My nine-year-old sister, one year my junior, remained visibly bored and broiled from the heat, perpetually daydreaming or peering into the sky, like an astronomer gazing for a shooting star. In her case, it was just a baseball.

My brother was a year older than me and because of his lone boy status, he felt in charge. You know how some children can be, give them a little power and some test what they can get away with. Whenever I'd hit a homerun, it forced him to cite some odd codicil of baseball regulation, which would subsequently strip me of my run. I claimed what I earned, in boycotting any further play. I read about unions and would take to picketing if that hadn't worked. It fertilized my hallmark tenacity that would someday become my marker.

I gained an inch one summer on the sibling rivalry, quite literally, growing one inch taller than my brother. It happened right around seventh grade. That drove him into orbit, while those baseball game innings that lasted an eternity did the same for me.

A little busy body is what I was as a little girl. While engaged in one activity, I'd have my eye on the next. To think that I'd ever miss an outing with my father to the local produce market was to ponder the unfathomable.

In the mid-1960s we swapped the 1952 Buick for a white Oldsmobile Cutlass, one with a maroon interior. Unlike the Buick, this car had no rust hole. Hence, the ride to the market wasn't as much fun, but I made up for it with my loquacious disposition. I talked to my father nonstop all the way to the market.

Coined the family fruit glutton, I'd go along to jam my cheeks and pockets full of cherries. My father got on to my game. It didn't take long before I learned that cherries were expensive and that excesses need to be contained.

It was an outdoor market with produce displayed in wooden crates. In a crisply ironed white sundress, tied with a big bow on the back, I'd follow my father up and down the aisles, skipping around, looking up to him. He'd rummage to find the best vegetables and fruits in each category, explaining what to look for in a cucumber or melon.

To the bottom of the pile he'd go, to find the freshest produce. Getting the produce weighed on silver scooped scales, and then labeling the bags as to poundage was my charge. I paid attention to detail. If I marked 100 on the brown bag instead of 1.00, we'd end up paying for 100 pounds of cherries. I'd get into trouble for that!

In between all this produce selection my father passed along his wisdom reiterating the omnipresent, "work, work, work, goals, goals, goals," in his Eastern European accent.

The conversation continued, "Only dead people have no goals." Imagine that one coming your way! While still trying to process this rapid commentary, I'd earnestly listen on.

"Don't let anyone ever tell you that you can't be what you want to be," he'd lovingly pass on.

To this day, tender moments continue as he accompanies me to the grocery store. I learned those lessons. I've replaced the white sundress with a chic pair of tight white denim jeans and those never to be without high heels. A lady in her fifties can be quite the dame.

Every summer, we'd spend the month of July in Union Pier, Michigan. We'd pack the trunk of an Oldsmobile 88 to the brim. When the final item, the ironing board, was placed on top, we were on our way. The ironing board invariably came along with my mother's devotion to us looking nice. No nannies, no housekeepers; my mother did the work and we helped.

A two-hour drive from Chicago took us to a motel, run by a Lithuanian proprietor. Year-in-year-out, we stayed at the same modestly appointed pine cabin. One bedroom housed the twin metal beds for the three girls. The scent of pine to this day triggers the memory of the very moment I'd walk into that room. I'd fall asleep to the music of crickets, then wake up to the sound of nature, smelling the fresh air. It became one of my favorite childhood memories.

We vacationed with the same Lithuanian families every year. After a long workweek, fathers joined mothers and children on weekends. Inevitably as the adults had their good time, they forgot our bedtime. We stretched the opportunity, playing hide-and-go-seek in the woods far enough away, so as to have a ready excuse for not hearing "it's bedtime!"

Childhood summers were like sliding into a cushy bed; only it's the bed of nature we found ourselves in, with time to cocoon, to leisurely drift into the beautiful world around us. Fantasy filled our days, as my sister and I lay on our backs watching the clouds go by, imagining what each one could possibly be. We'd chat about how the sky was like an art gallery where the Artist of the Universe was forever painting something new out of cotton-like clouds. In the evenings, we swooned over the beautiful stars, simply excited to locate the Big Dipper.

Ours was an uncomplicated world with few choices, few distractions. We prayed, we worked and we played. No computers, cell phones, just us together with a few books in hand and an outside world to explore; to be taken into our imagination.

A beautifully orchestrated world played out before me, no need to have another in its place. Creativity bloomed as we dreamed and found our own daily routines during lazy summer days, learning to keep ourselves active in the simplest of ways. Just a handful of TV channels to choose from for those few weekend hours we were allowed to watch TV.

Life unfolded gradually step by step, as childhood ticked away. It was the right mix of a little bit of everything for me within a cocoon spun by the love and discipline of my parents; no crowding out of a way of being. I packed a seal-tight suitcase of memories, ones that traveled with me along the road of life.

Beauty is what I discovered in my childhood. I'd carry it with me, never to let it go. It's like the little yellow sweater that hung in my closet. I moved all else around it out of the way to preserve it. Beauty waits at our doorsteps, sustains us at those crossroads of life.

What treasure do we live with forever?

The treasure that lies deep inside the chambers of the heart. I found the coziest of homes there, to visit, one with a flickering candle and shelves of memories. It's the home each one of us has to retreat to, no matter where we are.

As a child, I loved swirling in the snow with my arms outstretched, looking upwards to the heavens, as the snowflakes of the first snowfall of the season gently cloaked my face. I remember the quiet, the echoes as the acoustical nature of the snow blanket made the crunching sound of my boots to the snow more audible.

And then, there was the being on a swing. Seeing the beauty of the world around me, the kind that is so piercing that it brands the soul forever in feeling and memory. I'd hear sounds, as I'd propel the swing back and forth ever higher, until I'd almost reach the trembling leaves of the trees. The feeling of not a single care in the world, as if sitting on a cloud, as I'd close my eyes leaning all the way back with the wind in my face; how many before me had done the same?

Yes, those times we wish would never end; they do, when we hear, "it's time to go."

Where and to whom do we go?

We jump off the swing. As we move towards something else, the grinding metal chain sound against the empty thorny wooden seat becomes a fading sound and memory.

How many forget to return to the swing?

Chapter Two

Oh Fairytale!

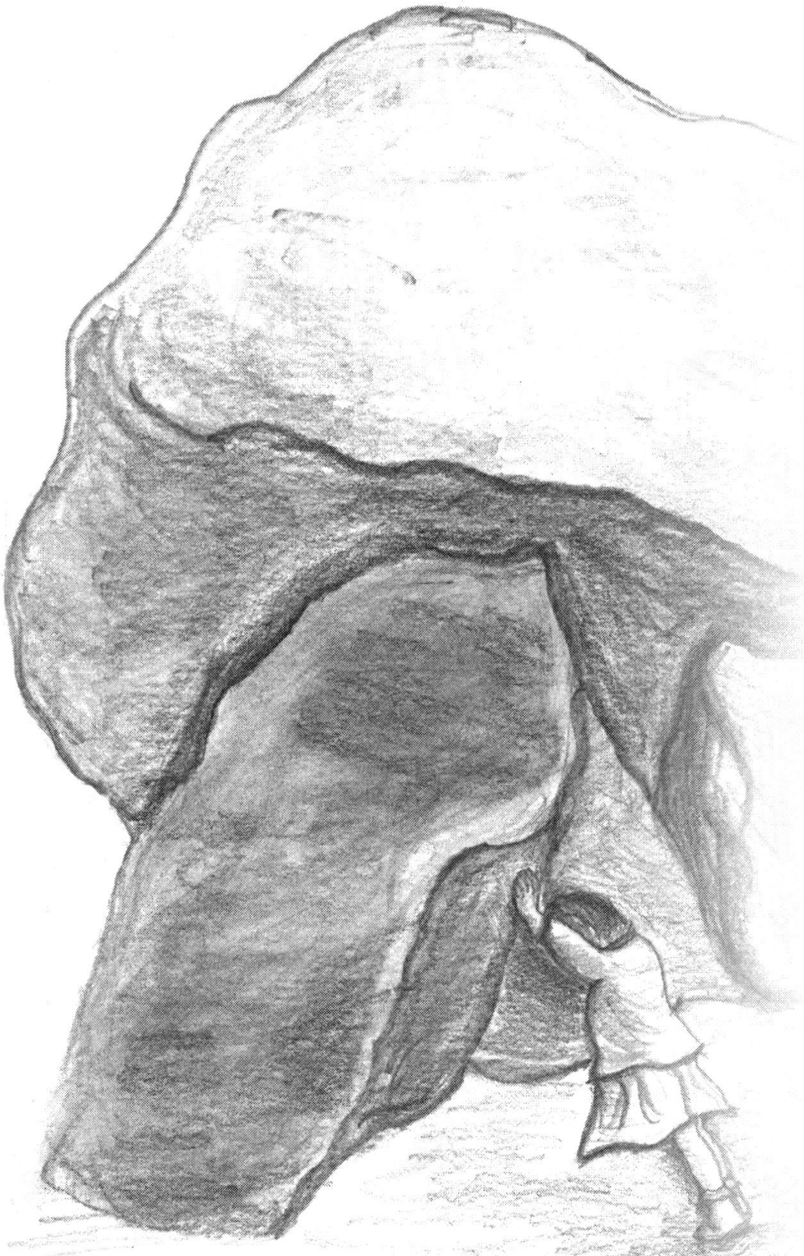

Fairytale of Amplification

December 13, 2008

Oh Fairytale, what are you all about?

You teach our children. You take us to a fantasy world where forces of truth and deception battle, personified in characters that represent good and evil. You don't age, you reveal truth as you create characters, that choose to endure and overcome obstacles, to stay true in protecting your truth.

Do you wish that we identify with characters, who choose to do good, stay true? Is this why you've the symbolic "happily ever after" to beckon that we act in a way that would have the intended consequence?

What if too many characters stray, act upon misguided intentions or amplify ambition to cross the line to the other side? Most certainly you, oh true fairytale, would try to awaken them from deep slumber, your truth to protect.

Did we create a fairytale, but one that doesn't follow fairytale rules…one that is faulty in its premises?

Subprime market loan defaults…bad lending practices… the trigger. Well, of course it would breed the toxic… why those practices?

Which of the two forces in a fairytale births scandal and destruction?

True fairytales have an order. Otherwise there would be

no "happily ever after."

Mortals unbridled…they like to conquer. Throughout history they have done so…the powerful and wealthy take their advantage. In the insatiable quest for profit and power in our modern day world, one could easily build a world of fantasy within one's reality if one runs out of ways to squeeze profit or attain power.

The conquer for profit and power in this day and age, easily enabled, through debt and complex financial engineering…the weaponry of our modern day era. For example, one may engineer fantasy products for profit. One may even engineer illusion through simple use of language.

With this weaponry, conquerors may grow mighty big… mighty powerful.

One can create fantasy in reality and make others believe it real (like a Ponzi Scheme)…create complex products (like elaborately packaged mortgages that become toxic)…create a market (like a credit default swap market in the trillions) — all of fantasy proportion, under the auspices of it being necessary, for growth and bigger profit. And before we know it, this necessary fantasy becomes an accepted norm as the unreal is spun to look real. With so many seduced by the seduction as the seducers' pots of gold overflow.

Oh pot of gold, do you then cajole those entrusted to govern, blindfold them as well, as they seek their power to retain?

Until, one day, it unravels…

If consumption has matured, capitalism in seeking profit has no place to go but to create fast, big or new fantasy products beyond our means and comprehension…with debt a beguiling friend to make that merry-go-round go round and round until it spins out of control.

I'm trying to figure out what really happened here… did we push it…pursue profit and power to such excess, in such novel ways, with tools that allowed us to so amplify, so as to create a feeding frenzy of fantastical magnitude…a kind of out-of-control "free-for-all?"

How did this happen?

We strayed from principles embedded in our economic and political systems…we deconstructed boundaries… allowed fantasy to flourish without limits…it's bound to create distortions and unintended consequences.

Conquerors, in their quest for power, take others into bondage with no accountability and remorse…without a heart they do so as they fail to see the human face of another. Anything is possible then.

What are the consequences of conquest in our modern day world?

Debt bondage…it comes with heavy chains…creates the unreal for us all…national debt of a scale that strangles and replicates itself impinges on our lives, liberty and happiness. It is a form of indentured servitude trickling into the nooks and crannies of our daily exis-

tence…increased taxation being just one heavy chain among many more.

Debt begets debt, which now begets more debt.

Intentions, choices, and actions…they set a stage to create a performance. The curtain rose, what fairytale did we see? As the curtain falls, how do we leave the theater…with hope to seek and protect truth or will we succumb to debt bondage with a haunting nostalgia?

The MBA - 1978 to 1980

How many of you stumble on to your careers?

Start out on a path and end up by a stroke of fate in a new direction that lasts decades?

Well, that's what happened to me.

I never took a single business course at the University of Notre Dame, graduating with a BA in English Literature in 1977. I thought business people were like the businessman occupying the Fourth Planet in Antoine De Saint-Exupéry's The Little Prince.

That businessman spent his life counting and owning stars being disturbed only three times in fifty-four years. I was saddened for him when I read that. He reminded me of Napoleon and the Romans, conquerors vast, who thirst for power and wealth, only his pursuit was directed towards such fathomless a conquest as counting the stars in the sky.

I had a Professor at the University, who left an indelible imprint on my life. I keep his class notes inside the drawer of my nightstand. He introduced me to The Little Prince, amongst many other literary works. One could hardly read any one quickly as they have beautiful simplicity in them. In their simplicity, they remain textured and ageless. In them, we too become ageless, forever youthful, as they keep us seeing life through the eyes of a child.

He taught a course in philosophy, but the kind that is a philosophy of seeing and living life with a heart. His class had windows that overlooked a tree-lined corridor, known as the south quad of the campus. He never changed the classroom's location, simply because there was a tree outside the window that he came to love so deeply.

Someone breathed life into my Professor's tree and as the Maestro conducted creation, he placed a heart inside each one of us with which to see. This tall, eccentric and absent-minded, yet brilliant man, with gray bristly hair parted in the middle, ever smoking a cigar, always in a three-piece suit, would start the class with a "Look at that tree just be."

He'd stare out the window and continue, "Beautiful, hmm?"

I did look and indulge. Wonder of wonders to think that perhaps this man thought like my parents, when they planted birch trees around my childhood home. That tree grew on me too as did the reverence for the culture of life. This simple tree had a purpose within the universe, ever more beautiful with each passing season, with a right to grow old, not to be cut down before its time. In the eyes of the sun all trees are the same, regardless of age, how they look, even if a little crooked here and there.

My Professor solidified the notion I grew up with, one that simply never goes out of style. The heart puts a human face before us in every engagement and action we undertake. And when we forget, many trees are around to help us stop and take notice, to "Look at that tree just be."

I took a year off after college to practice piano intensely, bidding *adieu* to countless hours of surrender, and that one key, whose spell I came under, lovingly touching it in the night. A professional direction would manifest itself and it did, like a shooting star out of the sky, only it was a little voice within me. Like the surprise cruise itinerary my parents delivered when I was a little girl, it pointed me right towards business school.

Math was natural to me, perhaps cultivated by the study of piano, which requires mental organization to understand music theory and memorize pieces. With excellent math skills in tow, I applied to what I perceived to be the best MBA School at the time, graduating in 1980 from the top-notch Kellogg School at Northwestern University in Chicago. If I was going to be a businesswoman, why I needed to choose the best school to prepare and create opportunities upon its completion.

What's the intent of MBA school?

It helps us get a job. But, there's a little more to it, isn't there?

I learned the basic principles of business.

What do principles mean if not applied, and why would that be important?

Business makes our whole economy hum, and with it, come jobs. It would naturally follow then that there is a common intent that business leaders need to concern themselves with. The health of our economy and society is in their hands.

Would it make sense then that political leaders need to keep an objective vigilant eye on those business leaders?

Together they are entrusted to safeguard our economy, our livelihoods. In that word I see trust.

Business is creation, an art form, like a symphony. Running a good business is just that. Bring the players and instruments together in synchrony — products, people, managements and boards — out comes the melodious.

We'd have case studies focused on what makes a successful business over the long run. I feel it's basic, as basic as good products sold by motivated and happy employees knowing what they're selling, who are supervised by vigilant managements, held accountable by their boards.

Like parents who set the tone for the home, political and business leaders do the same for our economy. Boards and managements are the shepherds of our corporations. Managements select board members, with the help of recruiting firms. How they shepherd makes all the difference in the world. It determines whether or not we have healthy companies that collectively make up a healthy economy.

Business leaders are entrusted with assets, both financial and human. A shepherd is vigilant, kind and loyal. The flock takes its cues from the shepherd. If one or two sheep stray, the shepherd pulls them back in and influences the direction they go, and makes sure they reach their destination the right way. Boards are the top parental level within a corporate structure ultimately responsible for overseeing it all.

We have freedom within our free market capitalist economy to choose wisely and responsibly; to be disciplined in the way we pursue profit. We accept a level of risk in return for a financial reward. How we balance risk and reward makes all the difference in the world when it comes to having a successful enterprise, a healthy economy.

Capitalism is about accumulating capital in private hands, creating wealth through private ownership. If companies accumulate wealth in too risky a way or mismanage their affairs, the principles of capitalism are designed to wash out those with faulty business models.

Freedom-to-succeed is the motivator. We all like to be rewarded and valued for our efforts. It feels good. Motivated people propel the economy. Freedom-to-fail is the restraint — keeping risk in the forefront of our minds when it comes to choices and decision-making. Together the two form the bedrock of a successful free market capitalist economy.

Knowing that one can fail is key within a free market capitalist system, to expunge excesses or flawed business models brought on by undue risk-taking or mismanagement. If we do not allow failure, the faulty goes on. If we allow the faulty to go on, to get big, without correcting it towards that which is sound and stable, it's bound to fail even on a bigger scale. Ultimately, we deal with the fallout; allow the faulty to fail through a painful and costly process, which breaks it up, eventually bringing back enterprises that are built on the sound and stable.

What is your concept of risk?

Risk assessment requires vigilance and discipline. It is key when it comes to determining growth and debt levels. Growth needs to be lined up with the demand side, as competitive and economic winds shift. How much should a company grow and how much debt should it take on, in the process, when demand may be unsustainable or the product is created in such a way as to be faulty from the get go?

Should we not also concern ourselves with risk mediation?

If we off-load or transfer risk, it should not be done in a way that creates risk, but rather done in a way where risk is assigned to those most capable of handling it. For example, issuing loans to those who may not be able to pay them back is not such a good idea.

Discipline and ethics help when it comes to juggling growth, risk and reward. If we turbo charge growth merely to accelerate profits, whether prudent or not to do so, we deny risk and may endanger an enterprise, even a system. We set ourselves up for danger, for failure. It's like accelerating a car to perilous speeds.

Now we all know that the performance of our stock market rests on corporate profits. How those profits are generated makes a difference. If corporate profits are turbo charged, generated in an unsustainable way, without sound underpinning fundamentals, why it's like building a house on sand drifts. Sooner or later, it crumbles.

Would you agree that some human beings look for opening spaces, those doors just slightly ajar wherein to take advantage?

And when they find them, in they go, some even with such impunity!

When individual ethics and objectivity are compromised, it should come as no surprise that the field is wide open to pervert a system. Of course, the self-interested would then push undue risks and costs on to others in the pursuit of growth and profit. That would not be a disciplined nor ethical pursuit of profit.

I also learned about our financial system. It is comprised of commercial banks, Wall Street investment banks or houses, and an assortment of other financial institutions. That assortment includes institutional investors like insurance companies, pension funds, bond funds, and hedge funds. Banks and Wall Street investment houses play a pivotal role in our economy as they flow credit from those who have it to those who need it.

Hence, the financial system is the engine and backbone of our economy. It drives everything, most importantly jobs and the stock market. Certainly then, policy, regulation and supervision of that financial system is of paramount importance. That's why we have regulatory bodies.

Good or bad policy makes all the difference in the world as to whether our financial system functions effectively. If policy is misguided, it might just cause problems down the line.

Who sets the policy stage?

We have Congress, our parents in Washington, who are responsible for lawmaking. The Treasury Department is the financial agent of the government responsible for financial, economic, and fiscal policies. It manages the "ins" and "outs" for the government. The Federal Reserve (Fed) is our big central bank. The Fed supervises banks and sets monetary policy, like whether interest rates stay high or low. The Securities and Exchange Commission (SEC) is the federal agency responsible for regulation and oversight of the securities industry as well as enforcement of securities laws. It sets standards for investor disclosure and aims to protect investors from fraudulent practices.

I'd begin to connect dots in those business school classrooms, like connecting dots as a child. Each entity and each person within our financial system has an objective to fulfill. Otherwise, it might just set a volcano rumbling.

For example, investors rely on credit rating agencies as the industry standard for credit analysis and rating. When credit rating agencies stray from credit evaluation standards, imagine the ripple effect.

I studied the hypothetical concept of what would happen if a company, regulatory body, system or even a government grows too big. I just couldn't see how big could succeed in the long run. Innately, it seemed unmanageable to me, as too much could fall through the cracks through layers. Layers may even create little fiefdoms within an organization. I'm thinking that might be difficult to manage.

Allowing some institutions to grow too big may actually jeopardize our free market capitalist system or even economic democracy. Monopolistic-like structures may concentrate power and wealth in the hands of few who may then exert political influence. The intent of true free market capitalism is to allow many to flourish and compete on an even playing field; where no single entity is allowed to grow so big so as to trounce competition, through economies of scale advantage.

For example, if financial institutions and markets are allowed to grow too big without checks and balances, it may impair the system causing competitive disruptions within the marketplace. Too big may simply lead to too-big-to-succeed, in its unwieldiness and inefficiency, which may lead to too-big-to-fail. That means that we could even have systemic risk, endangerment of the system if any one were to fail. And then what would be the whole point of growing so big in the first place?

On the other hand, my study revealed that big companies under certain assumptions could be successful. For example, those comprised of franchises, as the risk of running a franchise is not off-loaded. It rests with the franchisee bearing the responsibility for choices; keeping control over how the business is managed. It's like having a small business of your own. And then, it's up to the management and board to make sure they are living up to the expectations of the franchisees in running the conglomerate well.

I was leery of large enterprises. One may get lost in a big place and not even be noticed. Perhaps it had something to do with my heritage, my parents fleeing Eastern Europe during the Communist invasion decades ago. I came to respect freedom in all its forms. Some of our family members stayed behind, burdened by a big bureaucratic socialist system. Those who made their way into the inner sanctum of power were financially rewarded. They lived well by a different set of standards, while the masses suffered and struggled.

When it comes to growth of any kind, managements may get lost in numbers, without regard to what's behind all those numbers — people with real lives. Businesses may lose sight of the true purpose of their existence in the first place. I'm not saying we go back to barter, but mutual benefit is a needed consideration.

So, I think I had good professors who taught me basic business principles. I have my parents to thank for instilling fairytale lessons, like be true and honest; take fair pay for a fair day's work and take care of those who work with you.

It would be up to me someday to make my own individual choices in implementing that which I was taught, to contribute to my country. I think that if I were ever to run a company, I'd be nimble. I'd take care of those who work with me. I wouldn't grow too big, as it would be awfully difficult to keep track of everything. I wouldn't want to end up like the Romans or Napoleon.

"Pourvu que ça dure!" said Napoleon's mother to him, when he boasted about his growth and conquests. Of perspicacious nature, she was skeptical and aware that fortunes turn.

Translation: Let us hope it will last!

𝄞

You may wonder — what was business school like decades ago?

My fellow colleagues and I weren't entirely focused on "bucks." Seemed to me that career choices were dictated by interest in a business field rather than just the money. Not everyone wanted to be a hedge fund manager or investment banker. Plenty of other opportunities abounded in corporate Treasury, consulting and advertising, just to name a few. Careers in consulting were particularly in favor at the time. Imagine, a world where everyone just wanted to go into finance, we'd have a winnowing of talented people in other areas.

When it came to the world of investments, how different MBA School was decades ago, barely a course related to the subject. A scant two or so were offered; one covered money markets, the other commodities. The latter was considered fancy then. No telescope had wide enough a lens to encompass the universe of fancy instruments that would someday inhabit my world of high finance.

The investment world was simple back then, one of money market, stock and bond investing. And so, business schools took their cues, in offering subjects appropriate to that world at large. Neither products nor markets were developed in size and complexity, as they would someday be.

Investing was done the traditional way in those days. Stocks and bonds were bought for a commission or mark-up. You bought something lower and sold it higher. True free market capitalism is what I was steeped in.

Technological advancements would someday revolutionize the world of investing and set the stage for financial engineering; meaning the creation of new securities out of existing securities and assets. I lived in a world of typewriters; word processing was a novelty. The Kellogg School housed a few big computers that spewed punch cards. That was about it.

How did a South Side girl from Chicago with no connections eventually make it into the big league Wall Street investment banks?

Focus, perseverance and hard work, peppered

with a dose of humor; yes, of course, staple commodities, but it was more than just that. I planned, stayed vigilant, kept my antennae up, and was guided by people who came into my life at significant junctures along the way. Determined to do the best job, I needed to learn from those who taught well and were interested in helping me along. I sought out mentors in a world that still minted them.

I had good mentors. Remembering how much they helped me, I would for the rest of my career take time to teach or interview young people seeking to get into the business.

As years went by, I came to observe that many a "could have been" mentor or manager took on a little attitude, a tad bit "what's-in-it-for-me" persona. In fact, I perceived the financial world over the years to increasingly take on a few characteristics that if I were doing the parenting, a little scolding would have come its way.

I think about The Little Prince. Antoine De Saint-Exupéry talks about how much grown-ups are fascinated with numbers. Some don't look beyond them. I met a cadre along the way like that. They grew obsessed with numbers and spreadsheets managing their companies to the short-term. Upon falling short to meet quarterly growth and profit numbers, even by a penny, whether whisper or real or even made-up, it put Wall Street and the investing minions into a dizzying frenzy. Quite frankly, it left me perplexed to think that the world spins on a penny!

So what kind of mentor was I looking for back in 1980 as I embarked on my career?

A Sherpa. What does a Sherpa do?

A Sherpa guides one up a mountain in a direction that has safety in mind. He's sure-footed. We trust him, as one who has traversed many a steep terrain through experience, practice and vigilance.

I met a Sherpa in my second year at the Kellogg School, located on a stunning wooded campus, right along Lake Michigan in the heart of Chicago's North Shore. Interview season was in full bloom that spring. Top business brass descended like birds of prey, circling to pluck the best candidates. I was interested in general finance and commercial lending.

Life does throw us a wrinkle now and then. Fate intervened that spring by cancelling one of my hour-long interviews. I found another to plug the hour, an investment bank named Goldman Sachs. My interview would be with the head of the Chicago office that day.

The blueprint for my professional life unfolded. I walked into an austere interview room, resembling a drab storage closet with a blonde wood desk and two chairs. Sitting in one of those chairs, the stark contrast, a decked out man scented with the look of Wall Street and a hint of *Halston*. He wore a silky wool, dark gray suit, of subtle plaid. A cyan-colored tie adorned a white starched shirt, with French cuffs, pinned with glistening links. His silver hair, combed back, slightly wavy, matched the sparkly links.

No one in my family ever dressed that way!

He gets down to business right away, with a quizzical, "Do you know what you're interviewing for?"

"Not completely," I respond, "I just had an hour

to kill as one of my interviews was cancelled, and so I signed up for what was available. I didn't want to waste time."

My candor stumps him, as his expression reveals that his mind is the site of a debate, "Is she joking or truthful?"

He leans over a bit and proceeds to elaborate about high net worth brokerage. That means investing for wealthy people. It's a universe unfamiliar to me. I saved a nickel a week years ago and am now scrimping to get by in business school.

A lively ping-pong like discourse ensues, punctuated with an invite to visit their offices for a second round of interviews. I really didn't know what I was getting myself into, but had inkling that serendipity had visited me.

I shared this bit of news with my fellow business school chaps, who with astonishment remark, "Wow, you know how lucky you are?"

A cachet came with that second interview at those coveted Wall Street investment banks. An offer would pop, if you made it to the New York headquarters for a third round of interviews. And that was considered exclusive. I was never swept away by exclusivity gibberish. My upbringing kept me grounded and humbled, as I began the journey into the world of high finance.

I did a little homework before my second interview. What is an investment bank?

Many Wall Street investment banks existed back then, some even as private partnerships rather than public companies. Goldman Sachs was an investment bank that was still a private partnership. A Wall Street investment bank had three core businesses; investment banking/capital markets (deal origination and underwriting), trading (buying and selling of securities) and brokerage (brokering securities to investors). The core structure remained the same as decades progressed, but expanded to include new product and market divisions.

What does the fancy term, "capital markets," mean?

It's like a marketplace where those with money (like pension funds, bond funds, insurance companies etc.) come together with those who need money (like corporations, governments, agencies etc.)

Wall Street investment banks coexisted with the regular banks, known as commercial banks at the time. Both had a role to flow credit through the financial system, but through different channels.

The Glass-Steagall Act of 1933, enacted in the aftermath of the Great Depression, delineated what role Wall Street investment houses and commercial banks were to play in our financial system. It created a barrier. It's intent was to protect the banking system from speculative largesse and risk-taking endemic to Wall Street culture. So as not to jeopardize capital for the protection of lending and deposits, the Act prohibited commercial banks from engaging in speculative activities, like underwriting. Underwriting means the issuance of stocks, bonds and municipals, referred to as the riskier capital markets activities.

Like the little girl, going to the bank of her childhood, I'm gussied up the day I have my second round of interviews with Goldman Sachs. I wear a light gray linen suit, stylish but in keeping with the structure of female suits of that era. Nothing racy, essentially a suit constructed like one for a man.

The Sears Tower is my destination. Like walking up to the tellers of my childhood, I announce my presence to the receptionist. Out comes the Chicago office manager's assistant. A whole day of interviews is planned for me. Through a maze of desks, we go. The assistant keeps walking. I stop, stunned in awe! I'll never forget that "love-at-first-sight" moment!

What a frenzy; I'd never seen a trading floor before. A live ticker tape, operator-like phone panels blinking with lights, rows of trading desks, inhabited by agitated beasts as if responding to a female in heat, pacing with phones, crazed with intensity as they bear down at the sight of their prey. That spellbinding obsession with getting the trade done, those in the business know all too well, oozes from the nostrils of predacious alpha males.

At the sight of that room, a trigger goes off within me, "I could do this!" Something's implanted in me, gestating until that career is born.

Believe me, getting into Wall Street and lasting was no easy task. I liken it to scaling a palm tree. Not that I've ever tried; it just seems like an arduous feat. You don't get in on the first try. They want you to keep trying. They know you're hungry then. Hunger drives the business. Hungry to get in, to produce, to persist and it just doesn't stop there.

"Not tough enough" is what the pack serves up to my Sherpa after a day of devouring interviews.

I get the relay, then the send-off.

At first, I'm shocked, "where did they come up with the not tough enough part?"

I'm thinking, "Nonsense, but I'll go home and reflect."

Only two candidates nationwide would call this categorically unique firm, home. Hitting every interview marker to perfection is what it was all about. I did go home to reflect, but it bothered me. I couldn't take that flat out "no" for an answer without a more in-depth discussion. I called my Sherpa to arrange a meeting for the following week.

Something happened during that visit. It sprung a well within me, one of belief and fathomless calm, that I'd someday be very much a part of Wall Street. I just knew it. We connected, as a father to a daughter would, as my Sherpa kindly reminded me that I was only twenty-five years old with a bright future ahead.

He simply advised, "Why are you fretting? If you want to be in this business, you'll find a way in."

Very kind is what he was. He displayed a genuine compassion and interest in an obviously disappointed young person. Picking up on his paternal instinct, we stayed in touch.

In the meantime, I'd take to my chisel, straight to the opportunity spot on that marble of mine. Only in this case it wasn't marble sculpted, but those intangible "perceptions count in business." I'd work on conveying that "tough" part. We never really do stop sculpting. Fine-tuning and patience would get me there.

The Bank - 1980 to 1983

What is it about life?

Sometimes we get dealt a hand we may not like, yet it makes sense looking back as to why things unfold the way they do. I got dealt Option B, the bank. I wanted Option A, the Wall Street investment bank. I just couldn't get Wall Street out of my mind. So why is it that this stepping-stone was laid before me?

Like that second grade reading group, this is where I was to incubate for awhile until an opportunity on Wall Street presented itself. I tempered my youthful impatience, choosing to learn and imprint instead.

I take myself back in time.

Thick stone Ionic columns grace the entryway of this bank, supporting a triangular pediment with tympanum. What do these historic structures really mean? Are they meant to convey that these institutions are steady and solid, never age, with an impression of stability? Or are they meant to remind us that they may crumble and someday turn to ruins? Yet, this is no Rome, that eternal city. This is the heart of Chicago's Loop and Option B for me, not Option A. I certainly hope Option B does not turn out to be eternal!

The interior is magnificent, museum-like. I'm courted in an elegant way, one that takes me to their coffee parlor, more like a visit to *Versailles* than any coffee parlor I'd ever seen. I could've ensconced into a slumberous trance within a salon like this, simply with a book or a collection of paintings to view.

This is the place where officers of the bank convene with customers, to very simply have coffee.

"Appearances and perks" are what that first glimpse whispers to me, echoed by a "look official." That's all it took, in my opinion, to officially get the job.

𝄞

What was the business world like for women in 1980?

That's almost three decades ago.

Wow; it's a tome in itself!

We're the pioneers, still trailblazing Wall Street, decades later.

The feminist movement of the 1970s is underway.

My generation ushers in its own movement; and I, my own brand altogether. "Marching to my own tune," forging ahead to have babies and femininity in a financial world, where I felt like a solitary lynx.

It's 1977. I'm a senior at the University of Notre Dame. I am among the second class of women, only a few hundred, accepted into the University in 1973.

A unique group of women comprised that class. High ambitions and determination went hand-in-hand with a strong sense of family and social responsibility. I felt blessed to have shared the company of so many talented women. My colleagues went on to live extraordinary lives, paving the way for women to follow.

This was a watershed time for women. During senior year, I remember taking a leisurely stroll with a priest friend around the lakes dotting the campus. We talked about challenges ahead. It was one of many discussions. Before us were the crossroads yet untraveled. We were at the cusp of what would someday bring remarkable changes within family, society and the work world.

We'd soon enter the workforce with difficult choices to make. This priest's prescient thinking influenced mine; the way I'd prioritize. I'd build a career around a family. My family would come first. He encouraged me not to delay motherhood.

Working and mothering in the early 1980s wasn't easy. Throw in the wife part and wow I was busy. I loved being both a mother and achieving, and sometimes I felt guilty about loving both so much; what a dilemma, like choosing the pencil case in second grade. I was very obviously not alone in all this. Others felt the same. This duality percolated into a whole cultural movement at the time, a mantra, that all was possible.

Do you know of anyone who tried to have it all?

We freighted ourselves with the triple goal to have children, happy marriages and careers all at the same time. We believed it possible. How does one really juggle all those pieces?

They need to fall into place perfectly, within each category, but we know that life's not that way. And, because life's not that way, it's a persistent struggle. As professional women, we juggled those pieces, and the ones within our respective professions.

Back then; we were just dredging our way into business. Everyone was feeling their way through this new landscape, as a yet small army of women marched forward. Seemed like men were comfortable with women in the work force in a limited role, nothing too serious. Young men too were trying to adjust to professional wives; the older ones altogether wondered why we were at work in the first place.

How would this male and female tension eventually play itself out? Would the two worlds someday co-exist in a more balanced way or collide?

Strength in numbers is what we needed at the time, but it just wasn't there. The underbrush made it a difficult passage for many who attempted that triadic goal crossing. So, as careers progressed and children came, some of my female colleagues left the workforce.

It was just a matter of time before the sheer numbers of professional women would grow and infiltrate the business ranks. Girls increasingly excelled in school; were nurtured in a way so as to think about careers, to be self-reliant. That's how my parents raised me.

Being self-reliant didn't mean that I walked around all huffy. For years, I was within a small circle of women in the business world garnishing the type of earnings that could have easily given me a swelled ego. Instead, I viewed it as a conduit through which to actuate my potential in line with my ideals and objectives.

Self-reliance brings freedom and independence. It gives one a feeling of security. It's like food. It affects how we blossom, develop, the choices we make. It gives us a strong platform with resources to effect good.

I felt a calling to brave a new frontier, to pave the way for those to come. I always felt that women didn't need to be like men in the work world. Women bring a set of valuable attributes of their own, contributive to the health of our economy and society. Sooner or later the strong work ethic, competence and vigilant long-term thinking of so many wonderful professional women I've known, would lead to remarkable footprints within the business world.

Back in the early 1980s, copper-wired is what any businesswoman with children needed to be. The corporate infrastructure to support family life wasn't there yet. On site day care facilities, flex hours, a father leave of absence were not even on the radar within the world I lived in. The workday went on, regardless if your child was sick or the nanny didn't show up. And any company's maternity leave was seldom tested. Political correctness was not even in the vocabulary.

So, what did I do?

Forged ahead, with perseverance. Freshly minted out of business school, married and with baby number one shortly on the way, I joined Continental Illinois National Bank and Trust Company. Into their commercial lending training program I went. I'd soon learn how to make loans to corporations.

I was excited about finally earning an income. Though I did some part-time work throughout business school, I, like many others, came out of school poor with student loans. Half of my take-home pay would soon go towards a Lithuanian nanny. I didn't focus on pay so much. I focused on learning in those early years.

Considered one of the premier programs in the country, Option B was a great way to start out a career. Continental Bank was in the midst of executing a growth strategy to become one of the largest commercial and industrial lenders in the country.

In MBA School, I learned about risk. At Continental Bank, I observed what happens if not properly assessed and monitored, in the midst of growth.

Continental grew by focusing on the energy sector (piggybacking on the oil boom of the 1970s) and by implementing a more decentralized credit assessment system. What that means is that credit decisions, up to certain credit limits, were made at varying management levels.

Now, anytime anything is decentralized, I go "oh, oh!"

Why?

Growth creates layers, opening spaces for human foible to flourish if unconstrained. As the pyramid expands, those at the apex are increasingly removed, not necessarily signing off on every loan. The bigger the growth the greater the risk that indeed risk might be overlooked if robust controls aren't in place.

Do you remember as a child running to your mother or grandmother with open arms?

Open arms is not what I found when I slunk into this bank's training program with baby number one on the way. My pregnancy caused a stir as those preconceived notions came barreling down. I shook things up a bit.

Let's roll the tape.

How could she take a spot being pregnant and waste our resources? Is she going to come back to work? How do we handle this sensitive situation? How do we approach the topic?

Such poppycock!

I'm having the baby and feel up to the task. What's the fuss about?

It came as no surprise given the staid regimented nature of bank culture, more so the times. Anything outside the norm for a snoring bureaucratic bear was too agitating. I welcomed the challenge to find a way to navigate an environment unnatural to my own entrepreneurial spirit. It was a culture awash in bureaucracy, simmering with politics, and layers of managers. Jobs and coverage territories were neatly defined.

People were pigeonholed. I felt like a modern day vassal, in this world of organizational charts delineating who's reporting to whom, layer upon layer. It would take the finest of cartographers to navigate if this bank got any bigger. Such inefficiency, so much paperwork, and this was still a relatively small bank.

Dressing the part then, almost mattered more than the work. For women, the uniform, cotton shirt with a little bow tie, a made-over male suit with skirt below the knees and demure pumps. Oh no, I have to wear suntan nylons like Mrs. Mayfield?

I'd rip those clothes right off when I'd get home, slinking into one of my stylish frocks. As years went by, I unshackled male begotten female dress codes on Wall Street. I introduced feminine style and high fashion chic into the vaunted trading dens.

I swam through that training program like an athlete, tuning out the noise until my baby swam out of me. On an Easter Sunday, April 18, 1981, I was the proud mother of a blonde baby boy named Daniel Paul, forever grateful for the blessing, even though I packed on 50 pounds. Quickly shed, as my running routine launched me right back into my size six.

Having put the cobwebbed maternity leave policy of a venerable bank to the test, I returned, after a three-month leave, smack into the division they planned for me. As I looked up, the glass ceiling hovered atop my head. Dare to have a baby, take a short maternity leave and kerplunk, the ceiling dropped a few notches.

This mare stabled in the sleepy transportation division. Desired commercial lending spots, like the oil and gas division, where "growth" was taking place, went to purely bred stallions. Branded, I didn't stand a chance to be considered for an enviable spot like that. I took it in stride. Like I tell my children, the most important battle is the one we fight within. Win the battle deep down inside, believe in yourself. Then, a little noise from the outside world will be exactly just that.

Another reality made its way into the picture. Yes, the home and work push-me-pull-me tugged at my heart. In a world of mostly males who lived one world, I lived two. As "workingwomen," our hearts never leave our children.

I trained myself to tune out my work world when I came home, but learned to live two worlds by day, one visible to the outside world and one that lived within me. We don't leave our arms and legs at home, so too my heart was with my children always. They came first.

𝄞

So, what was life like in this lumbering group that lent to trucking companies, airlines, and the occasional yacht?

Too comfortable; I'm in a swirl of people, swirling around their desks, taking coffee breaks or moving back a row of desks in a pecking order based on years at the bank, rather than production, compensation similarly structured. That triage of three desk rows, undulating repetitively throughout those mesa-like bank floors, is bathed in buzzing fluorescent light. People get to work around 8:30 a.m. and then like clockwork, off to coffee at 10:00 a.m. I'm not used to working this way.

I couldn't wait to engineer an exit, as soon as an opportunity presented itself at one of those Wall Street investment banks. By now, I'd established a good rapport with my Sherpa, but in the meantime, I busy bodied in the land of slumber. I'd soon establish a close working relationship with the head of the transportation division. I was eager to help and learn.

My grandmother's lessons about adaptability came in handy. I immersed into learning. I not only did my own work, but offered to do legwork for the senior people in that division. I gave them all the credit and didn't mind it, as I was absorbing like a sponge. Like that second grade reading Group 3, this was my bus stop for now and the best I'd make of it, choosing to engage productively.

You know what it's like at those bus stops. You meet all sorts of people. You may choose to be helpful, to engage them kindly, to learn something about their lives and where they're going, not just where you're headed. Or, you can be prickly to others causing a hullaballoo in the process, shoving and pushing as you make your way first on to that bus, with a disregard for anyone else.

Respect for the process and belief in myself, cast a patina of perspective that helped me navigate through a career riddled with challenges. Toughing it out is what it was. Not just when it came to actual work, but also when it came to dealing with what today would be taboo. I'd be greeted in a room of men with, "when will the loan officer arrive?"

That was the reality women dealt with. A woman in business with a family was such an oddity back then. You were self-conscious about any corporate client inquiring about your personal life. With it came the dismissive thought, "oh she must not be too serious about her work." Prickly wouldn't have been a good attribute to have in those days; resilience was more *apropos*.

I sorted the important versus the unimportant, allowing the latter to just ricochet. Important was the analysis of credit and whether or not a loan should be extended to a corporate client. I analyzed creditworthiness, seriously. After all, I was committing some of the bank's capital in making a loan.

Loans stayed on the books of banks back then. There was no such thing as loan packaging to offload risk to someone else. Things were simple. As we move along through the decades, we'll see how we came to develop all sorts of investment instruments designed to shift loan risk to someone else.

I felt responsible for making those loans. So, I analyzed cash flows, tested future forecasts, questioned the customer about their assumptions and took time to really understand their business. That was my job. As part of the commercial lending program, we were also trained in understanding the principles of lending to individuals.

Here's how it was done then. One wouldn't have even tried to purchase a home without the prerequisite 20% equity down payment. Once we got past that, we'd allow no more than 30-40% of after tax income to go towards debt service like the mortgage and property taxes. The third leg of the stool was employment and income verification together with an accurate home assessment. If it all checked out, deal done.

I grew facile in reading financial statements, even understanding the devastating consequences that debt may wreak on a company's financial condition if not prudently managed. Turns out the sleepy transportation division became not so sleepy after all. When deregulation hit the industry in the early 1980s it triggered an onslaught of bankruptcies. Deregulation showed up who was managing their affairs well, who wasn't.

Hence, our division became understaffed. I rose to the challenge of taking on the work, but my division manager gave me the opportunity as well. I spearheaded intricate debtor-in-possession financings, as part of the restructuring of companies in bankruptcy. I worked directly with the Chief Executive Officers (CEOs) and Chief Financial Officers (CFOs) of transportation companies. I gained business sophistication and even learned a tad about executive suites.

The ubiquitous buddy system or club, flourished in splendor then and for decades to come, as a peacock fanning its glorious feathers. It was as visible as a ketchup splotch on a bright white T-shirt. Of course the clubs were all male and interconnected, from the board on down to management. They were well ensconced, well entrenched, and, I suppose, handsomely rewarded with "bucks" and perks.

What was the club atop this bank like?

They looked the same, in their mid-fifties, with slightly gray peppered hair, slicked back with a splash of *Vitalis*. You could tell who dyed their hair black. It resembled the jet-black shine of a black crow. Navy blue or dark gray pin stripe suits were the order of the day with white French-cuffed shirts. They fussed over their gold cuff links and pocket hankies while chomping on the ubiquitous cigar. On the rare occasion that one or two came down from their perch, to stroll a bank floor, they did so with dapper and panache.

What's with bank culture where managers are always in meetings, meetings, and more meetings?

The CEO reigned in his executive suite, equipped with an armada of immediate reporting managers, some fixers and troubleshooters, others heading up large divisions. They seemed to play up to the CEO, so much so that any subtlety was "thrown to the wind." Large division managers had other managers beneath them and under those, yet other layers of managers.

Just sitting at my desk, those MBA ruminations of mine, regarding big business models, would come to the forefront. I'd begin to telescope out what this bank could become if it grew into a monstrous brontosaurus.

How many fixers, troubleshooters and managers would need to exist, if this was all larger scale? How many private jets would need be deployed for managers to whisk around the world to stop by an office or two to say "hi" — at shareholder expense to maximize shareholder equity or someday make it even fizzle!

And how would people feel working within these structures?

Perhaps they'd feel like me, the poor lowly vassal doing the work, waiting to collect a miniscule year-end bonus, based on the most obscure of formula, one related to my desk row, within that pecking order.

Could this model someday grow to resemble the Egyptian pyramids, to rival even those of *Giza*? What would the apex look like? Could it grow with the size of the whole pyramid, such that the inner sanctum, surrounding the CEO, would be like an ever-rippling, ever-growing circle of manager bodyguards collecting some serious cash as a result of all this growth?

And who'd ever notice or even keep track of millions splattered, here and there, layers deep, even hundreds of millions, with a moat protecting them all. "Catch'em," those millions, lost and buried in those billions of revenue from growth!

Let's fast forward to 2008.

What is it that so many managers managing mismanaged financial institutions, collecting millions, within a mismanaged financial system, needing a multi-trillion taxpayer-funded bailout, really do?

I pick up *The Wall Street Journal* on July 31, 2009. The front-page headline story grabs my attention, Bank Bonus Tab: $33 Billion (By Susanne Craig and Deborah Solomon). While nine banks reported 2008 combined losses of some $100 billion, near $33 billion in bonuses were paid out in 2008. The nine banks received our bailout monies.

𝄞

A good grooming in basics is what I got at Continental Bank. Debt is deadly if not properly deployed. If debt backs shaky assets, watch out.

Lending requires principles and a sticking to those principles. Running a bank is not that complex, if one stays true to being a bank in the first place. Establish sound lending principles, implement and supervise, and grow for the right reasons. Bad lending standards and practices can lead to bad loans, which can seriously injure bank capital. If we experiment with new and fancy, well then risk assessment is of upmost importance. I come back to our shepherds. They have a big job to do as it affects us all.

Hanky-panky within some of the clubs, between boards and managements, let's not be fooled into thinking it doesn't exist. As a young rookie, I had a sneaky feeling that it'd be a toilsome task to penetrate a cloistered world of reshuffling and recycling for decades to come; with the seemingly fuzzy movement between the political and business worlds. They keep each other company, I suppose.

I sure hope in the meantime, like the bank of my childhood, the lantern's burning in a way that cares for our financial system, the backbone of our economy. In a simple world, a flub-up or two might not show up, but watch out if ambitions fly in a direction to grow ever bigger with more complex products and markets. It might just show up a thing or two.

Turns out that the most sought after commercial lending spots during my training program became minefields. Some shady lending practices were discovered within that oil and gas division. Apparently, a few loan officers got a bit sloppy or perhaps even knowingly strayed from those all too important lending principles.

An astute female loan officer discovered the problems in that oil and gas division. It took numerous attempts before anyone even listened. Rumor has it that a little "mind your own business" was at play. She persevered.

The subsequent loan debacle within the oil and gas division, (notably referred to as the Penn Square crisis), simmered and then grew big, eventually collapsing Continental Bank. It shook the financial system.

Oklahoma City-based Penn Square Bank engaged in risky energy loans, turbo charging its growth during the Texas oil boom in the late 1970s and early 1980s. Not so responsible lending practices collapsed Penn Square, shown up as the oil boom neared its apex. Continental Bank, on its own growth trajectory, wrote off some $500 million in loans purchased from Penn Square. Some purebred stallions were fired. This mare survived as the crisis unfolded.

Survive I did, gaining a little wisdom. It just so happened that this astute female loan officer was my training program mentor. Stand up for what's right is what she taught me. Through her example, I catalogued.

The $500 million loan write-off was considered monumental at the time, triggering concerns about a run on Continental Bank. In many respects, I view it as a smaller scale microcosm, of what would someday play out on a much larger scale. A chiseling of sound lending principles coupled with failure to control risk, amidst growth, led to the Bank's eventual demise.

It calls into question management; it calls into question whether bank regulators have the capacity to adequately assess risk within a financial institution. And, what if products and markets grow complex, and banks grow big, could regulators and policy makers even put their arms around it all to make sound choices? To what extent should a financial institution be allowed to grow, as a matter of policy, if it can create systemic risk or spillover into the whole economy?

Hence, the notion of too-big-too-fail was already on the radar.

What does this teach us?

We come back to the basic principles of free market capitalism. Being responsible in the pursuit of profit increases our chances for success over the long run. "Bailout" is anathema to capitalist principles.

You know, people are people. As a child I was taught that leaders should be held to higher standards. And yet, wrong choices occur at every level of an organization all the way up. If standards are compromised, that's a problem as standards may cease to exist. That may endanger a system, make it corrupt. If compromised standards persist for a sustained period of time, it may cause huge problems down the line. "Kicking the barrel" can only go so long, before it starts rolling back. And then, like anything else, we need to deal with it.

Behavior matters. A first-hand example in a mentor taught me just that, the importance of standing up, courage in action.

Truth's the lynchpin. How many of you feel the same?

It makes any relationship and any system work. It's like glue. When Ralph Waldo Emerson once said,

"The greatest homage to truth is to use it," the man knew what he was talking about. I've the *Kissy* doll incident of my childhood days to remind me as well.

Unmoored in truth, one no longer has a mooring. Shipwrecked is what happens when the storms come, causing confusion amidst all the destruction, as one may take others down. And all that wasted energy to fix what one shouldn't have been doing in the first place. Be out in the storm unmoored.

Life with Option B didn't turn out to be so bad. A few little extras were thrown into the teaching pot. Take every opportunity as it comes with an open mind. Sometimes what doesn't seem like it'll work becomes an important stepping-stone. Just by being in the game, things happen. Opportunities are always around us. It's a question of attitude.

Serendipity knocked on my door, one day, after the two year or so percolation. I got a call from my Sherpa, who left a message with my assistant at work. I took the day off to be with my son. Thumpity-thump went my heart, as the message was telegraphed my way.

Returning the call, I hear those wanting words, "I think I found a way for you to get into Goldman." I just knew it. I'm on my way to Wall Street!

The Investment Bank, Goldman Sachs 1983 to 1985

Swinging on a swing in the park is what my son and I were doing the day the call came in. The head of a Goldman division was in search for an individual to be his project person, a "jack-of-all-trades." My Sherpa thought I'd be perfect for the job. Knowing how hungry I was to get in the door of a Wall Street investment bank, he wondered if I might have interest.

"Are you kidding?" my first thought.

What he didn't know was that I was halfway into my suit already. I pounced on the opportunity. Look, even though my heart was still set on entering one of those prestigious sales and trading training programs, I'd figure it out later. This was the time to just get in the door. I set up an interview right away.

So, where on Wall Street did I ultimately want to end up and what went into the thinking process?

Not investment banking (the deal origination side) as it demands incredibly long hours and a great deal of travel. I had a family. A spot like those alpha males on that frenetic trading desk at Goldman Sachs was more like it.

Why?

Being a salesperson, a broker, fit my personality. Looking into the future, I'd lasso those workdays into the hours the market was open, once those initial few learning years were clocked. Markets close at 3:00 p.m. Central Time and back home with my children I'd be, right when they come home from school. Getting in any door, even the back door, of a top-notch investment bank, was a good first step. From there, I'd shimmy my way towards my goal.

Decades ago, the little girl with her prayer book had to keep much in mind. My goodness, I felt so confused back then, but those simple lessons stuck with me over a lifetime. Those little things we learn in childhood come back to help us along the way. As parents, sometimes we feel overwhelmed in raising children and working. But, know that what we teach them matters.

Getting into Wall Street took tenacity and patience. Surviving was simply Darwinian. I've often wondered how I persevered. I think it's because I was pickled in a childhood jar with a good combo of juices; ones that gave me faith and grounding from which came patience and the ability to survive adversity.

Eye-popping setbacks, a searing personal heartache and dealing with a clubby world, may have slowed me down here and there, but didn't stop me from going where I needed to go. I just felt a pull, something inside, to be in this business and to endure. All along, I knew it was for something else, that it wasn't my end-point. I braved jagged terrains, as I felt guided to keep walking and climbing. And so I did.

I had a strawberry garden as a child and you know how exciting it is for a child to grow strawberries. Something that one buys in a store can actually grow right in a backyard in a city.

It was a small patch, about 2 feet by 2 feet. I felt like I owned a little piece of property. Daily, I gave my garden a light sprinkle, appropriately adjusting the water flow on the spray of the green hose. That hose never did get a rest, as I'd even mischievously sneak up and spray one of my siblings. I'd let not a weed get in the way of bringing those sweet strawberries to fruition. It's the care and respect for something that makes all the difference when it comes to end product.

Tending that garden and practicing piano taught

me persistence and how to work hard. I came to respect the process, giving it, its due. The next several years taught me lessons that continued to lay the foundation for a professional life and way of being within the financial world, as I continued to connect those dots.

Connect I would. We lined up dominoes decades ago, ones that would ultimately set the stage for our current financial crisis. Each new decade brought government policy decisions, regulatory changes, market developments, technological advancements and cultural shifts. We were presented with choices as individuals and institutions.

Isn't every moment of life, every choice, like a trade?

There are two sides. If one pushes it, another might get hurt. If one seeks balance, both parties benefit. The whole has a greater chance of being sound. We're presented with those trades as we walk through life, and at those crossroads how do we choose?

Do we just go about life ripping off our neighbor or taking an easy ride? Or do we each assume responsibility to contribute to our country, to make it strong?

We can no longer afford to think parochially.

I think about *Romus* and *Romulus* suckling off the *She-Wolf.* You know, when the government gives, it doesn't come free. If too many suckle off the system, imagine where it all ends up. The *She-Wolf* grows exhausted, eventually running out of milk.

Little wonder that accumulated rip-offs made for a very big Rip-Off. It culminated in the onset of our financial crisis. Like a meteor, the resultant explosion in debt is coming our way with such impact.

Trades are all around us.

As a world, do we get along or fight?

As a government, do we rule with the interests of the nation first or that of self?

As a financial institution, is it profit at any cost or is it profit that takes into account the human?

As an individual, are we guided by a conscience, common sense, or by what we can get away with?

Do we stop and think about consequences as citizens, do we help others along the way or do we just charge ahead in a vacuum?

Choices and actions set a stage, a performance to make.

I remember the birth of the Internet. My children were young then. I deliberately made a choice to have no connection in our home.

Why?

I didn't feel like bringing the whole world into our cozy little hamlet. I wanted my children to explore the world, step by step, gradually with me doing the teaching. I followed the footsteps of my own childhood.

This newly discovered world, a fathomless frontier, was yet untested, but with potential to someday alter how we relate to each other as human beings. I wonder if Christopher Columbus was a little cautious when he first set foot on the shores of the New World.

We introduced something new into our lives that would someday have widespread ramifications, simply because of its reach and rapidity. Imagine how lives, livelihoods, and whole industries have since been transformed.

Whenever I sat down at the piano with a new

piece to learn, I'd quietly reflect upon how I would approach it's mastery; first the restraint and then the proper engagement. Progress towards instantaneity may not necessarily be true human progress.

Carte blanche acceptance of a new untested world within the confines of my home caused me discomfort. Understanding human nature and more so, my children, made the choice. Children may do dangerous things with tools, if not properly supervised. No doubt my children balked at the idea of not having the Internet or cable in the house. Riding their bikes to the library to use the Internet didn't harm them.

Choices make a difference when we deal with new tools. Do we choose to apply appropriately or misapply and do we think about consequences?

Someday soon the world would change, two worlds would co-exist, one real and one virtual. Capitalism would quickly jump on to the bandwagon to create products and industries within this world. Two worlds would someday influence each other and intersect.

Witness the companies spawned during the Internet revolution in the late 1990s. Some developed enormous capitalizations merely based on promises of future profits, profits that never materialized. Many eventually went out of business while some flourished. Price/Earnings ratios (P/Es) in the hundreds — way outside the norm — were used as a basis for investing. Yet, investors accepted *carte blanche* the introduction of such untraditional tenets of investing.

Excesses ended with the Nasdaq's near 40% collapse. The Nasdaq was created back in 1971 as the world's first electronic stock market, by technological advances that would someday alter the whole financial industry. The stock market collapse and the fallout from September 11, 2001, set the stage for a liquidity boom, engineered to stem an economic downturn. Easy credit put our financial crisis into motion. In averting a recession in the early 2000s, rather than allowing the natural economic forces to play out, perhaps we set the stage for bigger problems down the line.

Technological advancements would invariably push us into new frontiers. They'd someday enable all sorts of engineering, whether it'd be financial, genetic, or any other kind. Imagine the extent to which our lives could be altered, the limitless possibilities.

What of the consequences?

Let's fast forward to 2007, the onset of our financial crisis. Financial engineering facilitated the creation of complex securities so as to create triple-A (the highest investment rating) securities out of subprime mortgages and say even "liar" loans. "Liar" loans were made without verification of income, assets or employment, sometimes referred to as "low or no doc" loans. Little wonder that we created the "toxic." The word alone comes from the Latin *toxicum*, which means poison.

Trillions in toxic assets ultimately created a crisis. What are they?

They are both real estate loans (on bank books) and securities backed by loan portfolios (held by banks and other investors). The loans were originated in non-traditional and sketchy ways; many at the very apex of the real estate boom, the 2005-2007 period.

Toxic assets, lodged on the balance sheets of our

banks, obstructed credit flow into our near $14 trillion annual economy. The consumer makes up two thirds of the economy. One may well imagine the impact on business as consumer spending retrenches. Let's say a trillion of spending goes out of the economy. Businesses on the other side don't get the intake. They may shutter. It puts our livelihoods at risk.

Job loss sets a negative feedback loop into motion; consumers spend less, businesses lose sales and lay-off workers. Hence both may be unable to pay their mortgages and other debt, which then hits bank capital, further obstructing credit flow.

Did we try to convince ourselves that by packaging all sorts of loans together into new securities, slicing and dicing, some loans based on faulty premises from the get go, we could create newly "engineered" securities that were near riskless? What basis did the credit rating agencies use to assign triple-A ratings to securities created this way?

The ability to create complex securities eventually masked true reality in its application.

Some securities were even priced to financial models of our own making rather than current market prices where securities can be bought and sold. It's like fantasy. True value is more likely to show up in a market rather than in modeling within a financial laboratory.

Why did we price securities mark-to-model?

How else to price a created asset that may not be tradable, built in a financial laboratory, something with so many underlying variable loans in it, where value may become uncertain so quickly. Models rely on assumptions that may go awry in a human world.

There may not even be a real functioning market where prices could be realistically set. Rarely tradable assets are rarely tradable for a reason.

We let go of sound ways of lending, investing and pricing. It became an "accepted norm."

Technology accelerates everything as it collapses time; the exponential rate at which markets grow, the amount of money that could be made. Did we recklessly squeeze decades of growth and profit within the financial world into this last decade just because we could?

We may view financial engineering from the standpoint of technological engineering in car making. If we use technology in a way to make cars that accelerate to 300 miles an hour, we court disaster if placed in the wrong hands. I'm even thinking what's the point of such creation in the first place.

Financial engineering and debt were tools within the financial world managements used to push profits. Tools are not so much the issue. It's the envelope within which they find themselves. If managements are highly incentivized to the short-term, then it's within human nature to turbo charge growth and profits at any cost to that short-term, if unbridled by ethics and a robust regulatory framework. Bonuses are keyed off of growth and profitability.

If managements aren't careful about risk or are mesmerized by the razzmatazz of financial wizards, it'll trickle throughout the organization. Competing profit divisions within financial institutions may push it too as they myopically focus on generating short-term profit. Some market participants may not have the benefit of experience and longevity within the industry to have a frame of reference. The whole organization may end up getting carried away as it responds to distorted incentives.

The more innovative we become, the more behavior and ethics matter. Being inside the system, I'm not so sure that the financial world we've created can even be fully regulated. It would require a coordinated and centralized, anticipatory and nimble regulatory army, one that is a match for Wall Street. What's the likelihood of that happening?

We know there's disconnect between the archaic "out-of-synch" regulatory framework and the adroitness of Wall Street now enabled by technological speed. Because of this conundrum, it behooves us to look at behavior.

Can we afford as a nation not to pay attention to underlying behavior of market participants and those who regulate them?

I don't think we can. The bubble culminating in the 2007 onset of the financial crisis was no ordinary bubble in scale and reach. It cloaked us with trillions more debt as a nation, which in turn creates deep structural problems within our economy. The egregious 2009 deficit and the dislocation within the economy that the crisis created will ripple for maybe decades. We've not dealt with multi-trillion deficits before. It is foreboding. Servicing interest on the debt takes away monies for other basic needs.

I believe in incentivized compensation for performance as it motivates, but it works when those being incentivized behave. If they don't, then we rely on our regulatory bodies to protect the system, but is that even possible given the speed with which markets move and develop?

I speak from decades of personal experience as regards the importance of behavior. I was a commission-based broker. There were products I simply chose not to sell, regardless of fat commissions and/or pressure to sell them. Without an ethical framework, big money clouds and distorts business judgment.

I find intriguing a December 18, 2008 *New York Times* article entitled, Wall St. Profits Were a Mirage, But Huge Bonuses Were Real (By Louise Story). It delves into how big bonuses based on short-term profits encouraged traders to take undue risk to generate them. Hence, one can argue that they were generated in a way that made them unreal or unsustainable. In turn, risk managers and managements turned a blind eye to risk as their compensation was linked to short-term profits as well.

In a November 23, 2008 *New York Times* article entitled, Citigroup Pays for a Rush to Risk (By Eric Dash and Julie Creswell), the writers further explore the failure in risk management as the emphasis on growth and short-term earnings for personal gain took precedence. Accounting gimmickry enabled dodgy assets to be moved off the bank's books, freeing up capital to allow it to grow even bigger.

An April 30, 2009 *Bloomberg* update entitled, FASB "Close" on Off-Balance-Sheet Change, Herz Says – Update 1 (By Ian Katz), touches upon how bankers generated profits through the creation of off-balance sheet vehicles, some of which were conduits to disguise that securities were backed by bad loans.

We called this "fudging" in grade school. In the adult world, deliberate deception is called fraud. It feels *Enronesque* on a grand scale.

Let's look at the fallout. The cumulative effect collapsed the financial system and tattered the economy leading up to multi-trillion bailouts. Markets and credit froze. Whole markets that worked for years were wiped off the map as were the livelihoods of hundreds of thousands within the industry.

This spilled into the real economy with the destruction of over 7 million livelihoods. Line up 7 million people and those dependent upon them. Job loss continues at an alarming pace. With it come more home foreclosures and homelessness. Near $11 trillion in wealth vaporized out of homes and assets.

When we see numbers like this, it gives the financial industry a bad rap. Financial professionals who do a good job very obviously exist. But, it's hard for the general public, understandably so, to see the good parts of the business. Hence, the actions of few may spoil things for those within the industry who had nothing to do with the making of the crisis in the first place. It creates a reactive imbalance from many directions that may stifle entrepreneurship.

Our states and municipalities face budget crises from resultant revenue depletion. We'll see taxes rise. Things will start to look not so nice. Stressed welfare services may eventually collapse as the numbers of working-age unemployed and the indigent grow. Make no mistake, it takes time, but the devastation is manifesting itself in ominous ways throughout the country.

I came across an August 1, 2009 headline article in *The New York Times* entitled, Alabama Area Reeling in Face Of Fiscal Crisis (By Shaila Dewan). It delves into the economic fallout within Jefferson County. Jefferson County can no longer afford to bury public nursing home indigent patients; to feed children in their custody as cafeteria staff was laid off.

Let's go a step further. The problems were exacerbated by corruption surrounding a sewer project, and failed exotic municipal bond deals with swaps cooked up by Wall Street. Imagine the lines for municipal services of any sort when two thirds of municipal workers are laid off as the County runs out of money.

I am reminded of the family stories I grew up with. Within the former Soviet Union peopled waited in line for hours just to get a ticket to buy food. They waited in line, yet again for hours, to buy food. After waiting in line for hours, some were turned away as food ran out. Resources were deployed from productive uses for society to support an inefficient bureaucratic system and the huge arms build-up at the time.

My relatives lived within a system where all were supposed to be equal, but ended up within a system where unhappiness was shared equally by the masses, with no incentive to work and be motivated. Those on the "in" lived by another standard, indifferent to the population at large.

Where will our resources now go?

More Americans find themselves in a state of insolvency with no jobs, vaporized retirements and homes underwater, within a nation borrowing heavily just to pay its bills. Some older Americans seek work as their retirements and home values cratered. They trusted. They may not have skills to find jobs in which they can take pride. Some may even have compromised health and yet need to work.

If we don't truly reform the system, are we laying the seeds for a much larger paralysis or is Jefferson County already a premonition of things to come?

The potential for fantasy with engineering of any sort is limitless, as are the consequences. We can convince ourselves of anything for profit or power, and make it an "accepted norm."

Let's now go back to the call from my sure-footed Sherpa in 1983. I set up an interview, with the head of Goldman's asset management division with haste. Only there wasn't much of an asset management division back then. It only housed three money funds.

Asset management, what is it?

These divisions manage customer assets for a fee, on a discretionary basis; meaning the investment manager is responsible for making the investment decisions. In contrast to brokerage, which entails the buying and selling of securities for a commission with customer approval.

Fee-based asset or wealth management divisions at the time resided largely with money managers like investments advisors, bank trust departments and the like. People used mutual funds for their investing needs.

Goldman's asset management division, coined The Goldman Sachs Funds Group, was the stepchild or the "ugly duckling" of Goldman Sachs, back then.

Why?

Wall Street investment banks were all about brokerage, the mainstream business, and that's what I had my heart set on. Turns out the "ugly duckling" would someday grow into a swan, as asset management became a top growth priority for Wall Street. This division would someday house hundreds of billions under management.

So what was the interview like?

The Funds Group, located in a separate, somewhat run-down building, is just a few blocks away from Goldman's main offices in the Sears Tower. I do a double take, as I meet my future boss. He looks like a character from a Charles Dickens novel, in his mid-fifties with hair parted in the middle, long gray sideburns. Back a few centuries in time, I wasn't expecting to go. A cigar and twang-like voice greet me. How fitting, cigars and Wall Street, given the latter's penchant for puffery.

The office is cast in beige-like tone, all the way down to his bland *Triscuit*-colored suit. A gold-initialed ring adorns his pinky finger. He's wearing a French-cuffed shirt with sleeves, two inches too short for the right look. Some of you might recall the oatmeal-colored shirts from the 1960s. That's it. "It" is what he's wearing with a few small holes from cigar burns speckled throughout that shirt. Metaphors roll out of his speech that would elicit outrage from many an ethnic group today.

His ambulant corner office houses a stodgy cherrywood executive desk, equipped with moldings, outdone by the oversized leather chair, the kind that swings back and forth. Two big wing chairs, upholstered in taupe brocade, are in front of the desk at a slanted angle.

Clipper ship paintings hug the walls, ones draped in beige wallpaper, somewhat peeling at the seams. A wilted plant in the corner clearly suffocates from cigar smoke. Venetian blinds bend in every direction from the pummel-like dusting by the night cleaning crew. They're not straightened out, nor would ever be, by this somewhat absent-minded man, who sits at his desk working all day in a haze of smoke. The light barely breaks through the few open blinds. My emblazoned image of Wall Street is shattered.

I get it right away. He's a relic of the old Wall Street guard. Perhaps my own somewhat old-fashioned bent created an instant chemistry between us, bridging the older with the younger.

Five minutes into the interview, his wife comes into the picture. She's terrific by his account. He says something about retreads. Retreads are not tires, I learn. It means remarried a second time. I come from a family of long-married folks. Divorce was taboo, a hush-hush kind of thing when I was little. She's a vivacious Chicago socialite and, according to his account, a repository of social graces. I could tell where all this was going.

"Hmm...now if I hire this woman, will she fit in with my wife?"

I'm to learn from him, not her, but I take it all in

stride. That's what it was like then. The office environment had a family feel. Something I'd come to terribly miss as decades progressed.

He doesn't ask me too much about myself, occasionally casting an eye on my shipshape resume. He's too busy talking about himself. That's what the guys were like then. Their worlds took front stage. With interview sewn up, I'm to show up for work in two weeks. He assumed I'd say yes and how right he was.

As I walk away, I muse, "Is this man's eccentricity reason for why the Funds Group is housed in a separate building from the main offices of Goldman Sachs?"

I liked my new boss. Underneath rough edges, he seemed terribly in love with his wife and wasn't afraid to show it. It signaled a refreshing goodness about him.

So what was it that I learned from this walking history book of the previous few decades on Wall Street?

My new mentor was a visionary, whose views were not shared by others then, yet he telescoped out a vision of the future for me. Under his tutelage, I blossomed, took a peek at every nook and cranny of the industry. Within this budding division, I focused on marketing and researching new mutual fund product ideas. My office was just down the hall from his corner suite. His random way of assigning projects with a turnaround time of "now" made me think three steps ahead. My proclivity for efficiency took on yet another dimension.

He's smart and engaging. His company I thoroughly enjoy. We knit a close working relationship where I come to know what he's about to say before he even says it. Every assignment comes with a history lesson, whether I like to listen or not. I pretend I do, when it comes to be a bit much. He reminds me of my Lithuanian teacher, who taught me history based on her own personal experiences.

Tempest comes to mind when I think about this mentor of mine. That which he believes in, he vociferously expresses, in between cigar puffs. He champions the idea of expanding beyond the mere three money fund offerings housed within this group, to develop a family of funds, a broad array of mutual fund offerings.

He'd talk about technology someday making so much obsolete. The traditional brokerage model would become vulnerable to commission discounting. Diversification of the business mix would be necessary, away from dependency on trading and brokerage revenues. Asset management provided more steady fee-based income streams.

I observed many a tempestuous conversation regarding the subject. A personal crusade to move beyond money funds into more diversified mutual funds didn't convince the higher ups at the time. I admired his tireless resolve. As the future unfolded, one he so presciently forecast, the asset management business exploded on the Street over the coming decades. Not only within banks and the Wall Street investment houses, but in conjunction with the growth of new financial players, like the hedge funds. They'd come to define the new financial playground.

I'm a student, always, not only of fact, but also of human nature. At this man's doorstep, I watch

Shakespeare in play, the political sparring. Egos just grow bigger over the decades. I am reminded of my high school years. Remember the "who's got the good looking girlfriend and hottest car?" "Bucks" and power tower on Wall Street. Top dogs compete over such trivia. I think running a financial institution has not so much to do with brilliance. Tried and true common sense need not be trivialized. I think self-importance gets in the way. It may take one down a dangerous path.

What drives youngsters to pick up a book of matches and play with it? Is it that they don't understand the risks and consequences or do they choose to ignore them, thinking they won't materialize, blinded by their own childish limitations or ambitions?

𝄞

It's my second grade playground and it's a really hot day, the sticky kind.

I'm taking a break from running around, being the active type. I'm a little sweaty with red, red cheeks. I sit down on the bench. I begin to watch and think.

With their eyes on the prize, to be first on the slide, they "threw caution to the wind." Like rapacious wolves eyeing their meat, out of control consumed with the sight. Once they took hold of the slide, they forgot about anyone else, but fun with their friends.

What a ball they had as they hung off the sides of the slide, disregarding the rules, making up their own along the way. They'd make sure that no one else got in on their game, their power to retain. If anyone outside their pack came down the slide, why they'd walk up the slide, keeping their self-interested agendas in mind. What a problem they'd cause. If held to account, they'd point the finger at someone else. Imagine that!

Is this how we build fiefdoms?

Dominoes lined up decades ago to alter the landscape for the Wall Street investment banks. Like the dinosaurs, powerful and thought to be indomitable, what is it that eventually changed the terrain for the major Wall Street investment banks?

His smoke-filled office resembles an oatmeal bowl in color. I don't miss the cigar smell of my suits hanging in my closet, but I miss the world of long ago, the warm and open exchanges, the teaching. When he asked me a question, it was at face value, no need to wonder what the motive behind it all was.

Things were simple and easy back in the 1980s. A broker was a broker, as the word brokerage implies, not a fancy product wealth gatherer with a toolbox of Alternative Investments, the catchall category for fancy investments. We didn't have structured notes, credit derivatives, products with so many bells-and-whistles.

I lived in a world of stocks and bonds. One bought something at a lower price and sold it higher, homegrown true free market capitalism. The spread or profit was the money one made by buying and selling real stuff. If one bought a security, one would know who would pay one back.

My colleagues back then seemed happy making a decent living that way. Engineering profits from exotica, like exotic derivatives was not even on the radar.

What was investing like then?

The stock market was viewed as a conduit for the investor to own a piece of American business. The investing mentality was longer term in nature, more fundamental, rather than trading-oriented.

We didn't have today's hyperactive markets, with rapid-fire volatility. Quantum leaps in technological sophistication are taking us forward, we are taught to believe. I often refer to today's investing as video game investing but with fancy computers and proprietary trading programs. Whoever can push those buttons faster with the most sophisticated controller, wins.

Technology had not yet infiltrated the markets as now, where we have constant streaming news and information flow 24/7. We indulge in our devices, bombarded with data such that nothing seems new anymore. Hidden investment gems of the olden days find no shelter. Investing has become more about who's equipped with the most powerful technological tools.

The more the elasticity of time and information dwindle, the more the push to new frontiers. It was in the opening space, where information flow wasn't instant, that the old investing opportunities used to lie, where the old brokerage world of the 1980s lived.

While instantaneous information flow initially created opportunities for the average investor, over time I think it actually diminished true investing opportunities for that investor. Markets eventually morphed into casinos where powerful computers play.

Financial institutions increasingly came to rely on fancy technology for trading profits. Those with most ample resources pay millions to attract financial wizards. Fancy algorithmic trading programs that outsmart humans, even less powerful computers, are then deployed to produce millions, even billions for their financial patrons. It feels like a *James Bond* movie to me. You know, the moneyed with the power bug desire to dominate the world.

Have you heard of "high-frequency" equity trading?

It's trading powered by secretive codes run on powerful computers with capacity to transmit astronomical volumes at lightening speed, across stocks, markets and multiple exchanges. Visualize computers scouring the globe for fractional arbitrage opportunities. Think of it as high volume trading done super fast by computers within milliseconds to capture mere fractional profit opportunities across multiple venues. "High-frequency" trading makes up near half the daily trading volume of the US stock market. Meanwhile, you're probably thinking some financial institutions are mythical moneymakers, right?

They're "ringing in the cash register" from "high-frequency" trading. To think that galactic video game conquerors have infiltrated our markets. How unearthly that human beings suction hundreds of millions, even billions, on the heels of powerful computers. A billion made or lost in one place may just come out of another, as we are one world.

Looks to me like a two-tiered market, the empowered and us. Not a chance that an individual can keep up with split-second thinking and processing of powerful computers. Machines are pretty good at mimicking what used to be human trading on an accelerated and grand scale.

The old-fashioned providers of liquidity to our equity market were the traditional floor brokers and market makers. With their demise, proprietary trading desks of banks (banks trading for their own portfolios) and hedge funds, for example, have become the major liquidity drivers for our equity market. Imagine the power and control.

Institutions who've amassed the largest sums of money not only influence, but also seem to now dominate and control markets. Proprietary trading desks and fast-money funds fly in and out with their fancy computer acrobatics. They may drive and set asset prices at non-true value levels, swinging prices up and down. Add debt to the picture and all the more the distortion. Think about the potential for manipulation, colloquially called "pump and dump." Who gets hurt in the end?

Imagine; computer programs, not human traders, may create frenzy in asset prices that affect our lives. Commodity prices reached dizzying heights back in July 2008, before the stock market collapsed. It caused oil to spike and worldwide food riots. Policy makes a difference.

Today's faster and cheaper might just make us human beings obsolete someday, as computers rather than humans continue to trade with one another. That can be dangerous in its consequence, even for the mere individual who tries to play the markets.

And that's not all. We need now worry that rogue

traders may set off commodity price distortions that affect our daily lives. A July 3, 2009 *Financial Times* article entitled, Rogue oil broker triggered price spike (By Javier Blas), highlights how a rogue trader triggered the mid-2009 rise in oil prices.

You know how it goes. One action like that may set off a powerful computer feeding frenzy further escalating prices.

We may now even have to deal with invisible bank robbers who may become lethal with technology at their disposal. One could then conjecture that nowadays assets are subject not only to investment risk, but also stealth risk.

The term, "rigged" market, is making its way into our popular culture more than I'd like to hear. If one makes a stock investment as an individual based on sound thinking, one might even get singed as those in the know may create or engineer another reality. Can we even call this "our" market?

Free markets are meant to be free for all, not a free-for-all for those with money muscle to buy powerful tools. At the very heart of capitalism is competition. Codified in the rules of our markets are principles like fair and equal access. True value is determined when we have many participants within a market with a diversity of backgrounds and viewpoints, not just the empowered.

Do you have superfast powerful computers with fancy proprietary software sitting in your living room?

I don't.

Technology enables yet another trading practice called "flash trading." It gives those with fancy computers the ability to buy and sell stocks with split-second advantage before information is even made public to the broader market. This feels like the secrecy of my *Kissy* doll swoosh decades ago. Investor orders are "flashed" to select traders with superfast computers, a fraction of a second before it's made available to the rest of us; on our US exchanges, mind you. Does making money this way seem right to you?

The SEC is presently looking into "flash trading." Some exchanges may voluntarily give up the practice, but I'm wondering what else is out there that we don't know about.

Technology collapses time, but the mighty moneyed find ways to prosper between the cracks with complexity and secretive software. I don't know about you, but anything with complexity and secrecy on Wall Street makes me nervous. Sometimes it's hard to figure out just what is going on within our markets.

I remained puzzled during the April-May 2009 bank stress test period. All of a sudden, bank stocks ran up, some even with such ferocity. Then came billions in bank stock offerings to raise capital. What happened to toxic assets? Who kindles fires to maintain illusion?

With few dominating, just about any kind of market movement can be engineered, no?

The stock market is a reflection of collective consciousness. In its computerization, institutionalization, agitation, volatility and short-term nature, what is it telling us?

I think it's reflecting the trends taking place in our economy and society. Computerization in the markets facilitates marketplace distortions by the powerful if limits aren't set, generating casino-like compensation for few, at the expense of many. Institutionalization is what our corporate landscape (for example finance and healthcare) has morphed towards, with pyramid structures generating casino-like compensation for the few, yet again.

Sometimes, I feel inundated with agitating information, even with the sizzling and scandalous, don't you?

Scandals and investment scams have now become so ordinary in our daily news that it seems to desensitize us to its outrageousness, by its ever presence. Aren't you tired of hearing about corruption and fraud, even listening to the pontificating of those who presided over the making of a human crisis?

I'd rather have our news waves flow with the other force in the fairytale. When I keep hearing about how this and that executive or company misled the public, I have a hard time trusting it all. No amount of external regulation can stem a virus like this. One just doesn't know when the next shoe will drop. Yet the financial system relies on the need for seal-tight integrity.

Seeping through every cellular wall within us is osmotic information inundation. I don't think I want to know everything about everybody right when it happens. It gives me a headache. I even get confused when information is communicated. So many talk one on top of the other, like the *Tower of Babel.* The vivacious discussions even take me back to war movies of my childhood; only here we're using words rather than spears in the midst of a battle charge.

As I roll the film of my life in the financial world,

it feels like something changed this last decade. For lack of a better word, the "selfishness" astounds me; rogue traders, proliferation of investment scams, computer-triggered trading giving rise to commodity and asset price distortions that simply ignore the impact on humanity, the distortion of a loan packaging mechanism that facilitated the sale of dodgy assets to investors by "venerable" financial institutions. Then came bailouts in the trillions. So many walked away egregiously enriched crushing a nation with debt. Accountability?

Are opportunities in the markets increasingly diminished or not to be trusted, as we eliminate the natural out of our lives with man-made creations and yet, very naturally, we are human?

As a little girl, I once read that out of a simple "natural" mustard seed grew a mighty tree that endured. We can grow much without the much we think we need.

The movie *The Time Machine* comes to mind. It takes mankind through centuries, starting with the olden days all the way into a technologically advanced future only to return to a somewhat Stone Age existence through self-destruction.

How are we flying on the wings of innovation; where are they taking us?

Devices change how we relate to one another. They alter human interaction. In attempting to connect, I think they disconnect us from each other. Relationships are changing. Organizations are increasingly becoming isolative. Do devices create layers of processing, even an evolution of businesses to deal with the inefficiencies we've created?

Seems to me, in some cases, it was easier to operate in the world of time passed. What used to take a phone call and a few seconds, to say fix a simple fax machine, now requires the generation of layers of work tickets to be processed through yet another electronic channel. All this in-between stuff creates inefficiencies and actually slows productivity for some.

Are we undergoing a Darwinian-like evolution in displacing human character traits, replacing them with others?

Instantaneity breeds short-term orientation, the instant need for results and gratification. It even desensitizes us to the human. It spills into the way we look at life, the way we go about living our lives, the way we conduct business, how fast some desire to earn those millions, those billions. It affects how quickly we want to solve deep problems, like this financial crisis, one that doesn't necessarily have a short-term solution. Short cuts may be dangerous.

Are we thinking, giving thought to consequence or are we just accepting that which is getting pushed on to us *carte blanche?*

Back in the 1980s, our information feed was confined to the workday. We used the simple *Quotron*, a multiprocessor resembling a computer, that gave us stock quotes on line. We relied on the *Reuters* system for more comprehensive online market monitoring. *Bloomberg*, developed in the early 1980s, became the industry standard as Wall Street's multi-media market information service.

The mystery and fun were still in the game. Investors paid Wall Street investment banks and brokers for ideas and research. Technological advancements, decade to decade, were truly the double-edged sword that changed my world, as I knew it.

Technology eroded the traditional Wall Street brokerage model, the buying and selling of securities for a commission. Access and speed of information to the investor directly, price discovery and ease of trading made commission-based business ever less profitable, pushing Wall Street to find new ways to make money.

On the other hand, technology paved the way for the new ways of making money. It enabled the development of sophisticated program trading and financial engineering. It would lead to the explosive growth of complex investment products and markets, even facilitating the emergence of new financial players.

The future my boss and I talked about played out. Commission discounting took root. The traditional brokerage model came under siege, as the margin was increasingly taken out. Although, as an aside, within our current high-risk market environment, spread (the difference between where one buys and sells a security) has come back into the markets in a way it hadn't been in decades, if ever.

It wasn't just technology that would alter the world for the Wall Street investment houses. Competition from the banks was right around the corner.

How did it all happen?

The tug-of-war between commercial banks and Wall Street investment houses was some time in the making. Back in the 1960s banks were already lobbying Congress to enter the municipal bond business, the turf of Wall Street. Then in the 1970s, some Wall Street investment houses started offering money market accounts with check writing privileges, stepping on the turf of commercial banks.

There was plenty of business to go around, room for many to compete back in the 1980s. Maybe people were different. I don't know how some grew afflicted with a Caesar-like complex to become modern day conquerors vast, but they did. On to the scene came the aggressive banks, amassing an armada of banks within their fold. Smaller banks were gobbled up.

By now, you're probably asking why?

Was it to better serve you, or was it to compete in the global financial playground, or to create economies of scale to further trounce competition; was it merger fees or getting rich with profits from growth or was it simply *hubris?*

This *Little Red Riding Hood* has figured it out and soon you will too. The drool of conquerors never stops. Napoleon didn't stop at a nation or two either.

Some banks just wanted to get bigger, not just in their mainstream lending business, but through diversification into other financial services, even some of those not-to-be-touched speculative activities. The thinking goes like this, the greater the risk-taking the greater the potential for profit and reward.

Banks couldn't go speculative because of the Glass-Steagall Act. Now remember, the Act had a purpose, to keep banks and Wall Street separate in their activities. Think of it as a wall. Who'd want their bank to engage in financial speculation, bet with your money, right?

It could jeopardize bank capital and capacity to lend with implications for the broader economy. Hard to believe that a little coaxing of friends in high perches goes a long way to break down a boundary or two, but it apparently does. Back in the early 1990s, a major commercial bank convinced the Federal Reserve to allow it to nudge its way onto the turf of the Wall Street investment houses. This same bank would someday be at the heart of the development of the complex credit derivatives world. Our travels will take us to derivatives.

And so it happened. That commercial bank was one of the first to come back to underwriting stocks and bonds in decades. Congress repealed Glass-Steagall altogether in 1999. As I recall, the repeal had something to do with a mega-insurance company wanting to merge with yet another commercial bank. At that point, I started the countdown as to how long before divestiture or a "bust-up" would become a necessity.

Let's keep in mind that our forebears might have learned a thing or two from the Depression. Preservation of capital by banks for the purposes of lending and to protect deposits was essential to avoid future shocks to the economy. History repeats itself as mortal memory fades for expediency.

I often pondered if the "big bank" engineering marvel was constructed in a conference room. You know how it goes. A few congregate, then birth a nifty idea to make a lot of money from growth.

Banks, Wall Street brokerages and insurance companies had been "stepping on each others toes" already, for years. The repeal of Glass-Steagall made the creation of the too-big-to-fail financial institutions all the more possible. A tidal wave of consolidation unleashed ultimately creating the big diversified bank goliaths of today, involved in underwriting, brokerage and insurance. They spouted the cross-selling mantra — "We'll do it all!" with one-stop shopping.

The complete elimination of Glass-Steagall was a critical moment. It completely broke down the boundaries between Wall Street investment houses and banks, but the playing field was uneven.

Banks had access to cheap funding sources (through their vast deposit base) and a liquidity back-stop through the Federal Reserve discount window (where banks can borrow from the Federal Reserve). The Wall Street investment houses had neither. And yet, both came to compete in the same markets.

Banks had lower capital costs. Lower capital costs gave banks an edge, allowing them to be more competitive on say underwriting and deal pricing. It paved the way for what would someday be an inordinate amount of risk-taking and leveraging (taking on of debt) by the two as they competed in this uneven playing field. Leverage or debt is used to amplify profits.

As I sat at my trading desk watching this play out, I had a feeling that it was just a matter of time before banks would cause competitive distortions in the marketplace trouncing the Wall Street investment banks. The stage was set for the transformation of the financial services industry for decades to come.

Competitive forces set up a horserace between Wall Street investment houses and the big banks. It put pressure even on the small community banks. In order to grow, some became increasingly aggressive in taking on risk. Wall Street banks would eventually seek SEC approval in 2004 to raise leverage capacity 40 to 1 from their traditional leverage ratio of 12 to 1 (that means for every dollar of assets one can borrow up to 40 times that). I'm astounded that any management or board would allow such leverage.

With all this, the roll of the traditional broker transformed. The 1980s was the era of the "star" broker. During the late 1990s, Wall Street brokerages began to push brokers to become fee-based asset wealth gatherers rather than commission-based brokers. Gathering customer assets became the game in town for that steady fee-based income. It created a feeding frenzy amongst financial institutions to garnish assets. Banks and Wall Street investment houses vied for brokers with assets, paying handsome upfront bonuses for the brides with the best dowry.

The roll of the office manager transformed as the business changed. Recruiting supplanted mentoring. The organic — grow your own brokers — seemed to take too long in a world of instant and now.

Managers were increasingly paid not just on the production of the office, but on the number of new recruits. Brokers jumped from firm to firm for substantial upfront bonuses. Once contracts were up, some kept shuffling around. Institutions got on to that game. The contracts grew longer with more restrictions. Brokers were even pushed to work in teams. Securing assets for the institution became priority number one.

The star legendary broker of the 1980s who made it through that one last decade in the 1990s, lost "star" status. I feel "team" is proxy for the institution. We erected big, opaque financial pyramids, ones that would someday cause a problem or two.

Even with the too-big-to-fail issue in the forefront with our current financial crisis, some big banks grow bigger even still, feeding off the fallen. I find it puzzling, do you?

History is replete with conquerors colluding. They remove weakened competition and consolidate power by cherry-picking choice assets of the fallen, discounting the rest.

The powerful may dominate trading, asset gathering, control borrowing costs, fee setting and exert even more political influence. I'm thinking that a few financial oligarchies have clearly emerged as dominant in a democratic nation with a free market capitalist system. Fewer banks means more pricing power, maybe even bigger stakes down the line. Concentration of banking amongst few spells risk, control and power.

If the financial system is the backbone of the economy, does not common sense thinking call for diversification of banking amongst many rather than few to mitigate systemic risk?

I think so. Policy matters. Yet, the fantasy waltz

continues, but with fewer players. Fewer players may continue to cause competitive distortions in the marketplace.

Diminished competition enables record profits for those remaining, and that secures record bonuses. Debatable compensation structures, based on short-term profits, incentivized undue risk-taking in the first place. Stacking incentives to the short-term naturally fosters management of businesses to the short-term. It facilitates a "take it while you can mentality." What's really changed?

One may can even go so far as to say that big bank debt may be a safe investment as it carries with it an implicit or explicit government guarantee. We now have fewer even bigger players that the government could ill afford to let fail as they are too-big-to-fail. So, the taxpayer may continue to be on the hook for systemic risk. It's like having a contingent liability hanging over our heads. In the meantime, small banks are failing at an alarming rate as they too caught the growth bug deconstructing lending standards in order to grow.

I'm not impressed that few big banks make record profits. Afterall, competition is reduced, cost of funding is near zero with low interest rates and raising debt capital came with a government guarantee. With pricing power muscle, banks can take fat spreads, between where securities are bought and sold, as customer business needs to be done. Even those within the financial industry have taken notice as I took notice of a July 22, 2009 *Financial Times* article entitled, BlackRock chief attacks Wall

ST. banks' "luxurious" trading profits (By Henny Sender and Francesco Guerrera in New York).

There's yet another wrinkle. I came across an August 3, 2009 *Financial Times* article entitled, Wall St profits from Fed role (By Henny Sender in New York). In order to stabilize the financial system during the crisis, the Federal Reserve (the Fed) bought securities in massive quantity from banks. In other words, the Fed (in effect us the taxpayers) took securities on to its balance sheet to provide liquidity to the system.

It continues to do so. Think of the Fed as being a customer of Wall Street. The Fed announces which securities it's going to purchase ahead of time for the purpose of transparency. If banks know they have a ready buyer, think of the potential for trading profit. The article notes that the forum enables securities to be sold to the Fed even at inflated prices. Making profits trading with the government (in effect, us)?

You know what I think?

Institutions have gotten so big and opaque, markets so complex, that it feels out-of-control. First comes the simmer, then the bubble up, like those complex mortgage securities that buried bad loans. The toxic cookery or voodoo was some time in the making before the top came off the pot, scorching all of us. When we start down a path where we let go of principles and limits, anything goes and who knows where it all ends up.

Is this good for America?

For a moment, let's put aside the power and control over our lives that big conquerors bring. I think we let go of something within our work environments, perhaps basic human warmth. Imagine a land strewn with big institutions where we cease to feel and be valued as unique individuals.

This is not the America I grew up in. I was raised in an America with small and cozy efficient businesses in my neighborhood; where a proprietor did not make tens of millions, where customer service meant a human voice, not a machine; where short lines or no lines were *de rigueur;* where making an appointment took a minute, a simple phone call with a person, rather than a computer generating a chain of emails.

Someday what we are allowed to say or do as ordinary citizens may even be institutionalized. How does all this feel to you? What will our young people look forward to as they filter through pyramids or laterally slosh around within them, with little mentoring and movement, where advancement and reward exist for the few, those on the "in," atop the apex? Or are the young programmed to think that this way of being is *de rigueur?*

Well, let me tell the young folks, this is America founded on principles and ideals that aren't necessarily being upheld. I feel there's something quite amiss about a system that flushes the young and old.

Motivated people drive the economy through venues where they can blossom; venues that foster competitive drive with an opportunity for reward. Our people, over 300 million, can power the best economy in the world, but not through big inefficient structures and bureaucracy, where rewards are limited to few, holding back many.

Stars in the sky glisten every night. As a child, I'd try to reach them on my tippy toes. Who's clouding the skies for all those children to come?

Children thrive on dreams and seeing the stars in the sky. No matter what decade of life we're in, each one of us desires to be valued and to be of value to society. The pursuit of happiness is one of our "inalienable rights." It flourishes with hope and the ability to see a future.

I think about the family stories I grew up with. Within the Eastern European countries during the Communist era, massive bureaucratic structures ruled. Getting anything done was frustrating through layers of logjammed bureaucracy.

I don't think any one of us wants to feel like a robot, as worker or consumer, marching through big inefficient structures for all our one-stop shopping needs, from banking to healthcare to what next?

My life would become difficult in an institutionalized world. I'm used to the simplicity and warmth of the way it used to be. I liked walking into a small bank where the tellers knew me by first name. There's a reason why banks were called community banks. I liked my doctor knowing the history of my life and that of my children, the personal connection, the quality and accessibility of care, the freedom of choice. I liked making a phone call and talking to a human being.

I think the unbridled push for growth and profit created inefficient monstrosities, delivered into the hands of the government, some in need of bailout. Hence, a yet bigger government bureaucracy emerges spawning new departments with new regulations. We allowed faulty models to just grow bigger over time. One could argue that deep financial crises have the capacity to alter economic and political systems.

I've been in the business world for several decades, in effect running an entrepreneurial business within a larger structure. I'm all for small business as it is where true capitalism blossoms, where we as a people prosper. Pride of ownership and participation in the reward is the essence of unadulterated free market capitalism. Growth in the economy comes from entrepreneurship, small business and us simple hard-working folks, from the bottom up.

Policy makes a difference in protecting economic balance. I think about CIT and the company's difficulty during July 2009; no bailout. CIT serves small businesses. Small business provides about half the jobs in the private sector. Yet, big banks found government shelter through unprecedented backstops in the trillions. I'm not a fan of bailouts, mind you, but I'm trying to make sense of the selective pruning as to who lives (through bailouts), who dies.

Even some community banks that we're now shutting down, at an alarming rate, might have survived had big banks not trounced them, had this emphasis on growth been more balanced. As local banks close we may shut down the credit lifeline to small business.

Big banks eviscerated competition, even eliminated consumer choice. Corporate takeovers disrupt lives and take away livelihoods. Economic and societal imbalance follows. This financial crisis has shown that when allowed to run amok, big bank conquerors cause competitive distortions within the marketplace, even a ratcheting of risk-taking by the competition trying to survive. Unbridled growth has been a costly experiment to the citizenry, further polarizing our society. When few benefit at the expense of many, I, for one, think this is not true free market capitalism.

Let's fast forward to the present for a moment. I fell upon a June 3, 2009 article in the *Financial Times* entitled Lessons from the Rise and Fall of a carmaker (By John Kay). It relates to GM. It sheds light on the interplay between technology and growth. Technology enabled growth and mass production, but it took something away from workers feeling pride in product quality. Growth created layers of managers, spawning a complacent bureaucracy and competing fiefdoms. We all know the outcome, massive bailouts.

I think the GM example could be compared to what we've created in the financial industry.

Financial engineering enabled the mass offloading of risk through securitization that allowed banks to grow bigger. It encouraged, in part, a lack of concern for the financial products that were sold. Growth created layers of managers whose razzle-dazzle short-term bonuses, based on growth, fostered complacency when it came to risk management and risk mediation in the marketplace. The big diversified one-stop shopping model spawned too many profit and loss centers, competing fiefdoms. Generating short-term profit for personal gain trumped generating profit in a way that maximizes shareholder equity, maintains financial stability for a healthy economy and society.

What did we accomplish with, say, big auto and bank models?

I wonder if the interest of the consumer, amidst all the self-interest, was even in the equation.

Are big bank business models out of synchrony with true free market capitalism and the amorphous nature of life?

Imagine if a city crumbles, nature asserts itself. We find nature in the cracks and crevices of city streets. I've come to believe that true free market capitalism is in synchrony with life, when risk and responsibility rest with the purveyor of the product. It goes hand-in-hand with our basic human nature. It fosters vigilance in how the business is run and concern for the types of products sold. When we take out risk and responsibility, it fosters the opposite, even fraud and neglect.

Simple values, like responsibility and respect, matter. Simplicity may just be simple enough to keep us out of trouble. When we live in a growth economy, where profit trumps all (where financial institutions even manufactured complex fantasy product to drive growth and profit) we as individuals and investors, need to be vigilant.

I like to ask questions and be informed. I scour and question every fee that shows up on statements by financial service providers. Financial institutions make money off of us. So, think about how much power we as informed consumers and investors have.

I don't like debt, I don't like fees and I like to save. I'd rather pay in cash than use a credit card. I feel empowered when I say, "no thank you" to fee-laden services that are being sold.

I like my "ins" to equal "outs;" to live within my means, to simply take the responsibility to say "no." I keep extra cash in my checking account to avoid exploitative overdraft charges.

Basic family values — like honesty, sharing and respect for each other — transfer into society and how we run our institutions. Fall short on the most basic, and out come distortions and unintended consequences. The financial world and regulators may need to take a deep breath, go into repose for just a tad. That "presto" (fast and lively) tempo of the last decade may just need to go "andantino" (move moderately), as we "poco a poco" (gradually) morph into that which is "sostenuto" (sustained).

What we face today goes beyond what a single individual can solve. It is a systemic problem in the system that has evolved over decades. How we came to an economy so driven by profit at any cost and political influence befuddles me. So many had a hand in forging the heavy chains that now weigh us all down.

We may continue to witness failures until we morph toward what is sound as individuals, institutions and government. An economy based on services and consumption, finance and debt is unsustainable. Reigniting consumer spending with debt will not lead to a sustained recovery nor will uncontrolled government spending with heavy taxation. It prolongs the inevitable.

When the *She-Wolf* runs out of milk, how will *Romus* and *Romulus* suckle?

Witness simply the status of California. Budget slashes hit the daily lives of the masses with impact. Imagine the fallout from a reduction in welfare spending, education, state job losses and prisoner releases. It has enormous societal ramifications. Further, note the expected freeze on 2010 and 2011 Social Security cost of living adjustments.

We have a choice to self-correct or it may one day be imposed upon us. Do we use technology as a tool to keep creating complex fantasy instruments benefiting few or technology as a tool to restructure our economy to create goods and services additive to the daily lives of many, where many compete, with incentives for small business development?

I recall painting moldings on the walls of my home years ago. One can't just keep painting over as cracks show up. Time comes for the scraping, to get the job done right.

When we encourage small business, we encourage our greatest resource, our people. Big bureaucracies and big financial enterprises may just be like the big empires throughout history that ultimately failed. They worked for awhile, but then imploded. Empires have an Achilles' heel. They hold back progress for many, but the human spirit cannot be held back. Truth and human spirit prevail throughout history. They cleanse out the users and abusers to start anew.

What led to the ultimate failure of the Roman Empire?

It grew big and unwieldy, an enormous bureaucracy difficult to manage; hence the split into the eastern and western empires. The Romans kept conquering, even fringe kingdoms that maintained their own disparate social structures.

It created the opening spaces for the barbarian Visigoths to infiltrate. Bureaucracies and inefficient big structures create opening spaces for Visigoth-like infiltration, a feeding off the system across the board. TARP alone, which was originally part of the solution for the financial crisis, has now sprung investigations of fraud in its application. It makes one wonder about the true roots of the financial crisis and where we are going.

The Visigoth menace made itself known for a sustained period before the final ransacking of Rome. And yet, those Romans just ignored the signals blinded in the pursuit of power and wealth through growth.

A growth economy cannot function over the long run without ethics, sound business models and robust regulatory controls - in it, and in its component parts, and in balance together. When profit is hypertrophied for the benefit of few at the expense of everything else, even basic common sense, it throws out of whack all the components and the system. I don't think this is what capitalism was meant to be all about. Seems to me it has been within the envelope of the undisciplined. Hypertrophy in medicine is the enlargement of an organ. It causes harm and is not to the benefit of the whole person.

What are we after?

A promising career in the burgeoning asset management field was mine for the taking in 1985, but I experienced that "love-at-first-sight" moment on the Goldman Sachs trading floor. I kept my dream alive.

The brokerage side was mainstream Wall Street and that's what I had my heart set on. I liked its frontline rapid-fire nature, interacting day-to-day with people. If you made it into and out of one of those prestigious sales and trading programs, you'd write your own ticket. I just needed a catalyst.

Back in the mid-1980s, my husband and I had our sights set on moving to New York, if an opportunity were to present itself. We both loved the heartbeat of that city. I fell in love with its European flare upon a first visit in my mid-twenties. We were determined to move there. It was the nexus of finance and for a highly ambitious young couple, those early years were the time to dream and explore.

We met at the University of Notre Dame. We were united by our love for learning, our love for intellectual pursuits; so much so that we'd sit outside on a bench, in front of the Administration building, in the middle of winter, freezing cold, until the wee hours of the morning, engaged in deep discussion of Jacques Maritain (a French Catholic philosopher), Friedrich Nietzsche, even Shakespeare. We'd end with yet another round of discussion sorting through classical music. I must admit, we were a bit competitive with one another. Why did we sit outside?

Anyone who's ever visited the Notre Dame campus in the wintertime knows how magical it is. The snowflakes cloak the campus with a blanket, giving it a warmth and echo that lives within the chambers of the heart forever.

Late spring 1985, my husband was offered a promising capital markets opportunity with a major New York bank. That was my opening space to seek acceptance into one of those six-month sales and trading programs. They were all domiciled in New York.

Why didn't I apply for one of those programs earlier?

I couldn't just go to New York, leave my son with someone else in Chicago for six months. It wasn't in me to do so. When the geographic opportunity came knocking on my door, I enlisted my boss' support. He understood and helped. At age 29, I was ready to shimmy ever closer to my professional goal.

Chapter Three

Vision

Dreams

February 4, 2009

On one of the ledges within my soul, a memory…I dust it off.

My sister and I are lying on the grass in our backyard… it's a beautiful sunny summer day…we hear the lawn mowers going in the background…our white terrier is running circles around the cherry tree…two little girls, dressed in simple lime-colored dresses, just looking at the clouds imagining what each could possibly be. We talk about what we want to be when we grow up. We have dreams as we look into the future.

My mother and father had a vision for their children when they came to this country…for "life, freedom and the pursuit of happiness." They stuck to principles and discipline within the home, defined boundaries that we came to respect, as with a loving hand we were guided into the future.

What if the sky was no longer blue, the clouds no longer white, the sun decided to rise and go to sleep at odd times?

Oh laws of nature, you keep things in their place, each one of your components has its true intent. When something rumbles, out of the ordinary, what destruction it leaves behind. And yet, everyday you bring us the sun, to give us vision, the splendor and hope of a new day.

What if mortals act upon misguided intentions, in such a way, that it may dim sunlight for years to come, what would our beautiful world be like?

Intention, do you matter and what are you all about?

In your purest form, you beckon us to stay true in word, choice and action. True to objectives…true to our families, others, our professions and ourselves…true to taking responsibility…not straying from fulfilling that which has been entrusted to us.

Leaders are like artists painting a portrait…each stroke is linked to how healthy our lives day to day will be.

If vision stops at self-interest, what of our nation?

Isn't there such a thing as staying true to intended purpose and unified in the ideals upon which our nation was founded, which guide choices and actions, keeping things intact, rather than in disarray, greatly influencing the direction we go for decades to come?

I think it's cool and hip to be idealistic…in this day and age…or any age…as it is the fathomless universe that's worth counting the stars in. Our forefathers gave us a common ground in those "inalienable rights," regardless of our differences. Isn't that what we desire for our families and ourselves?

Upholding our ideals as a nation...it unites us as we are one in this together…and in that the excitement, the splendor of a new day, our hope.

"Where there is no vision, the people perish." Proverbs 29:18

The Investment Bank, Salomon Brothers 1985 to 1987

As a little girl, I had an eye of an unswerving lynx. True to it I stayed, as I started this next chapter of my life.

I had as my professional goal reaching the pinnacle of my field with that "Do Your Best" inscribed above the front door of my mind. But, like walking my sister to my grandmother's after school in second grade, I focused on learning the business the right way, staying true to my ideals with others in mind. And so like the lynx, not known for its speed, but able to make astounding leaps when its time is right, I climbed a jagged mountain slowly in my own solitary way.

In all this, I was blessed with yet another mentor – let's call him Max, his favorite name. He passed away suddenly of a heart attack on July 25, 2008, at age 63, the day I finished the first draft of this book; Max encouraged me to write.

I was out of the country on an island doing just that, writing, when the news arrived. It rained that day, after many consecutive days of sunshine. Max was unique, a man way before his time in the support of women within the financial world. He came to be a treasured and loyal friend, my "fairy godfather." His lessons still ring true as a blueprint for business conduct on Wall Street.

The Training Program

So how did I end up at Salomon Brothers?

It's spring 1985 and my husband accepts a position with a major New York bank. The family would soon move to New York.

Spring was not the best time to interview for one of those sales and trading training programs. Candidates were already selected. I tried anyway with the help of my Funds Group boss. He paved the way for an interview with the head of Goldman's training program in New York, but made known that true to the survivor culture of the industry it's up to me to take over from there.

I'm now expecting our second child. Well, that calls for a little creative thinking and creative dressing, adding a tiny wrinkle to the interview process. It was so different then when it came to being pregnant in the business world. It was an issue.

True to my gut feeling, but also ethos of Wall Street culture, the head of New York recruiting came up with a "before we make an offer, we'd like you to also interview with other firms and line up a few firm offers."

Polite way of saying, "you're pregnant and that's an issue" or is this the hazing process, testing the mettle?

Doesn't matter, I'm giving this my best shot. My grandmother made coats out of army blankets to survive in a displaced persons camp in Germany. I'm from that bloodline. I've got to find a way to wiggle in.

I arrange interviews with a handful of investment banks in New York. I completely block out of my mind that interview season is over. Next, I buy a boxy style interview suit, as I'm three months pregnant. Doused with conviction and confidence, I fly to New York, determined to deliver those job offers. And I did.

Having spent a whole week there, my last interview is on a Friday with Salomon Brothers, one of the *crème-de-la-crème* Wall Street firms of the time. A grueling day of interviews was planned for me, with three department heads. By now I had nailed the "perceptions count in business," that lesson I learned when initially interviewing with my Sherpa. I wasn't going to miss anything this time around.

During the first interview, I encounter one of those people who inexplicably come into our lives. This man, the head of the municipal bond department, took to me for some reason. He told me exactly what I needed to do to get hired.

"Tell everyone that you only want to work at Salomon, there's no other firm for you and don't leave the premises without having an offer in hand."

I must have looked like one of those children, with puckered lips, going "oh!" with my hand over those lips. I recovered from the serendipitous encounter; peeling off one "thank you" after the next.

The interview process proceeds late into that Friday. I end up in the office of the head of recruiting.

"Everything went very well and we'll be back to you on Monday," he remarks.

I respond, "Everyone liked me, right? How will the weekend then change anything? Why don't you offer me a job right now and I'll accept, just like that," as I snapped my fingers, like I once did in second grade.

He said, "Ok, you're hired and we'll be back to you with details."

This time, my lips pucker up with two "oh, ohs!"

The dream becomes reality. I immediately walk to

Goldman's New York offices to inform the head of training that I'd be joining Salomon Brothers. His stunned expression revealed wonderment on how I was able to engineer a few offers, pregnant, at the end of hiring season.

Experience and sophistication were already under my belt, but most importantly, an ironclad belief in myself, deeply grounded in faith, helped me walk the high wire. I had the most amazing Friend with me and with Him I felt secure.

Few women populated the ranks of Wall Street in the mid-1980s. I walked away from this experience knowing what was ahead. Unswerving in commitment and better than my male counterparts is what I needed to be for a chance at success within this peculiar world. Climbing the ladder rung by rung became a way of being even as your fingers were stepped on. You just kept going. One doesn't survive several decades on Wall Street as a woman, without a few bruises and learning how to look the other way.

I played my own melody nonetheless, the piano concerto of my life. Have you ever listened to one?

The orchestra comes in and out as the piano plays. Maintaining the integrity of the melody throughout the piece is what makes the whole concerto come together so beautifully. We each have our melody as challenges and obstacles come in and out, in the pursuit of our objectives, as responsibilities are entrusted to us. For me, it always came back to my prayer book, my family and music, as I made my way up the path with little cracks and crosses.

𝄞

I would soon enter the New York Salomon Brothers training class of July 1985 with about 125 fellow trainees, comprised of a handful of females, possibly seven or eight. Our class was immortalized in Michael Lewis' book, Liar's Poker.

I bumped the norms out of the way on Wall Street back then, being the first ever to have dared to enter and complete that Wall Street training program, proudly in such fruitful a condition. As such, I had to make a special trip to New York, before the program commenced, to advise Salomon that I'd need a few weeks off in December close to my baby's expected birthdate. I invited the head of the recruiting program to lunch, thinking it would soften things up a bit.

As I take myself back in time, I grow nostalgic for the cachet of those bygone days of the 1980s. To me, it was the era of President Ronald Reagan. It was quite the start to a business career. He inherited an economy plagued with high unemployment, high inflation, interest rates north of 20%, high income taxes, and over-regulation.

Nonetheless, he rallied the country forward with his infectious optimism and idealism. President Reagan cut taxes and moved to reduce the government's role in our daily lives. The emphasis on freedom of the individual and small government set the stage for the economic growth and resultant stock market take-off for decades.

There was something raw and natural about Wall Street back then. It wasn't stilted. It was a fun work environment. A greedy few existed, but nowhere near what I came to witness over the last decade.

Ambition versus greed; it's another one of those trades, two sides of a coin, isn't it?

Now, we all know that greed has always been a part of Wall Street, but back in the 1980s at least it rested with a smattering of individuals epitomized by the corporate raiders, like Gordon Gekko in the movie *Wall Street*.

I think Gekko went institutional in the last decade.

What do I mean by that?

Greed became institutionalized, a credo and entitlement of the embedded clubs, layers deep residing within our financial institutions. Compensation simply followed the growth and profit turbo charge. That's how those bonuses became so big. The bigger the growth, the bigger the money.

Well, we can convince ourselves of anything, as if it were normal. Annual compensation of $40 million, $100 million, is "normal"?

If maximizing shareholder equity is a goal within our capitalist system, money may be returned to the shareholder in the form of dividends.

If bonuses are based on real honest profits based on true growth, additive to the success of a company and our economy, I'm all for productive pay. When king-sized compensation is dispensed in the midst of losses or even in the aftermath of a financial meltdown that splinters throughout the daily lives of many, one can't help but ask, what afflicts leaders?

I lived within this world, watched compensation of the absurd dispensed, suctioned to the top of the funnels, as the worn out and dated cliché, "we have to recruit and keep top talent," was sold to the American public. Denizens of financial cloisters, "crony capitalists," strolled porticos, with devotion to maximizing shareholder value, yet they drained money and perks out of their companies; some even drove their companies into the ground.

I don't begrudge anyone his or her fair due. It's how the money is made that matters. If one invents, starts a company of social usefulness or has genius talent, it's unique. I believe "crony capitalists" are unique in being just that, "crony capitalists." Did they truly concern themselves with capital formation?

So what were the alpha males of the 1980s like?

They were enamored with themselves; cruised with attitude and moxie. I felt comfortable amongst them. A competitive brother and a practically all-male University prepared me. It felt perfectly natural to live within a world of men. I just accepted the egos as part of the theater of Wall Street. Whenever they bragged, I'd listen. I'd let them indulge in their *braggadocio,* then I'd turn away to chuckle.

They made a lot of money. Some just threw their checks into a drawer, like $25,000, $50,000; cashed them when they felt like it. I was just a rookie when one of them opened a drawer full of those to-be-cashed $25,000 checks.

Money flash showed up in their attire. What they wore epitomized who they were. They fussed and matched suspenders to stiff white collared blue striped shirts, with the ubiquitous collar stays. The relic is still worn by some today. And who could forget, the slicked-back hair, aviator glasses, and silk hanky for some of that hanky-panky that never seems to die.

When it came to female attire, femininity had not yet knocked on the Wall Street door. Suits made for men were transformed into a female version with the simple application of a skirt below the knees; no deviation from the original male form, no funny collar. Cotton shirts were in; any cleavage was out. Anything away from the standard attire, even in the most modest application, was simply risqué.

An enforced dress code made us live with the ever present, "Is this appropriate office attire?"

Like the *Kissy* doll incident, I confess! I pushed the envelope when it came to Wall Street dress, much the way I did in having those babies; no harm in trying to blaze a few trails. How could I possibly keep the feminine side of me, the love for style and high fashion chic, bottled up all day?

I didn't!

When mini-skirts came back in style in the mid-1980s, I wore one to the office. Even though mini, then, was merely a few inches above the knees, it was a departure from the tried and true mid-calf length of the mid 1980s. So, with aplomb one day, I wore high heels and a charcoal gray mini skirt that rose three inches above my knees. All gussied up, I showed up for work that day.

I was the *belle of the ball!*

The production of a predominantly male office fell short of its daily quota. A stare of disapproval made its way from the high perch, but that didn't stop me from trying to be feminine within this male world.

You know, I learned to participate in the Wall Street razzle-dazzle, but it was just theatre, not real life. Real life was home, my children.

So, let's go back to the lunch date with the head of recruiting.

Well, I had to do a little educating, enlighten the guys that the world was changing, that the most natural would someday be naturally a part of the business world. What better format than one of those fancy French restaurants that were the rage of the day.

French frill was in back then. Formal china, silverware and ornate glassware flecked the white tablecloths. A single rose occupied a delicate patterned vase. What table you sat at, and with whom, mattered. The chic restaurants of the day took either the form of snooty and quiet understatement, or that of a lively, but very well-behaved buzz.

We had lunch at one of those French restaurants. I got down to business right away and enlightened my lunch guest, the head of Salomon Brothers' recruiting, that having a baby is a perfectly natural part of life.

He ordered *vichyssoise* for an appetizer. The spoon fell out of his hand, into the bowl, splattering all over those French cuffs. I offered to help out, to dab a French cuff, with a splash of club soda. In the meantime, I secured my maternity leave and went on to enjoy my *potage* at this quietly understated place, on my way to the *crème-de-la-crème* of Wall Street!

𝄞

I joggle my memory a bit. It all starts to come back. I hear the fluorescent buzzing lights of the lecture hall, the bustle of footsteps and papers, the rush to our desks. It's 7:00 a.m. and the day begins.

This is one of Wall Street's fertile breeding grounds, spawning sales and trading warriors, those agitated beasts. The program is designed to be brutal in nature, testing commitment and stamina, true to its objective of molding survivors. Some of my fellow colleagues never became gladiators, falling by the wayside as the program progressed. If you made it here, you'd make it anywhere. The future Wall Street titans brimmed with ambition to reach the apex of their respective fields.

Like my second grade, I secure a seat in the first row, from day one. A few Japanese colleagues join me. The pranksters occupy the back row, torturing the lecturers much the same way they must have their teachers as they were growing up. Yes, those future financial leaders were in their twenties and thirties, but that didn't keep them from launching paper airplanes and rubber band darts.

The auditorium looks like the typical lecture hall with the theater-style incline. It's a drab, dated room with windows floor to ceiling along one side, with the New York canyon-like view of building after building. The gray outside blends with the tone inside. Rainy days make it all the drearier. After awhile, looking out the window was like looking at a black and white TV set. Inside the lecture hall, the carpet is so worn out;

hard to figure what the original color was.

The front of the room has a plain blonde wood desk, chalkboard and the overhead for the never-ending slides. The whole room is awash in ubiquitous buzzing fluorescent ceiling lights. Every morning two-foot high rectangular chrome coffee dispensers are trucked in; Wall Street's notion of trainee hospitality.

The daily grind is engineered to stay true to the overall ethos of the business, all the way down to the austere setting of our daily home for the next six months. It's a "sink-or-swim" culture on the Street, such that "baptism by fire" starts on day one, no exception to the rigidity of the daily routine. If you don't cut it at this level, you aren't going to make it in the jungle of the trading floor.

Class starts around 7:00 a.m. daily. We're stuffed with bond theory and an intensely jolting investment curriculum until about 4:00 p.m. or so. At that point, we're free to roam the trading floors with the goal of finding a job once the training program is completed. No way that any job would show up in our lap. It's ours to find. Entry into the program did not assure a position with the firm. A percentage of the class never found a home on one of those trading desks.

You had to absorb the grind, the inundating workload. Any speck of doubt or lack of confidence was to be left at the front door long before you ever got there. It was a business where you were constantly shot down, had to get up, dust yourself off and get back into the fray. The training was a microcosm of the afterlife on that trading floor we'd all experience someday. You needed to develop the skills to get the job done through any type of work environment and market cycle.

The class sizzled with competitive ardor. Imagine a room full of smarty-pants, each with their own peculiar story on how they engineered getting into this elite program. It was an eclectic group; the standard MBAs, a former pilot, a ballerina, the Japanese, and then there was me, pregnant. This was a survivor reality show in the making, rolling way before its debut.

The female entourage, in true 1980s style, was immediately catalogued. When the good-looking ones presented in front of class, it was the whistle brigade from the back row that never subsided. None of us gave it a second thought. It was just banter, all in the spirit of humor to add some levity in between option theory. At first, no one knew I was in my fifth month of pregnancy. The guys later admitted that they catalogued me as "beautiful, but too bad that she's a bit chunky in the waist!"

As news about my pregnancy spreads, many fathers and mothers kindly remind me to drink the milk placed right next to the chrome coffee dispensers. I even give the back row their *raison d'être*. Three lotteries originate from the boisterous breed; birthdate, size and name of baby number two. The yellow pad circulates throughout the lecture hall, row to row for continuous market updating, until December 8, 1985 — the Feast of the Immaculate Conception — when baby Gabriel Luke graces the world and is appropriately named to celebrate the Feast.

Names, they have a special meaning for us don't they?

Don't we all wonder how we were named and why?

My mother named me after the main character in the movie *Quo Vadis,* based on a novel of same name by Henryk Sienkiewicz. It is a love story set in the time of Nero between a Christian woman, Lygia, and a Roman patrician, Marcus Vinicius. My mother viewed the movie while she was expecting me. She was taken by the character's strength. And as life went on, I was taken by love stories.

My middle name, Rugile, is Lithuanian for cornflower. I was so named because of my mother's fondness for the azure blue flower, so much so that as a little girl she embroidered the border on one of her mother's dresses with tiny cornflowers. It was a surprise gift for Mother's Day. The flowers were embroidered in such a way so as to reflect the various stages of the flower's blossoming, from bud to full bloom.

What is the story behind your name?

No surprise that my fellow colleagues missed on picking the name Gabriel, entirely, but two lucky lottery winners guessed the date and size — closing those trades and collecting their commission from that overflowing dollar bill jackpot, "deep-in-the-money".

A lively underworld coexisted with serious lecturing, allowing us to decompress with an eye to what the next prank would be. Sorely needed for reprieve, after bludgeoning episodes on trading desks where traders basked in beating up the rookies.

So what were lectures all about?

Sleeping, for the Japanese in the first row and that was a good thing. Otherwise they'd have skewed the grade curve. Salesmen and traders from each department — equities, bonds, mortgages, high yield, security analysis etc. — taught classes. Classes were naturally designed to intimidate, culminating in grueling weekly tests.

Superstars existed within this Wall Street culture, legendary salesmen who had a reputation for cleaning out the inventory. Their big accounts swept the traders dry. Their amplified persona put us rookies in awe. They were the mythical gods, the unadulterated true brokers who bought and sold securities for a commission.

This is how I first hear about Max, one of the top bond salesmen at Salomon, a legend on the Street, domiciled in Chicago. Rumors about him swirl within the training class, something about a guy who makes those around him squirm, a man impossible to work for. There was no such thing as political correctness in those days. You worked "for" someone, not "with" someone.

With a stack of index cards in hand, Max shows up one morning in the drab auditorium and stands out, like me once wearing a *Chanel* suit, after a symphony concert, at a *White Castle* hamburger joint.

My eldest son commented on the *White Castle* incident, "look at mom trying to blend!"

So what's my first impression of Max?

Max is a big guy, with a big personality. He stands tall at 6'4," ever so slightly heavyset, with slicked-back black hair. He's in a navy blue suit with a vest; a suit with a sheen. Wire rim aviator glasses frame his face. He's got those slightly heeled black shoes, in high shine. Bright gold cuff links speckle the French cuffed shirt.

The giant diamond and gold ring tops off the look.

He kicks into his "How to Sell" lecture, with a delivery that's unique to him, deliberate and loud. Every word is enunciated. Off he goes in an orderly manner.

"I'd like to share with you my selling principles. Abide, implement and never forget them." It goes something like this.

"First, your word is your bond and your reputation is everything."

"Second, never sell anything you don't understand."

"Third, make sure you are talking to the right person and decision maker who pulls the trigger before you start selling anything."

"Fourth, know your customer — get as much information about the customer to assess need and appetite for risk."

"Fifth, you'll have a higher close ratio if you do number four and then match the product to the need."

"Sixth, put the interests of the customer first — disclose all pertinent information before executing any trade."

"Seventh, the customer is always right, but don't believe when they say they have no money — they always do if you show them what they're looking for."

His sincere delivery stays with me. I like him. While earnestly passing on his wisdom, he endures taunts of the back row. His, were my guiding principles for the rest of my career. I passed on the same to those who worked with me. Simple basics, practiced daily, were my base one. They touch upon nearly every aspect of the business.

I hear rule number one.

"Your word is your bond."

What is a bond based on? Trust, truth?

It doesn't get more simple and basic than that.

Max says if we don't abide, we get entangled and things go haywire.

Why have we lost confidence in our system?

It's amorphous; rules to the game shift and bend, even break. We can't believe that what we are being told today won't change tomorrow. Word waltzing makes me dizzy. Plain old communicating is like reading hieroglyphics.

The trust lynchpin; it's a constant that never ages. It simply doesn't go out of style; believe me it stays in vogue, even if not worn for awhile. There's something to it, to keep systems intact, as years go by and markets change. Credibility in anything simply comes from integrity.

Truth is like glue. It's supposed to stick; it hovers and tickles the conscience. Into its stirrups, from the frontline, to managements to boards, to leaders, it beckons we go.

And why not?

Imagine a world of mistruths, nothing holds.

Max's eloquent soliloquy is delivered with authority. He doesn't mince on the vital element of self-regulation and trust as the foundation of this business or any other business. He talks about a regard for suitability in governing sales choices rather than commissions or mark-ups.

We all know that there are two types of regulation,

internal and external. We look to our regulators to give us some protection, very obviously, with updated regulations and enforcement. Their job may just get bigger, as everything keeps getting bigger. More may fall through the cracks, with big consequences.

For example, no sooner have we come out of the gate with TARP (Troubled Asset Relief Program) and already a Special Inspector General overseeing the bailout program has opened criminal probes related to fraud and abuse. Will we now have to start regulating the bailout programs?

We talk about regulation, but what kind, directed at whom and how to enforce?

Those within positions of authority chose not to regulate or even chose to chisel away at existing regulations. Outdated and absent regulation or a chiseling away of regulation through political influence, led to what feels to me like legalized lawlessness within the financial world. Can we blame only those who are greedy and hubristic, as we all know they exist, if our system enables it, allows them to get away with it, to such an extent that it has brought the financial system down and economy right with it?

Let's keep in mind that it's the highly regulated institutions that failed or required bailouts — Fannie Mae, Freddie Mac, Wall Street investment houses, big banks. It says to me that there's something else at play.

Some thirty years within the financial world and learning at the side of some pretty wise mentors, have taught me that both internal and external regulation, continuously updated, go hand-in-hand. It's simply impossible to regulate everyone, everywhere, all the time, no more than we can regulate everyone who wants to drive a car way over the speed limit, causing danger to others.

We rely on market discipline within our free market capitalist system to keep markets functioning. What is market discipline, if it is not rooted in individual ethics?

Adam Smith in his The Wealth of Nations, talks about the "Invisible Hand," that self-regulation, whereby in the pursuit of self-interest through profit, one may aspire to raise the common good. For that "Invisible Hand" to work, I think it presupposes a certain level of ethics, and commitment within leaders and market participants to adhere to that vision. Without self-regulation, external regulation of any kind will be but a screen door only, trying to keep water from coming in.

Financial players find ways to wiggle through opening spaces. It makes external regulation somewhat always behind the "eightball," playing catch-up. We can have all the external regulation in the world, but if not appropriately coordinated, implemented and enforced, backed up by ethics, what does it mean?

An auditor once came to ask me, a few years back, not just for a list of customers, but the memo authorizing me to send my customers *Godiva* chocolates for Christmas. There are guidelines as to how much we could spend on a customer per year. I'm perplexed. A $65 billion Ponzi scheme came to slip through the cracks while whistleblowers brought it to the attention of our enforcement agencies. Chocolates may add calories, but they're not destructive.

Can we even descend into a modern day Middle Ages, as things keep getting bigger and even more complex?

I am reminded of William Manchester's book, A World Lit Only By Fire. The feudal lords within the Middle Ages ruled with power and wealth as civilization declined into a morass of infighting and corruption. Human life was devalued. A world without a moral compass is frightening.

If self-interest or self-interested agendas, like "what's the deal for me" is the guiding intention well then, who keeps the whole together? Could anyone of us feel safe, in the markets or anywhere else?

Could it be that some who got lucky enough to sit in the executive and board suites of our financial institutions, come dressed in suits, riding on the legitimacy of a corporate structure, rather than animal skins on horses?

Internal regulation matters.

What is it?

Some would think it's a debatable subject. For me, it's rooted in those simple moral ethics and conscience.

Boy, did I learn about internal regulation when I cruised in that 1952 Buick decades ago. I had one of those intense temptations, to stick my foot through the hole in the floor of our car. Something inside told me to behave. I cocooned within a cocoon of ever-present external parental regulation.

"Actions have consequences," my parents would say.

If I got a little naughty, they'd get me back on

track to take personal responsibility with a verbal lesson. Even Napoleon's mother told him a thing or two, when his ego swelled.

And if that didn't work, my parents even took away my allowance, which meant I suffered, with such pain, in not being able to buy my *Tastee-Freeze* dip-top ice cream cone.

Our *Pledge of Allegiance,* "One Nation Under God, Indivisible," reminds me that it's not just me in the world. I exist as a part of a whole, in relation to others. Martin Buber, a philosopher, further explores human interaction in his essay, I and Thou. How do we encounter one another — as two human beings within a relationship inherently requiring respect or as a conduit to advance self-interest or something in-between?

Sheep may go in all sorts of directions if not properly guided by their shepherds towards a prudent common direction. To whom should regulation be directed, the shepherds or the sheep?

Misdirected external regulation may stifle entrepreneurial spirit and motivation, of those who had nothing to do with the making of the crisis in the first place. It might even put a damper on our free market capitalist system. It's not the sheep necessarily that need the regulating.

When toxic ruins are strewn in the trillions, across the books of our financial institutions, so consistently, we can't help but ask the question, is there a malady?

Now, the debates are as varied as the some three hundred million people in this country, as to how so many big structures, products and markets, even fraudsters, were allowed to flourish within a legalized system in a disorderly way, but suffice it to say they did.

We spawned a global financial hydra of size and complexity, constantly morphing, in its rapidity and complexity.

Is there even a regulatory framework that can now be designed to keep up with the size and complexity of what we've spun over the last decade? What exactly are we embarking to regulate and are we going in the right direction?

An international regulatory body may now come to oversee systemically significant financial institutions; ours included; instruments and markets as well. How did we get to a point where we are on the doorstep of something so novel; why did we grow so big and complex in the first place?

We tore down boundaries, innovated in a way that proved destructive and in the process created a system so complex, global and big that we may now be relinquishing regulatory control in part to the globe.

I learned from my Lithuanian teacher decades ago that the heartbeat of a nation slows, when it loses its sense of nationalism. Lithuania was a mighty power in the 16th century. It was its unification with Poland under the Union of Lublin in 1569 that marked the beginning of its descent back then. Staying true to ideals and protecting them, gives any nation its true identity and strength.

I think about what Max would do and say about this mindboggling conundrum, this matchbook with uncommon risks and consequences.

Too big across the board, as we've lost control?

I hear rule number two.

"Never sell anything you don't understand."

Securities too few understood were peddled. "Top talent" put to motion a funnel that spun bailouts for our nation as they took us into a world of financial engineering on steroids with undue risk-taking.

What is financial engineering?

In the extreme, I think of it as voodoo. By definition, it's the creation of new financial instruments off of existing financial instruments and assets. In a financial laboratory, it may work. In the real world, one might just be surprised how it goes, if unbridled.

A *Frankenstein* was created out of a simple mortgage.

Can you believe it?

Frankenstein One came to life — a few trillion in toxic assets, illiquid and non-performing real estate loans and mortgage securities originated at the apex of the housing bubble. Right next door, *Frankenstein Two* was in the works — credit derivatives, financial instruments whose values derive from an underlying financial instrument or asset. We will come back to credit derivatives later in the book.

Financiers created, salespeople sold and investors bought.

What was it that was being sold — computer entries backed by bad mortgages?

I wince. Imagine the potential for lawlessness within an unreal world of no boundaries, if it exists in our real one, one that has boundaries.

Truth is like glue. It's impossible to live without, as it is impossible within an innovative limitless frontier to regulate and enforce the regulation of every product, market and human being. Yet, there are no victimless consequences when we embark into new frontiers. Engineering of any sort takes the human race in a direction, yet unimagined.

Max talked about reputation — a jewel. Once lost, it's hard to regain. An insider trading scandal years ago was big news. Nowadays, the repetitive ongoing insider trading scandals barely make the news as a vast ocean of scandals pounds our shores.

What will financial history write about the last decade?

As the century turned in the year 2000, financiers made fortunes, tens and hundreds of millions, even billions, through debt-financed speculation in self-created complex paper. They gambled in an interconnected virtual casino that bet a nation's future.

The law of the jungle ruled — to win, players needed big money behind them, the fanciest trading systems and the best mathematical wizards that money could buy, and some friends in high perches. They called it innovation, but came to create a financial *Jurassic Park*.

Reputation, what kind do we want to have?

More on Max later.

𝄞

It's early Monday morning. The school bell rings.

Mrs. Mayfield is getting ready to take attendance. I quickly straighten out my green plaid uniform and white crisp cotton blouse, and then shimmy into my desk. The last name is called.

I'm excited! I get up, out of my wooden seat for my favorite part of the day. I put my right hand on to my heart and I begin.

"I pledge allegiance to the Flag of the United States of America, and to the Republic, for which it stands, one Nation Under God, indivisible, with liberty and justice for all."

Birth of Securitization

Here I go again, 1985 and in the heart of yet another trend, but now at my dream spot on Wall Street.

MBA School instills the principles of business and capitalism. Continental Bank teaches me about lending standards, the dangers of too much debt, and the risks associated with growth. Goldman Sachs picks up from there to introduce me to the world of asset management.

Technology begins to alter the financial world. A new financial services landscape is taking shape. The financial industry consolidation is around the corner. Community banks and some Wall Street firms would someday fold into the big banks of today.

The stage is set for a very competitive landscape and the development of new products, markets and financial players. Alternative Investments make their way into the world of investing, the term used for new fancy investment products. This world of mine would someday grow into a global and complex interconnected financial world in the hundreds of trillions.

Hedge funds explode in size and influence within the next two decades as independent entities. Banks and the Wall Street investment houses even offer their own hedge funds and private equity funds within their rapidly growing Alternative Investment divisions.

Now I'm at a firm where the first financial engineer gives birth to securitization, the loan or debt-packaging vehicle that would come to drive lending and Wall Street's earnings for decades to come.

What in the world is securitization?

It's the process of packaging loans into securities. It's the liquidity vehicle through which our financial institutions came to fund loans, so much so that in the last decade near half of all lending became tied to it.

Traditionally, banks funded loans through bank deposits. Loans stayed on the books of banks; banks were required to maintain certain capital levels against potential loan losses. Securitization opened the spigot for loans to be funded through the capital markets. By taking loans off banks' books, it freed up capital to make more loans, thereby giving banks the capacity to grow bigger.

I see my grandmother, my *bobute*, with her iron meat grinder, affixed to her kitchen countertop. I watch her put all sorts of meats, fat and the like into the top of the grinder. She begins to grind. *Voila*, out comes new looking meat, to be packaged into all sorts of casings. Here come the sausages, all kinds, as I grab them one at a time. Sausages full of fat may be tasty, but they're not good for you, like those toxic assets.

My *bobute* was like a financial engineer!

Over the last decade we threw trillions of loans

— for example, mortgage, credit card, auto and commercial real estate loans — into that securitization meat grinder to come up with newly engineered securities that were packaged and assigned credit ratings (many triple-A, the top investment grade rating) to be sold into the capital markets. Mortgage-backed securities are packaged mortgages. Asset-backed securities are other packaged loans, like credit card and auto debt.

How did all this come to be?

Salomon Brothers created the mortgage-backed security in the late 1970s. It's sort of like a bond, but instead of paying a coupon a mortgage-backed security is backed by cash flows, like interest payments, coming from a pool of loans.

How did Salomon create a mortgage-backed security?

They figured out a way to pool home loans, those originally on the books of lenders, into say a bundled vehicle. This vehicle then issued securities with different cash flow and risk characteristics.

Salomon Brothers underwrote the first issue of mortgage-backed securities in 1979. The mortgage-backed securities market subsequently exploded in size, so much so that it eventually even dwarfed the Treasury market.

Why did the mortgage market work for so many years?

Credit standards were maintained. This, of course, is key to a sound functioning mortgage market.

Remember Continental Bank and loan standards?

When mortgages stayed on the books of lenders, lenders paid attention to the borrower's creditworthiness. For example, there's a reason why we called banks community banks. They got to know the borrowers within the community. It's the simple "know your customer" rule.

When default risk shifted from the lender to an investor in the capital markets, it created one of those opening spaces. Securitization put distance between the borrower and lender. When two parties directly share risk, they work to ensure that the deal is sound, basic business. Taking direct risk out of the equation removes responsibility. Anytime we off-load risk, I go "oh, oh!" It would invite abuse at some point, given human nature.

As the decades progressed, lenders increasingly sold home loans they originated to Wall Street to be securitized into mortgage securities. With the transfer of loan default risk from the lender to investors in the capital markets, lenders grew less vigilant about the underlying borrower's creditworthiness.

So how did we get carried away?

A confluence of events, but government policy paved the way.

The Community Reinvestment Act of 1977 (CRA) encouraged banks to meet lending needs of all borrowers within their communities, including the needs of low to moderate-income borrowers. The Federal Housing Enterprises Financial Safety and Soundness Act of 1992, required the government-sponsored agencies, Fannie Mae and Freddie Mac, to allocate a portion of their lending to affordable housing.

Monetary policy played a pivotal role. When it's too easy, it naturally encourages speculative behavior. In the aftermath of September 11, 2001, the Federal Reserve slashed interest rates to stimulate the economy. Low rates encouraged borrowers to take on debt. To lure borrowers, lenders created exotic mortgage products.

Borrowers took on all sorts of mortgages on the faulty premise that real estate prices would continue rising. Plentiful credit and loose lending standards fueled the unsustainable rise in real estate prices in the decade leading up to the financial crisis that began in 2007.

We can't fault someone for wanting a home. It's a natural desire. But, do we tease and prey upon another? Do we disregard, as individuals, affordability? Do we stoop to even fudge the facts as lender or borrower?

Profit trumped common sense, even common decency. In some cases, consumer wants trumped common sense when it came to affordability.

Good times don't last forever. When the Federal Reserve embarked on raising rates in 2004, it naturally filtered through the system. Those luring loans, like the sirens of *Ulysses,* caused more than a shipwreck or two. Subprime mortgages, among others, would reset at higher less affordable levels, eventually triggering defaults. Payment shock, speculation and fraudulent practices made for a potent cocktail.

So what does this look like?

Those who operated the securitization meat grinder profited at the expense of those at opposite ends. A vehicle that was initially meant to provide liquidity for home financing and risk diversification for the banking system was compromised in its application.

Not just regular and subprime loans, but other faulty loans, like "liar" loans were increasingly put into the grinder. When it's all mixed in there together, who'd notice the dodgy stuff, right?

Not so, at the very heart of the crisis and mortgage collapse is the creation of triple-A rated securities out of subprime mortgages and "liar" loans.

Those who assumed too much debt lured by exotic mortgages and those victimized by predatory or reckless lending practices provided the "feed" into the grinder. The toxic asset sausages that came out the other "end" went to investors in the capital markets, our banks included. Faulty loans on the way in make for faulty on the way out.

Can we believe that loans and securities created without sound lending standards, in some cases, outright fraud, will be liquid and perform; what do you think?

In the end, our banks became victims of their own excesses and risk-taking, to grow in this securitization business. They even leveraged up their balance sheets with low borrowing rates to buy the high interest paying mortgage securities they created, to simply play the spread. They got stuck holding their own creations, those trillions in toxic assets.

When we stick to standards and objectives, it works. When we stray, it doesn't. And when we cross the line where the intent starts to shift as to why we're doing what we're doing, that's the danger zone.

The intent of facilitating lending and home ownership, where maintaining credit standards is key, switched to the intent of generating volume and fees. Some Wall Street firms even established their own mortgage origination subsidiaries to provide the steady feed of loans to securitize. The integrity of the securitization model was compromised as enablers were incentivized to push profits with little to no risk.

I am reminded of my children's grammar school band concerts. Each year the band sounded increasingly cacophonous. I suppose many relied on the next individual to do their job to make it all sound right. When you have many acting that way, it just doesn't quite come together. It takes sticking to a standard, the discipline of practice by individuals, to make the whole work.

Any kind of loan or mortgage regardless of its creditworthiness was put into the meat grinder, to securitize as this boom neared its apex. By the year 2006, a sizeable portion of the mortgages securitized never even made their first mortgage payment. I wonder if the commercial loans that were securitized in 2007 would even qualify for refinancing through the traditional channels of bank lending today.

That's how we created toxic assets, bad loans and securities backed by shaky loan portfolios. Hard to know how much of this paper is out there. And, as the economy weakens we face imminent defaults from trillions in yet other residential and commercial whole loans sitting on banks' books.

Bank losses and write-downs already exceed well over a trillion (through May 2009). Any number of sources put the forthcoming global loan and securities write-offs in the trillions, if economic conditions continue to deteriorate. And yet, the total capitalization of the banking system is nowhere near that to absorb such losses.

What happens when illiquid assets and loans of such magnitude sit on the books of banks?

It clogs the banking system. Illiquid and non-performing assets impair capital. Banks need to maintain capital against assets and loans. If bank assets fall in value, it impairs capital. If capital is impaired, there is no credit flow into the economy. Capital is needed to make loans. When credit doesn't flow, business stops. We lose jobs.

Illiquid means the securities are unable to be sold; no functioning market where someone wants to buy. If there's no real market, there are no reliable prices, like the worst stuff in a garage sale.

I've been in the markets long enough to know there's a reason why a market is illiquid. External economic and credit market dislocations may temporarily freeze a market. An investment product may have few buyers that traffic in a type of paper. Or, something may be innately wrong with the product and market.

It's hard to price the illiquid. Within a frozen market, one either fire sales or waits till things thaw for buyers to emerge. But, what if there's something truly wrong with the product; it may have little value. Assessing true value of bank assets is key to confidence, a normal functioning banking system and economy.

So what are toxic assets worth?

Even though some may generate cash flow, what

they're worth, I guess, depends upon how our economy goes and/or what the underpinning loans are all about. That would shed light on whether our banks are sitting on truly rotting assets. With the significant injection of liquidity into the financial system and if credit markets truly recover, some toxic assets might even get a boost. Whether short-lived or sustainable is anyone's guess. Initially the bad loan problem was confined to subprime mortgages. The contagion spreads as people lose their jobs. Plain vanilla and commercial mortgages, and other associated assets like credit card debt are at risk. The problem compounds.

So, how are banks valuing toxic assets on their books?

Accounting standards were relaxed. FASB (Financial Accounting Standards Board) changed the accounting standard in April 2009, to allow banks to mark toxic assets to their own models rather than mark-to-market. Banks carried these assets at mark-to-market values (prices at which assets can be bought and sold in the market), which would mean that if value deteriorates, bank capital takes a hit. Mark-to-model got us into trouble once upon a time. It did not reflect true value. This brings us full circle to transparency issues and trust within the financial system.

Can we sell toxic assets?

Well, there was talk at one point about setting up a "bad bank" to take toxic assets off banks' books and place them into a "bad bank." That was scrapped.

Then came the Treasury's PPIP (Public-Private Investment Program), introduced in March 2009 to restart toxic asset trading. PPIP was designed to encourage private investors, in conjunction with the government, to purchase as much as one trillion of toxic assets from banks, with cheap government financing. The Treasury's PPIP toxic asset clean-up plan appeared to essentially be a slow transfer of toxic assets off of banks' books onto the government's books at taxpayer expense.

I find intriguing a June 2, 2009 *Financial Times* article entitled, Toxic Assets 'bridge too far' (By Krishna Guha). The article gives insight, coming from the President of the Philadelphia Fed, as to the difficulty surrounding toxic assets; simply that they are difficult to price and liquidate.

PPIP has been in a kind of "on-again-off-again" mode. As of July 2009, a handful of firms were selected to participate in the program.

Toxic assets and bad loans remain. But, Wall Street finds ways to repackage even the dubiously repackaged yet again.

You know what I'm thinking?

The financial industry may have simply grown up, reached full maturity. Seems to me that financial innovation is increasingly synonymous with packaging and repackaging for fees, even burying souring loans and dodgy created securities through multiple layers of securitization. No surprise that our banks malfunctioned with such broken asset creations based on false premises.

I'm trying to figure out how big our bad loan problem really is. A decade or two ago, the folks in Japan sat in a room and figured out just how much their bad loan problem would end up costing its citizenry. That means they had to come clean on what their questionable assets were truly worth. As I recall, I think some $800 billion in loans were written off, launching them into a multi-decade workout.

I think in musical terms as I always come back to my beloved music. Disney's movie *Fantasia* with its musical backdrop comes to mind when I ponder our current financial crisis. It reminds me of the sorcerer's apprentice when the Master sorcerer goes away. Do you remember the broom and water pail scene?

From the get go, the apprentice tinkers with magic that he's not completely trained in, to get a broom to carry the water pail for him. He doesn't know what he's getting himself into. It leads to water sloshing all over the floor.

In an attempt to fix the problem, the apprentice then breaks the broomstick, which leads to the creation of multiple brooms out of the splinters, with pails sloshing even more water all over the floor. The sorcerer's apprentice desperately tries to bridle the forces that unleash from magic gone badly, but to no avail, until the Master sorcerer appears.

This crisis has a mind of its own as the forces have been unleashed, rippling through our economy and around the globe. Can we hazard a guess on the outcome, or craft a quick solution for the unprecedented that has no quick sweep? Hence, can it be possible to think the unthinkable for expediency now that trillions in bailouts, backstops and stimulus have drained our nation of valuable and much needed resources?

Engineering and technological advances may

take the human race in a direction yet unimagined.

I loved my grandmother deeply. She played a role in my life. She was like my Professor's tree, ever more beautiful with each season, ever more priceless. I would not be what I am today had it not been for her influence. She sacrificed with bravery to bring her children to this country for those "inalienable rights." From her sacrifice came a large extended family that contributed to this country.

I shiver over trillions of bad loans, the losses, the write-offs, all those billions in the news. Broken trillions reverberate. They create a slosh whether the broken is passed along from one pail to the next through labyrinthine pathways or even repackaged through "financial innovation." A trillion moved or lost in one place comes out of another.

Labyrinthine solutions, revisionist accounting, trying to earn one's way out of a collosal problem, or sequestering bad assets into quarantine may not do quick magic. A multi-trillion toxic monstrosity was created based on the dubious.

When we wipe off the cosmetics, the legacy here is the ominous legacy of debt that looms on our horizon, a swell of over $11.5 trillion in national debt. Add $9 trillion in cumulative deficits projected over the next decade and our national debt skyrockets to over $20 trillion in the year 2019.

Have we hit an iceberg?

On June 10, 2009, ten banks repaid $68 billion in TARP monies. I see it as barely a dent to the multi-trillion deficits they created and the some half trillion annual interest paid to service our national debt. In the wings wait all our other obligations.

Shall we hazard a guess as to the final tab of our current financial crisis both in dollar and human terms?

I posit that it is immeasurable.

In the meantime, bonuses return as if all's swell. The author Lina Saigol further highlights the return of bonuses in her June 1, 2009 *Financial Times* article entitled, <u>Seeds of another pay furor.</u>

For every taxpayer dollar earmarked to correct malfeasance, for every dollar borrowed or printed to fill the shortfall, it's a dollar taken from productive uses for our society. I am a mother. I think about the lives of our young people. I love them and my country.

Like a "thief in the night," debt comes to rob us. If we print money to pay debt, it debases our currency. Increased taxation and spending cuts to stem deficits will ripple through our daily lives.

I watched a TV interview on April 3, 2009 with Congressman Paul Ryan (Republican, Wisconsin). He discussed the ominous taxation that faces our children if we continue on the current budget and spending trajectory. We have many entitlement programs and services to fund amidst the growing national revenue depletion and working-age unemployed.

After watching the interview, I reflected upon how many have been thrust into indigence worldwide as a result of this crisis.

"Financial innovation?"

Hunger throughout the world is the outcome of the self-interested. Its roots are planted far before it infiltrates a land. When we grow desensitized to the human face of another, the writing of a dark chapter begins.

Who were the players executing the trades and choices at crucial opening spaces?

Elected officials, regulators, mortgage originators, banks, Wall Street investment houses, lobbyists, insurers, credit agencies, appraisers, brokers, investors, and each one of us as individuals, some in taking on too much debt.

Vultures circled to feed. Do you remember the scene in the movie *Zorba the Greek* where the old woman lies on her deathbed?

Before she even passes, people come into her bedroom to take her furniture and belongings.

As we move along we will see how some financial institutions profited enormously from the foolishness of those institutions that took on irresponsible levels of debt and risk to grow in the booming securitization business. Wannabe investment geniuses employed various investment strategies to take advantage of the foolishness of "regulated" institutions run by "top talent." A few big banks scavenged in the process and grew ever bigger. Managements and boards of fallen financial institutions destroyed the assets and livelihoods even of their own employees as they self-destructed.

I think about my Professor at Notre Dame and the reverence for life.

I take myself even further back in time. Moonlight seeps through the bedroom windows of my childhood home as if to beckon that I cast an eye outside. I jump out of my bed to take a peek. I see the swaying birch trees and hear the rustling of the leaves. They tremble underneath the moon that swells through the clouds.

I return to bed and close my eyes into silence. I see a label marked, "Cherish and Preserve," sitting on a ledge within my soul, lit by a flickering candle. In the dim of light, I read the beautiful words.

Life and human dignity, freedom and truth.

I'm sitting at my wooden desk in my second grade classroom, scribbling on a piece of paper and rolling a piece of my hair with my index finger. It's one of those lazy late Friday afternoons, where I'm a little tired, like I can't wait for the weekend to begin.

I'm watching the clock, as the hand moves in ever slow motion. Filler time, as I'm sure Mrs. Mayfield can't wait to go home. She's just trying not to show it.

My head is tilting over into my right hand, with elbow on my desk. You know the feeling?

I don't really want to finish reading this, but I do.

by William Tyler Page

"I believe in the United States of America as a government of the people, by the people, for the people, whose just powers are derived from the consent of the governed, a democracy in a republic, a sovereign Nation of many sovereign States; a perfect union, one and inseparable; established upon those principles of freedom, equality, justice, and humanity for which American patriots sacrificed their lives and fortunes.

I therefore believe it is my duty to my country to love it, to support its Constitution, to obey its laws, to respect its flag, and to defend it against all enemies."

-Written 1917, accepted by the United States House of Representatives on April 3, 1918.

"The American's Creed"

I stop at "all enemies," as the school bell rings. I'm thinking that I want to be a Patriot, to carry on the vision that all those people had for our country.

They sacrificed their lives and fortunes for us. When I grow up, I will sacrifice, to uphold our principles so that my children may someday live a happy and productive life.

On The Job

Do you have gut feelings coming out of nowhere that guide you?

Well, I am having one of those feelings.

I'm slated to join Salomon's budding high net worth brokerage group in New York, upon return from maternity leave. It's December 1985, near a week since my dear little Gabriel made a splash into the world. I stop by the New York office to complete some paperwork.

What a beautiful sunny day and yet, an uncanny feeling is astir within me. I make way towards the main trading floor. Perched from above a wraparound balcony embracing the trading den, I peruse the view from a distance.

I hear phones, shouting and bustle of that trading room. It's captivating, yet at the same time diabolical. It's regal; this room paneled in dark cherrywood with ceilings soaring some thirty feet high. This labyrinth of interconnected trading desks houses beings; half man, half bull. Yes, that's it, a room full of Minotaurs.

Swirling, yet sequestered within them and that room, are the brute forces of power and greed. The insatiable pang for money runs through their vessels. Minotaur spew, testosterone driven energy is directed towards trade execution.

The bulk of financing for the US Treasury passes through this floor. At the altar together, kneel those who die for the trade, in worship of mighty "big buck." It's a game where they all want to win, but there's always the other side. Someone loses and maybe big.

Like a meteor coming out of nowhere, I feel disturbed. What's this feeling inside me?

How fleeting and risky is all this? If I stay in New York, will I be beguiled, like them? Bets in one direction or other could get bigger and bigger, and what would happen if it all blows up?

This is a dangerous game without proper controls, from within and outside; just think, potential financial Armageddon, encapsulated in the emotions of this one trading room. How many get carried away with it all?

Money breeds a need for more, and the power that then comes with it. How many before and how many after succumb, counting those fathomless stars like the businessman on the Fourth Planet of

The Little Prince?

Imagine if markets grow big, develop in complexity or people change and vigilance diminishes, with no force to bridle that which might unleash, could there someday be a big game played, the likes of which we've never seen, with far reaching consequences spilling brute disorder outside this room?

Like the sirens of *Ulysses*, voices beckon those ships only to cause them to be shipwrecked. Forget the sirens of *Ulysses;* mine are going off in every direction. I need to stay on my mooring. Some force is beckoning me to leave New York. Perhaps it's Gabriel's birth, but I'm seeing this all through a different lens.

So what was I thinking at that very moment?

I'm a mother and mothering I'm going to do first; no career is consuming my life. I'm not falling for all this. I'm taking my wares to a regional office, a bit lower key than New York. I'm competitive and Type-A, so I need to stand guard. I trust my instincts to change course. I'll request a transfer to a spot in Chicago. I'm going home.

For those who chose to find home in New York, it meant relinquishing much measure to the firm. It would come first. For many, the money and allure were irresistible. It came as a shock to my fellow colleagues that I'd dare chance a gear switch so late in the game, but I did. Some weren't even placed into jobs upon completion of the program.

I took that leap of faith and you know what happened?

A stroke of serendipity was right around the

corner. The head of the Chicago short-term taxable money market desk was looking for an individual to grow the corporate cash business. Spot on, I was hired; didn't even need to interview.

You know what helped this time around?

"If she could get through that program pregnant, she's tough enough for me," remarked my future boss to the head of training.

𝄞

The family moved back to Chicago. After a few weeks of maternity leave, I reported for work that January 1986. A truncated leave was about all the business afforded.

The Salomon Brothers regional office was a smaller scale version of New York, perched up high within the Sears Tower. Now among those elite Salomon rookies, trained and hungry, I'm ready to go and live my professional dream.

On that first day, I emerge from the elevator, right into elegance with lobby of champagne patina, colors gentle to the eye. Blonde wood hugged walls draped with oil paintings, ones hanging at a slant. The tastefully appointed twelve foot high lobby, flecked with Chippendale furniture throughout, atop demure oriental rug of Impressionistic nature, chants that Wall Street is alive and well.

A set of double doors, at the entry to the trading floor, stands proud with carved lettering above with the inscription, Salomon Brothers.

"Oh my," bemused I stand, "how grateful I am to be here!"

This must be what an athlete feels like upon a medal win.

Those imposing doors breathe welcome as I make my way into the trading room. A rectangular trading floor houses three long linear trading desks, evenly railroaded throughout the space, surrounded by floor to ceiling windows.

The first desk houses the folks involved in the eurobond, mortgage and institutional equity markets; the second, those trading corporate and municipal bonds. The mortgage and junk bond desks keep adding people, taking up a larger part of that room. Both markets continue their explosive growth during the 1980s. The third desk is my home, housing money markets, commercial paper issuance, foreign exchange and corporate coverage.

Well, guess who's my boss?

Max! Yes, the same Max who lectured our training class on "How to Sell." I almost fainted; I'm so petite next to him!

Yes, Max Hansem is my boss, and together with another gentleman, let's call him Larry, they run our desk. Max and Larry sit at the helm.

A bird's-eye view of the trading room easily reveals how conveniently the industry was gender-segmented. In a predominantly male room, our desk houses the trading room's female population. Women found their way onto the money market and short-term taxable desks back then. That's how it was. Had we, as females, not yet developed the cognitive function to understand corporate bonds?

We had some representation on the municipal

desk and one female on the ever-growing mortgage desk. There are about six of us on Max's desk, kindly referred to as "Hansem's Harem," within a total team of fourteen or so.

True to form, my baptism is one of fire. I secure a seat at my trading desk and am immediately assigned the bank portfolio side of a major commercial bank. They call in to do a trade. I hear $100 million of some Treasury.

"Max, what do I do?"

I'm in a panic!

Max yells back, "Come on, are they selling or buying, bid or offer?"

I couldn't recall. Max proceeds with just about every expletive in the book and "I'm" getting irritated at what's rolling out of him. Into the game I go.

I call the bank back, "Look, I'm a rookie on the desk and if you want to get your trade done, please repeat the order, as there's no one else to answer the phone right now. What do you want to do, again?"

Trade done.

This imposing, chain-smoking man stands towering at his trading post when he's not pacing back and forth. His boisterous spill of profanities fills the trading floor with revel. He loves to put me on the spot, to see how long before I cave. Provoked intimidation I'm not about to feed. I'm a lynx, I see what he's getting at!

I fling the balls right back. I take out one base after the next, developing skill and toughness. Like Continental Bank, I let the noise just ricochet. I focus on the work. He repeatedly tests me until one day I'm simply baptized.

A gentle man, gentleman included, lives underneath the bodacious veneer. The gruff rough-and-tumble manner is just a disguise. The gentle giant comes equipped with kindness and generosity. He's respectful and an adamant supporter of women on Wall Street.

Hence, I overlook the ostentatious gold and diamond ring, the glaring trademark. It traveled with him wherever he went, Las Vegas included. No surprise that this naughty city might be a favorite. Only in truth, it was all "boys talk" for him.

No posturing is what Max was all about. He was genuine. What he said he meant. And it was meant to teach us, not put us down, nor make us part of some larger mercenary agenda.

He honed in on our skill set, placing us in positions synchronized with our talents. I was "the closer," effective in marketing, able to get business in the door. As such, I was placed in charge of the Corporate Coverage group, growing the corporate cash investing business for the Chicago office. That means investing monies for corporations. I prospected, but also worked directly with the investment bankers, who originated underwritings, to secure the resultant cash business.

Individual autonomy, but respect for the team goal, flourished under Max's wing. We soared as he taught us to fly the right way. Teaching with a heart was his motivation and as such, he brought out the best in us.

He was the mentor of mentors, the breed that sadly disappeared from the financial world as decades went by. I still have my first performance review. He saw me and my skill set as I saw myself. The time and detail that went into the review stunned me.

Women during the 1980s had a hard time making it on the Street. Few made it in, some left under the stress of being in the daily boxing ring. Max mentored. He showed us respect. It laid the groundwork for the catapult that launched me into the upper production ranks of Wall Street. Max armed me with tools to survive the next few decades.

Thank you Max!

𝄞

How do you feel about your work environment? Do you have fun? We had fun with Max. On that desk, bantering went on all day, but in a kind whimsical way.

En route to the lunch carryout, I'd say, "Max, what do you want for lunch?"

The yell, for the whole trading floor to hear, "I want you for lunch in a negligee!" All in jest, of course.

It became our trading desk's daily Cab Callaway question and answer. No one made a big deal about it. It was part of the culture.

When calling the commercial paper trading desk in New York to do a trade over the "hoot" — Street parlance for the firm intercom — the flirtatious head of the desk picked up with the opener, "Welcome to my boudoir — " for the whole firm to hear.

On one of Max's birthdays, the guys hired a stripper that posed as a customer. Max had a unique way of addressing customers with appreciation and fanfare; the big "appreciate your business" sales pitch delivered in a theater-like manner. We put him into action. The whole trading floor was in on it.

Here's the setup. We present this young lady as the head of trading for a Midwest regional bank. We'll call her "Susie from Pakosie Bank." In comes Susie around noon that day with big blonde sprayed hair. A colleague escorts her to Max's desk. She's wearing a trench coat and platform heels that took her to Max's 6'4" height. The introduction takes place.

Max launches into his spiel, "We appreciate the business and we so enjoy working with you. If there is anything we can ever do for you, please let us know."

She responds, "Well, as a matter of fact, there is, I'd like you to help me take off my trench coat."

She turns on her boom box. Into the strip routine she goes, all the way down to her negligee. Max collapses in his chair. He confesses wonderment as to why a customer carried a boom box. The trading floor roared.

I miss the relaxed nature of the work environment. We didn't worry about every word we said, if someone was looking over our shoulder. We stuck to the basic principles. Amidst all this, business was getting done, customers were happy and so were we. Traders and salespeople trusted each other. There was the free flow of information so vital and necessary to get business done well.

We had our day-to-day routine. Every morning during the firmwide conference call, our CEO reminded us that, "to be in this business, you need to feel like you want to bite the ass off of a bear everyday."

The economic update from the chief economist followed. Then, each trading department reviewed "axes of the day," security positions looking to be bought or sold. By 7:30 a.m., all was wrapped up and the phones started ringing.

A blank trading sheet stared at us every morning, replacing the one from the previous day. Nothing mattered in this business, but the scorecard at the end of the day. No one wanted to hear about what trade you almost did, missed or could have done. It was black and white.

Every morning felt like the start of a horse race. After the ritualistic daily call, we'd bolt out of the gate. Production objectively measured by a trading sheet created intensity to the day that defined the business. I liken it to being a performer on stage every day. That accountability and daily ritual stayed with me for the rest of my professional career.

𝄞

Dress codes on Wall Street; unshackle them I would. So let me tell you about the day I wore red lipstick and a dress, instead of a suit, to the office.

I'm in the mood to wear red lipstick. I generally don't wear makeup, but for lipstick. It's *Lancôme's* signature matt red, eventually discontinued, much to my chagrin. Just when you fall in love with a color, it's invariably replaced with something new. Since then, I've bought backups when I grow fond of a color, just in case it happens again.

To go with the red lipstick, out of the closet comes one of my *chichi* favorite dresses, a gold colored silk with tiny black polka dots.

"Too slinky?" the thought crosses my mind, soon dismissed by that "not at all" feminine side of me.

Not very tight, falling loosely, but nonetheless the dress outlines the silhouette of my very trim and shapely figure. I'm in my early thirties at the time and athletic, running a few times a week. It's modestly mid-calf in length and buttons up to the neckline with a tuxedo-like bib styling on the front. The tiny silk buttons take forever to button all the way up.

Well, "it" and the red lipstick cause quite a stir in the office that day. Suits are the norm, although a few of us begin to wear dresses. I'm determined to add a little flare to the office environment.

Our trading desk is located right outside the glassed-in office of the office manager. Max and Larry are summoned into that office back and forth all morning long. Max looks perturbed, to a lesser extent Larry.

The morning trading rush subsides. Larry calls me into a separate conference room. Awkward and uncomfortable, Larry's about to deliver the message ordained from up above, the glassed-in office.

He stutters, "It's about...it's about your...it's about your lips..."

My female sensitivity takes hold of me, "I think I'll spare the poor chap the anguish."

"Let me guess, it's about my lipstick and somehow I look like a lady of the night?" I retort.

In a relieved tone he proceeds apologetically, "Yes...ah no, that's not what I mean and it's not me. I like it, I mean it's ok, but it's coming from...from..."

My remark, "the office manager?"

Once again he sighs with relief, "yes, yes," and then, quickly and quietly he sneaks in "don't wear that dress again."

I'm told at that point to remove the lipstick, but not the dress, thank goodness; with the box of tissue conveniently located on the table of the conference room. Max pulls me aside immediately, to relay his displeasure over what had transpired, in his customary manner of expletives I dare not repeat. I take it in stride and keep focused on my work.

Focus and goals are what got me through many a tough moment throughout my career. I looked at my profession as an art form, like playing a long piano concerto. As with the study of piano, I implemented all aspects of my training into practice, learning the products and markets thoroughly. I studied and restudied bond theory until it became second nature and learned how to trade the relative value of the yield curve under Max's supervision.

Then I practiced and rehearsed how to market effectively to source business. I set prospecting goals and, in typical Catholic fashion, reviewed what I did right and what I did wrong at the end of day. The rigor continued throughout my career. I simply put my heart and soul into being the best at what I did and loved taking care of my clients. As decades went by, I taught my associates like Max taught me; always believing that the smallest smidgeon of good anywhere, anyplace, could spark more good.

Have your parents ever said, "Mistakes are good teachers, but a lot of heartache can be spared by observing and learning how others act or don't act?"

Mine did.

Job mobility existed back in the 1980s. The industry was largely fragmented into many Wall Street investment houses and commercial banks. Salomon bred salespeople that the Street coveted. Those with training in the mortgage-backed securities and junk bond markets were in high demand. It wasn't uncommon that after a few years of training, the Salomon broker moved on to other houses, lured by king-sized upfront bonuses.

The mortgage-backed and junk bond (or high yield) markets were the high margin growth areas for Wall Street in the 1980s. The junk bond market developed under the leadership of Drexel Burnham Lambert. It allowed less creditworthy companies to access the capital markets for financing. Those companies traditionally relied on bank borrowing. Junk bond or high yield issuers are those companies whose credit ratings are below investment grade.

The access to capital markets by junk bond issuers unleashed a wave of takeover battles that raged across America during the 1980s. Drexel was in the heart of it all.

Some of my colleagues succumbed to the lure of Drexel Burnham. It was "the" junk bond house of the time. The million dollar sign-up bonuses were too good to pass up, but the jobs didn't last. The investment bank collapsed in February of 1990. Drexel concentrated its business almost exclusively in the junk bond market, ultimately becoming a victim of its own excesses, its own risk-taking.

Drexel Burnham epitomized the telltale signals that inevitably lead to a crisis or collapse. We come back to management. We come back to miscalculation of risk amidst growth through financial innovation and debt usage.

One can draw parallels to our current financial crisis. Turmoil in the junk bond market started with defaults. Defaults were the result of excessive debt usage or irresponsible corporate borrowing by junk bond issuers. This calls into question credit evaluation. Cracks in the junk bond market showed up in the late 1980s. Even in the face of a weakening junk bond market, Drexel continued to underwrite what some considered chancy loans.

Turmoil in our mortgage market started with subprime loan defaults. Defaults were a result of borrowers taking on too much debt and credit standards being disregarded. We continued to lend and securitize in the face of loan defaults and a weakening real estate market.

Witnessing the implosion of an investment bank and the lives of people shaken, taught me some valuable lessons. Anything is possible in this business. Growth requires robust controls, ethics and sound business models where risk assessment is key. Without those fundamentals, it can lead to dire consequences.

I looked at my career as a vocation, a long-term profession. It was not an avenue for "getting rich quick." I've observed over the decades that as new products and markets develop, money sirens beckon. The money lure is irresistible. Opportunistic bandits invariably push it. Things get out of control. Excesses get wrung out as someone takes the death spear.

A spear, in the hand of one warrior does damage on a limited basis. As we tinker with unknown spears, products and markets of size and complexity, the field of consequences grows ever wider, ever deeper.

Managements are not always right in the choices they make. "Keeping eggs in one basket," as investor and company both, is not prudent, especially when markets turn. If growth is fueled by excessive debt, watch out. And yet, this happens repeatedly.

Few geniuses exist; so too in the investment world. Some get lucky for a stretch or until the discovery of just how those returns are generated. "Too good to be true" is just that.

Right around the corner, there's yet another valuable lesson. Let's go back to the Fall of 1987. Just before the October 1987 stock market crash, someone leaks a story that makes its way into a newspaper over a weekend. Salomon plans to exit its municipal and money market businesses.

Why?

The bull market is losing steam; cost cutting is necessary.

"Yikes," our group; no warning?

Imagine that. All this over a weekend, effectively code for "I will not have a job on Monday if indeed all this is true."

I'm mortified!

Hard to believe that something like this could happen. I put in the prerequisite rookie time. I was just about to break out to the higher levels of compensation. I got into the coveted training program, then on to a desk and zap, just like that, gone?

So what happens that Monday morning when I take my seat at the trading desk?

My worst fears are affirmed. I feel "cut off at the knees!"

I'll deal with the feelings later. I spring into action to take care of my customers. The phones are just ringing off the hook. I navigate those waters trusting my instincts.

I'm involved in commercial paper issuance, working with traders directly, to help corporations fund themselves. Commercial paper, unsecured promissory notes, funds corporate day-to-day liquidity needs. My corporate clients needed help that morning.

I just knew that the traders would scamper to look for new jobs, within hours. I field one call after the other amidst the chaos. I tell my accounts to line up other dealers, to secure their channels for funding right away.

This is my first brush with the reality, of what was just a feeling. A feeling, when I viewed the Salomon Brothers trading floor shortly after my little Gabriel graced the world; the fleeting nature of this business.

I learn what "lay-off" really means.

The whole municipal department was let go. Within minutes of their dismissal, some return to their desks. They assemble their belongings. Something uneasy goes off inside me, over what is taking place, the rapidity of it all. People leave the premises with their personal items, never to return, after years of work, day-in-day-out.

They left, but the silent movie of those laid-off played. I am left with the vision of the empty seats on the trading desk, once occupied; the voices, the phones ringing, and laughter, all gone, replaced with silence. Those I made connections with over the last few years, will not come back the next day.

Then, a sadness; Max is approached by the human resources person asking for his ID. It's a signal that we'd soon take our leave. He was one of the largest producers. It didn't matter. This was a cost-cutting emergency for the firm at the time. It was done based on which markets drove the most growth, the widest profit margins. Max would land on his feet, as would we, but a tight group so beautifully created was gone forever.

This word, "lay-off," is such an "accepted norm" in our culture. Yet, I have a hard time getting comfortable with the word and the concept.

Do we no longer value loyalty?

Companies seem to want loyal customers.

Once upon a time, managements took care of their employees as if they were family.

What does a lay-off do to a human life?

It's demoralizing for any human being. Health and financial consequences show up immediately. Yet, the emotional disruption it creates within the fabric of family life and marriages few talk about. Imagine the feeling, when a provider or anyone else comes home to tell a family that a job has been lost.

Lay-offs create deep scars.

"Business is business." What does the oft-used phrase really mean?

Everything is personal because we are human beings. There are two sides to every trade. Filling coffers to excess in one spot empties them out of another. I'm struck by headline news during this crisis referencing that not even lay-offs can do much to prop up balance sheets and stock prices.

How illusory is this world of Wall Street that maintains its own illusion, this fantasyland desperately in need of demystification. Its inhabitants pay themselves what they can because they can. Perhaps we're approaching the point where Wall Street's illusions may soon peter out as our nation finds itself in deep fatigue.

Wall Street is neither secure, nor safe even for those who don't even know they're in danger. It swallows and washes up lives. For those seduced, they blindly graze in dollar bill-laden pastures, building sandcastles, until one day, position, title or income so readily disappear. It's kind of like a dandelion; you know the type that you just blow once and "poof" the flakes vanish.

I decide to do a little engineering myself having been trained by the birthmother of securitization. I'd take to creation that would give me more time flexibility to be with my children.

I don't easily give up, no matter what the obstacle, but I, like you, struggle within the battlefield of life. A long time ago, I made a choice on what side of the battle I'd be. A soldier commits to a purpose with copper-wire resolve. When in battle, one grafts one's will on to that purpose and takes the shots.

Sometimes, pushing up boulders gets tiresome. There's no other option, but to do so as the journey has its own time, only then, to end. Heartaches and teardrops come unexpected for all of us, right when we think the coast is clear, even at points when we're weakened and tired. It is then that we're tested. If Someone, some 2000 years ago, was tested and tempted as a Man after 40 days in the desert, then what of us?

Heartaches bring us gifts of fortitude and perseverance, even though it may not always be visible. They cloak our hearts with empathy for others, in giving us that "walk in another's shoes perspective."

What one considers painful, another might not. Heartaches hit each one of us differently, as we have different priorities and come from different experiences. A searing personal heartache during the Salomon Brothers training program, chiseled me to the bone. It took some time to work through, as it hit where it really hurts.

Chapter Four

The Crossroad

Teardrops

September 3, 1985

Oh rainy night, why do you thrust such a thorn through my heart? Why do you test me so? I'm six months pregnant, with a four year old and in such a rigorous training program. I'm afraid and overwhelmed by the emotions.

Will I now be alone in the world with my two little hearts? Why do you disturb the flow of life, the pursuit of dreams? You leave me now exhausted....away from my family back home, with little in the way of financial resources.

My mother and father want me to come home...I'm staying to complete the training program, to stay the course. I feel something within me to stay, painful as it may be.

Change back the time, return the morning or tell me this is only a dream...

We're sitting at the metal table in the tiny kitchen of our modest apartment in Brooklyn Heights. Devastation doesn't even begin to describe the emotion. I was to be happily married forever!

It's around 6:00 p.m...I see teardrops, not raindrops... they're coming down the kitchen window...just streaming down...you know the type of rainfall I'm talking about?...I freeze, as I stare out the window feeling pushed into a vaporous barren room of gray cement floor.

Out of desperation and pain, I run out of my apartment

barefoot on that rainy night, with my four year old running behind me calling "mommy, mommy!" Grabbing him close to me amidst the thunder and pouring rain, drenched in each other's clutches, the emotions flow. We just run together hand in hand. All the way to the waterway in Brooklyn Heights where we find a public phone to call home…the powerful and massively lit New York skyline in full view.

We stand together in the stillness of the night…enveloped in the mist of that evening, as if Someone's arms are trying to give us a hug. Life goes on all around us. There is visible beauty around me as I'm breaking inside. I'm heaving with tears and emotion…I can't stop…this can't be happening!

A tugboat sounds its horn in the distant background. The beautiful arrowlike rain continues its dance on the pavement…I stand motionless with my son. I'm processing what has just taken place. He looks up at me with those beautiful blue eyes that pierce through the tears in mine…I need to persevere for him and his unborn brother, where life is taking place as I'm dying inside.

I'm digging…to find something to hang on to where all feels shaken, crushed…my melody, where is it as I fight back the tears? Please keep me together…just something beautiful for those few minutes to absorb the pain. I reach into the ledges of my soul, near my heart. I close my eyes and I hear the beauty of the searing piercing violin in Rimsky-Korsakov's "Fantasy on Russian Themes."

I find calm, as I listen, hearing the whole piece in my mind.

The night begins to grow quiet. . . I press my son close to me, hug him, stroke his curly blonde hair, as time stops...I feel frozen, wondering what to do next as I'm still in shock. . . slowly we begin to walk. . .home or a new reality? My faith, my two children. . . this still the same. . . they give me strength. Yet, I'm struggling to find footing. . .

How do I accept this piercing sorrow of betrayal?

So unexpected, I've no preparation for something like this, right now, right here, at this moment. Why now? How in the world do I push through this?

How do I go on day to day. . .how to take care of my son and the life that's within me, while at the same time, make it through this brutal training program and not let on that anything is taking place. . .

Those first few weeks. . .days blur, one into the next. I feel just seared inside...as I walk towards the subway from my apartment every morning at 6:00 a.m. with a tethered heart. . .across the way is an old outdoor parking lot, owned by a Greek man. . .he's out there every morning. . . .as I cross the street backwards waving and blowing kisses to my son until we fall out of each other's sight, I pass this man.

With a Greek accent, he says the same thing every morning, "There goes my girl again. Goodness gracious, when will you take some time out to have that baby?"

Every morning. . .he says the same...if only he knew that he's helping me string my days together. He's gentle, *kind…with the warmest of smiles…just sitting out there manning his parking lot. I look forward to seeing him every morning…this complete stranger in my life, who gives me encouragement to go on. One word, one glance, one action…*

I then retreat into the corner of my heart woefully wondering how to make it through the next few hours, the day, and then the next. I live two lives. As I stand in the crowded subway train every morning, the noise around me goes silent as the new reality within me grows. Hearing only the train stop…rushing through the doors, up the underground escalator into the morning mass of people all the way to class.

I'm in the training class, drifting in thought, with the lecturing a distant muffle in the background. How does life change so rapidly or do the rapids of life take us into change…I'm struggling with the range of emotions…what could I have done differently, fear, anger and loss….

With me everyday, this Greek man's human touch…. piece by piece we come back from sorrow…with moments, seldom noticed in the rapids of life's accelerating rhythm…

Strength and comfort come…from Someone who comes to prod me along the way, every step He takes with me.

The Last Investment Bank, First Decade 1988 to 1998

Doesn't life sometimes feel like rolling a boulder up a hill and just when we're almost at the top, it comes tumbling down and we say, what happened?

That's what I felt like, when things ended so abruptly at Salomon Brothers early Fall of 1987. Dreams within my personal and professional life shattered. I had to find a way to pick up the pieces at age 33. It was a crossroad. I just moved forward, accepting and believing that this was part of a larger plan.

Have you ever listened to Abba?

I like to listen to Abba's *I Have a Dream* as part of my exercise routine.

What were those initial days like? What was the thinking that went into the process of looking for a new opportunity?

I took a few months off to be with my children. My Salomon business family, close in work as well as outside the office, I sorely missed, especially Max. Those human connections that we all make day-in-day-out are what make any job loss difficult.

Being at Salomon Brothers gave me a pedigree. Just about everyone wanted a Salomon trained broker at the time. It was like having an MBA from a top-notch school.

I had plenty of job offers to consider, but it was selecting the right one, consistent with my priorities. I wasn't carried away with the bait of big salaries and upfront bonus guarantees. I looked beyond for an opportunity where I could last, a niche within the system that would give me some protection, some security within a world of little.

Experience had taught me that I'd stay away from riding the risky product and market growth areas as they may come and go. I'd seek to remain true to being a broker within the traditional fixed income bond business. It's a world I easily understood, one for which I had the best training, mathematical acumen and sales skills.

Being my own boss and running my own schedule were the reality I sought. Time flexibility was priority number one. My children would have breakfast with their mother every morning and she would be there when they were home from school. She would be off on days they were off.

I'd continue to focus on sales, but not within an institutional division, like my job at Salomon Brothers, as I could get cut again. I'd seek out opportunities within the high net worth or retail sales divisions, which house commission-based brokers that cover high net worth individuals. But I didn't want to just cover individuals. I wanted to cover corporations and smaller institutions to leverage my Salomon experience. I perceived a sizeable opportunity in this area.

In the aftermath of the October 1987 stock market crash, many brokerage firms dropped coverage of the smaller accounts to focus on the larger. It was more profitable to do volume business with larger accounts as commissions were eroding. Someone would have to pick up the coverage of smaller institutions, as they still needed to do business.

Brokers in the institutional divisions were compensated based on salary plus bonus, a fixed cost for a firm. They were, as such, susceptible to cutbacks. They didn't own their accounts, the firm did.

On the other hand, high net worth brokers were on a commission-based structure and, as such, had control over their destiny, paying for themselves. Like a doctor, you build your own business. With this opportunity, I saw the sky as the limit and I'd be immune to any future Wall Street cuts. I just had to find an entrepreneurial thinking firm, consistent with my nature that would give me the opportunity.

Jobs at major elite top tier Wall Street investment houses came my way, but I decided to dig a little further. I explored opportunities at what were considered the smaller second tier firms at the time. They were more nimble and entrepreneurial, even revving up for growth. I could grow with them.

I wasn't interested in a big firm, nor any firm that had a culture that was susceptible to being bought out, in effect, management looking to cash out. The consolidation within the financial industry was already afoot.

With a little bit of the adventurous within me, I took my time to explore. Like the little girl, who went on an archeological dig in her Lithuanian teacher's bathroom, I was curious as to what else was out there besides the staple firms. I liked to push the limits, but in a good direction.

So, I set up an interview with a somewhat venturous firm. It just so happened that the day of the interview coincided with the day of the October 1987 stock market crash.

Can you believe it?

I showed up nonetheless, only to be greeted by the frazzled office manager running out to the lobby holding his head, apologizing that we'd need to reschedule a week later.

Well, I show up one week later; no stock market crash this time. Fresh off the elevator, I walk into a lobby where things don't look so fresh. I couldn't figure out what the decorator of the lobby meant to convey.

Bordello or funeral parlor?

Black molded wood framed the walls with an occasional section done in forest green fabric panels. The floors were stained dark, looking worn for wear. Occupying the largest reception desk, slightly offkilter to one side of the lobby, was a somewhat manly looking, heavyset receptionist. The colors in the Oriental rug, perhaps a spare, had nothing to do with the hues of the rest of the room. As elegant as the lobby of Salomon Brothers was, this was its antonym.

With sensory stimulation in overdrive, I barely notice the office manager when he comes out to greet me. A bit burly, balding with granny glasses halfway down his nose, he seems congenial. As we move towards his office, I'm struck by how plain and simply worn out the back offices look. The place whispers, "cost containment." Ubiquitous beige blankets the outfit. Glass window offices surround the perimeter of the floor. An open area in the middle houses desks linearly arranged for rookie brokers.

We sit down to chat in his corner office, appointed not unlike that of my previous bosses. Clipper ship paintings speckle the walls and a yellow chintz patterned Chippendale sofa sits in the corner.

He starts the conversation, "Do you have a book of business that you can bring over?" Back to the dowry.

"I have solid corporate relationships and know how to build a business," I reply.

This firm didn't have a short-term investment desk at the time that could accommodate the needs of my corporate clients. That didn't stop me. I needed a spot to set up shop according to my priorities. Hand me a key that would open the door to cover the world, any bond account that was not yet covered by them.

Salomon taught us to be aggressive, how to go after business. In this sleepy place, I had a feeling that I'd shine with my training and work ethic. Once you've learned how to build a business in this industry, the principles are the same. A lack of perks, guaranteed income or not having a book of business to import didn't bother me. All I needed was a phone and a desk. There's something exhilarating about starting out with a blank slate and creating something. I love the challenge.

Traditionally known as an equity trading shop, this investment bank had already begun to build out the infrastructure to become a player in the fixed income bond business. Perfect, I'd grow with them. The firm was making its mark in the municipal bond underwriting market. That's good, as I sold municipals at Salomon Brothers. Their mortgage-backed securities business was growing, someday to make them one of the top in mortgage-backed securities underwriting.

Next, I learned that they had recently gone public with the same management team still running the firm. That appealed to me. Perhaps it conveyed stability, entrepreneurship and risk management. When Wall Street firms existed as private partnerships, their own capital was at risk. When it's one's own money, one looks at risk differently. I was hoping that the partnership culture would continue in the management of this firm.

Well, I saw no roadblocks here, only opportunities. Any obstacles, I could circumvent. And I certainly wasn't going to think about them if I wanted to achieve my goals.

The interview progressed with the remark, "Since you don't have a book of business, all we can give you is a desk and phone, see what you can do."

His challenge alone almost made me say yes that very moment, but not quite yet. I could do this, but was this really the place for me?

I requested to meet with a few salespeople and various sales managers. There was a somewhat tripartite structure for advancement in the high net worth or retail division of this firm at the time. You started at the bottom rung, the calling room. If you made it there, you graduated to the main retail trading floor. Last stop was an office if you met the production targets. There was no doubt in my mind where I was going.

That day I did meet with the sales manager of the calling room. He was a Milton Berle look-alike, with a big gold pinky ring.

What is it with all these guys and their rings?

I was beginning to think that I should don one. I don't know what I conveyed when I first met him, but he didn't leave me alone until he single-handedly engineered my hire. He called me everyday for almost a month until I said yes. And it was always the same question, "did you make a decision yet?"

I felt a bit overqualified for the position, but I saw tremendous upside. Seeing the opportunity to grow through hard work and be rewarded, that upside, makes all the difference in the world.

It was lunch at the company's fancy dining room one day – equipped with full kitchen, tuxedoed dining staff, white tablecloths and a head chef – that sealed the deal, after this sales manager's tenacious pursuit. With exasperation to get the trade done, he pointed to a broker at the next table, leaned over and said, "If that broker can do $750,000 gross a year, you can do four times that and have the time flexibility to be with your children."

Poor chap; he was trying his best to close the deal. Not necessarily for my sake, but his own. He ran that calling room and made money off the production of his team. Honing in on my maternal instincts, he was true to one of Max's rules of marrying the product to the need.

We struck a deal that afternoon. When negotiating the draw or base salary, I'll never forget how tight he was with the money. Cost control in the name of profit wasn't just endemic to him; it was the way this firm was run. But, I was already moving beyond the miniscule salary draw as I knew deep down inside, I'd far exceed those numbers. I got what I needed, the opportunity, with the go-ahead to fly.

While he thought he cut the deal, it was actually

my own homework. Nothing gives you a flavor for a place than talking to the people who work there. I'm of the belief that cracks within any institution and its potential for a fall show up on the main floor, long before managements even get wind of it. If employees are not motivated, feel unhappy, or if ethics are compromised, sooner or later it bubbles up.

I previously sought conversation with the top multi-million dollar brokers, as it'd be just a matter of time before I joined their ranks. In this business, I believe that if you languish at a production level for years, that's where you seem to stay. Those who excel seem to do so exponentially.

I found the top five or so brokers within the Chicago office engaging and bright, each with a unique approach to the business; uniformly focused on consistent execution of their business strategy, in keeping with their interests and personalities. This appealed to me. I just knew that I'd be successful, within what seemed to me like a very entrepreneurial place as long as I had a plan and did the work.

Max initially wasn't too thrilled that I wasn't joining one of the top tier firms, but as time passed he came to understand why I did so. I had my priorities, time with my children.

I'd catapult quickly at a place that was growing their bond business, where so many accounts were yet uncovered. I was extremely well-trained in that area and knew how to source business. So, I simply went to work.

This calling room was a small drab room with around twelve of us on the second floor of the two-floor space the firm occupied. I began to wonder what it is about the culture of this business that décor outside the New York headquarters never seemed to matter. Variations on beige and worn out carpet went together wherever I went. We were tucked away in a corner right next to the water cooler.

The rest of the floor housed the institutional sales department with the usual railroaded trading desks. Equity sales and trading dominated the floor, the firm's main business at the time. Followed by the municipal desk. And then there were the growing corporate bond and mortgage-backed securities trading desks.

It wasn't easy getting started within this firm. There was a cultural adaptation that needed to take place. Many in a calling room don't last. Some stay, some leave or simply burn out. The sheer daily grind is a deterrent.

I started in the calling room from scratch, quickly developing traction and landing a few accounts. I just called every type of account for bond business that was not covered by the institutional desk; day-in-day-out, 100 or so calls a day. This business is a numbers game. Back then, for every 100 calls or so, one would have about thirty conversations. Eventually, a handful would become accounts.

Building a book of business is all about disciplined work, mental fortitude and follow-through. One simply has to be one's own cheerleader. As a woman in this business, hard work was the only way to make it, no leads, and no handouts.

I built my business at my desk with a phone and a *Quotron*, the quote machine of the time. That was the extent of technology. I wasn't going to travel and be away from my children. I had no choice, but to rely on my phone skills. It's amazing what one can accomplish through sheer will power.

I stayed true to Max's "How To Sell" principles. On that first conversation with a potential customer, I'd extract all the necessary information, so that when I made the next call, I wasn't wasting anyone's time. I learned to assess need and if the firm's product was an appropriate fit for the customer, matching the product to what the customer was looking for. I set criteria and cardinal rules for myself when it came to prospecting and selling. It had to be an investment product that I felt comfortable selling and thoroughly understood. I was conservative, developing an account base aligned to my nature.

Within a few months I hit the production markers that would move me away from that water cooler. I didn't miss the calling room as I graduated to the main retail trading floor. Once I left that calling room, I said good-bye to the last mentor I'd ever know in this business; my calling room manager took a little time to mentor.

I was now on my own, a revenue generator and that's all that mattered here. If you produced, you were left alone. I came to affectionately call this place "the outfit."

So what was life like after I left the calling room?

I moved to the floor that housed all the retail brokers. Glassed-in offices around the perimeter of the space surrounded an open area with rows of desks.

It was quieter than the calling room, where a bunch of young eager folks were trying to make their mark. There was a flurry in that room, not this one.

Let me tell you about this population. I was in the front row as you entered the floor, dead center between two guys who almost drove me out of the firm. To the right, one never quit talking about the divorce that he never got over some twenty years ago. He was around fifty years old, thin and slightly bald with gray frizzy hair. He kept his sleeves rolled up and pretty much spent the whole day reading his newspaper, when he wasn't complaining.

My other neighbor was to the left, in his sixties at the time. He reused his dental floss daily, a five-inch piece, stored in the top drawer of his desk right next to the pens. Without fail, it came out at the same time everyday after lunch, only to be reused and restored to its original location, the top drawer. When I first witnessed the ritual, I couldn't believe it. I always wondered if that piece of floss went with him when he retired some twenty years later.

Right before moving into an office, I had yet another colorful neighbor who kept talking about how much he wanted to be a restaurant entrepreneur. I wondered why then was he a broker. Like my former neighbor, he never stopped talking.

One day I finally told him, "For heavens sake and mine, just do it!" He eventually became a successful restaurateur.

Believe me, in that room there were many days where I thought, "What is this all about? How does this firm make money? What on earth am I doing here?"

At Salomon Brothers, I'd look around and there'd be two or three people I could learn from. Compared to the daily rigor I was used to, this place felt like a country club.

So how did I survive the cultural shock?

I kept my mind fixed on becoming one of the top brokers. I was determined to be one of them, but only after I suffered serious doubt as to whether I should stay here or not. But, you know, the Salomon Brothers training program taught me that any doubt had to be left at the front door. If you were to make it, it's because you worked and believed in yourself.

Imagine, graduating from the Kellogg business school and having been at the "hot spot" firm of the time, thrust into this environment. I don't know how I made it through those initial months, but I did. For one, I didn't have the ill placed self-importance that so many in the business have. Humility helped. The egos I just never understood.

I learned to largely tune out the surroundings, the noise, focusing like a laser on the work. Even if a loud marching band had walked through the floor, I probably wouldn't have looked up. I told myself that within five years I'd vault to Managing Director. I went from Associate to Vice President to Associate Director to Managing Director in short order. To keep myself focused on the goal, I took my business card with the title of Associate on it, scratched it out and wrote Managing Director in blue pen. I put the card in my wallet and to this day it is still there.

The pinnacle last spot, that of Senior Managing Director, was an altogether different league. Not that I couldn't have done that quickly. I chose not to for my children. It would have required far too great a time commitment. I sacrificed advancing as quickly as some of my male colleagues who started at the same time I did. That wasn't easy, as I'm competitive, but I had my priorities. It's about balance and the big picture, which way we want to go.

I sculpted a sizeable fixed income commission-based business within those first ten years, never had a loss month and always made money for the firm, becoming a multi-million dollar producer for years to come, purely on my own merit. I worked efficiently, didn't waste a minute, as I had a limited time slot daily to get my trading and prospecting in.

I had one time around with my children, no repeats. My pumpkin turned into a coach daily at 3:35 p.m.; only in this case it was a train carrying me to my children only to become a pumpkin the next morning around 8:30 a.m.

The first decade was the entryway, the antechamber of the firm. I got a feel for the landscape. I climbed the ladder rung by rung, making it on my own, while account referrals were dispensed to my male counterparts. Although I was putting up big production numbers, I felt visibly invisible.

As the second decade began, the bilingual little girl became quite fluent in reading two languages within this world; one of the mind, the other of the heart. It helped me sort the real and the unreal, and to act upon the real.

𝄞

During the decade 1988 through 1998, I rebuilt my personal and professional life. As I look back, I sometimes wonder why is it that I felt an underlying calm amidst all the struggles and changes that were taking place in my life?

Perhaps it had something to do with being able to make the difficult choices, fulfilling responsibilities and accomplishing goals in spite of obstacles. Couldn't we liken just about anything to a trade, there's always that point, the crossroad, where how we chose makes a difference in our lives and that of others.

I was established in my profession and at the same time thoroughly enjoyed life with my two boys. The three of us explored the world together in thought and travel.

I made the heart wrenching choice to end my marriage at the start of 1990 together with an annulment. I struggled for years with it, but, I felt deep down that it was the right decision. It was one of the heartbreaks of my life, in so many respects, particularly as I so desired to have more children. I felt like something deep was taken away. It was difficult, but I drew strength from my faith and those we look up to, who endure adversity. I had a great aunt who survived the harsh Siberian *Gulags.*

And so, I joined the sisterhood of single mothers raising children. I understand how they feel, the range of emotions and daily struggles that come their way. Raising and supporting two children on my own was not easy. It kept me busy "round-the-clock."

Being a mother was the most important part of my life. I made the deliberate choice to remain single until I raised my children. It was a decision based on my own personal belief that once a mother, your life is not your own, and any decision, need take into consideration first the well-being of your children. And so it was.

And yet, Someone did send a special someone into my life, who waited near a decade, with amazing patience, until I raised my children. In the meantime, when he visited, into the family fold he went as he participated in tennis, golf and crew meets that my competitive boys filled the decade with. And like children, they learned to even game the system a bit in taking advantage of Francois' fluency in multiple languages.

When my eldest composed a poem for his French class, his teacher remarked, "Why Daniel, if I didn't know any better, you think in French!"

And Daniel's mother remarked, "I'm on to why you leave your French homework, for when Francois comes to visit."

Gabriel simply continued the tradition paved by his brother.

𝄞

I started the first decade at my last investment bank with the October 1987 stock market crash. I ended it with the collapse in 1998 of the hedge fund Long Term Capital Management (LTCM). LTCM's fall led to a sizeable unwind and a bailout shaking the financial system at the time.

I witnessed yet another crisis, the Savings and Loan debacle during the 1980s that was years in the making. It showed up how policy decisions make a difference in prolonging or exacerbating a crisis. Hundreds of savings and loans failed, culminating in well over a $100 billion government and taxpayer funded bailout, leading up to the 1990-1992 recession.

Unlike the Savings and Loan bailout, the hedge fund, LTCM, was not a taxpayer funded bailout. It was a bailout orchestrated by the Federal Reserve and funded by a consortium of banks and Wall Street investment houses.

The collapse of LTCM in 1998 was considered monumental then; the bailout was under $4 billion, just ten years ago. Bailout came on to the radar, for a financial institution engaged in financially innovative proprietary trading strategies with high use of debt. Perhaps LTCM gave us a glimpse into what could potentially happen when we start introducing fancy trading strategies and high debt usage into the investment world.

Was it a crossroad and did we read the signals? Was the unwind a simpler version of the AIG bailout? And what is it that the AIG unwind is telling us now?

LTCM signaled the mutating of the financial world. Technology was very obviously driving the speed and way in which markets were developing. Financial engineering, complexity, derivatives, high debt usage, globalization and systemic risk were already on the radar.

We were becoming globally interdependent. LTCM's collapse was tied to the collapse of the Russian ruble and the Russian government defaulting on its own debt in August of 1998, brought on by the Asian Financial Crisis of July 1997.

The Asian Crisis started in Thailand with the collapse of its currency, the Thai baht. The Thai government could no longer support its currency in the face of too much debt, partially driven by the real estate market. In effect, the country was bankrupt. This then spread throughout Southeast Asia and Japan, causing their respective currencies to fall, stock market and asset prices to decline as a result of too much debt.

Was LTCM a precedent setting moment of choice and action?

You know, if you let it pass, next time might be worse. Didn't we have faith in our free market capitalist system and its principles to allow normal market forces to play themselves out without a need for bailout?

Failure cleanses the system, expunges flawed business models or high-risk practices within our free market capitalist economy. It rids the system of those who don't know what they're doing, but think they do, or those who do, but endanger the system with their high risk-taking.

I come back to the family as a nucleus and the importance of boundaries. If children are not taught responsibility due to parental bailout as parents turn a blind eye to irresponsible behavior, imagine the outcome.

Out-of-control behavior?

Let's fast forward to the present.

In growing big financial enterprises and markets, in chasing profits through complexity, even based on unsound fundamentals, in breaking down barriers and discarding basic principles, did we create an unmanageable fairytale with our fantasy creations?

This fantasy might just have been restrained, if we had stayed true to the principles of free market capitalism all along; one of which is to allow failure, another to restrain any one institution from growing too big in its size and complexity where it may endanger the system at large.

The simple notion of respect and responsibility keeps coming back, nothing too fancy; the sticking to principles that form the blueprint for a system and the harnessing of human ambition by an ethical and robust regulatory framework.

We all know that capitalism is about accumulating wealth in private hands and maximizing shareholder value, but is there not such a thing as a soul in business?

I think there is. Leaders are responsible for maintaining a healthy economy and society. Being entrusted with that responsibility, should take them beyond mere short-term profit and power. It's the soul within business that might have just averted our current crisis. For example, do financial institutions pursue profit at any cost, or in line with maintaining financial and systemic stability over the long-term?

Some financial enterprises have obviously done good things for business and society. But, it makes one wonder, doesn't it, the extent to which good is erased given the sheer scale and cost of our current financial and human crisis.

If we chase growth and profit in disruptive ways,

we disrespect the system of capitalism in such a way as to eventually lead to its demise. Colossal complex financial structures and markets developed, but they were enabled. We blurred the lines between banking, brokerage and insurance where a financial *Jurassic Park* turned on us. If it doesn't quite get us this time, next time the dinosaurs won't be so friendly.

I happen to think that the traditional banking model, where banks take in deposits and lend is a good model; not enough money in it for some. And so, we allowed things to grow big, complex, and out-of-control. The only way out for some of the too-big-to-fail casualties is through government intervention and ownership, whether back door or front door, which by "definition" suggests socialism. Monstrous structures had nowhere to go, but to be pushed through the front door of the government right on to our couch.

Bend the rules and before we know it, we end up drifting in a direction where we lose control, of our own economic and social freedom, even democracy eventually. Inordinate national debt, in and of itself, is a threat to freedom. Perhaps, there is something to the way this country's free market capitalist system functioned for decades with many small and personal businesses that had a human touch, where there was a stepping in of government to disallow or break up monopolistic-type structures.

So what happened?

A financial system was allowed to flourish in a disorderly legalized way in scale and magnitude, the cumulative effect of which created a financial and human crisis worldwide.

Where are we?

Our nation is in debt lock-down. We have a wobbly financial system. Credit isn't flowing as it should.

With all the mergers and bailouts, we've created even bigger bank structures. It makes one wonder if after all the talk, we've done much to mitigate systemic risk.

What is even more disturbing is that for all the brouhaha about "bad bankers," not much has changed, some say. I thought for a moment that I wasn't seeing straight when I came upon a June 27, 2009 *Financial Times* article entitled, How fading political will has let banks off the hook (By John Plender). My parents never stopped talking about will power.

The writer notes that banks are still plugged into a central bank liquidity feed as a lack of trust lingers in the markets. The value of toxic assets is still uncertain. Changing mark-to market accounting rules for valuing toxic assets may even facilitate the creation of "zombie" banks; meaning living banks that are insolvent. Regulatory reforms still leave much to be desired. The modern day bank business model remains.

We sit on a national debt of over $11.5 trillion. A near $1.6 trillion 2009 deficit faces us. It ballooned as a direct result of the financial crisis. We added some $1.2 trillion (in stimulus and bailouts) to the $400 billion deficit that was already there at the start of 2009. Such deficits are unsustainable without sustainable stable growth within the private sector and the abatement of deficit spending. And, worldwide calls for a new international currency mount.

A deficit is the difference between "ins" and "outs." If we run annual deficits, they create a national debt. National debt is the cumulative amount of debt created over the years by annual deficits.

Debt may be financed in any number of ways; 1) Borrowing, which means we pay interest on our Treasury bonds; 2) Collecting and/or raising taxes. 3) Printing money, which devalues a currency. When the gold standard was eliminated in 1971 (where gold backed our currency), it opened the door for the printing of money to manage financial crises.

Pumping trillions into our economy, as a result of the crisis, created the gaping 2009 deficit. This deficit is to be funded by money we don't have. This means we need to borrow, raise taxes, cut spending or print money.

Of course, pumping trillions into an economy may make it and even the stock market pop in the short-run. It may give it a fleeting boost. Stimulus intends to jumpstart the economy to eventually plug the deficits. But, here too, the stimulus needs to laser in on stimulating the economy in a way that will generate sustainable growth within the private sector with job creation, rather than one-off band-aid application.

What of the long term consequences as we dig a deeper debt hole for ourselves?

We are not only oil dependent, but dependent upon the world to finance our debt.

Why is all this troublesome?

We trespassed into a danger zone. Not just because of all those trillions in debt generated by bailouts and spending, but because we chiseled away at our free market economic system and its principles that have made us unique in the world.

Individual freedom and small government are embedded in the founding principles of our country. In the process of bailing out our financial stewards, we created an even bigger government and bigger debt. Is our freedom and happiness now being threatened by not only big inefficient institutions, but also an even bigger government because of the choices we made in the last decade to grow unbridled for profit?

If the government is taking over so much of the private sector, who will work to support the government? And if the financial component of the private sector misbehaves while innovating, how can we innovate, and where does this put us as a nation?

So much of what has caused our current financial crisis, is embedded in so many other worldwide previous crises — mismanagement, lack of fiscal discipline, lack of timely checks and balances, miscalculation of risk, and too much debt — crises that prior to our current crisis, have been contained to a specific institution, market, country, or currency. As we've gone global and moved towards big everything, everything gets amplified as we stray, thereby making the consequences much deeper and wider.

Why should debt of an amount close to our GDP (Gross Domestic Product) concern us?

Our fiscal health determines if we remain strong or grow weak as a nation.

What makes a nation or any individual strong?

Self-reliance.

Imagine what happens to a household burdened by excessive debt. Debt is a yoke, stealthy indentured servitude. It has the potential to strip one of freedom and power, whether an individual, family or nation. It may even make access to basic necessities difficult. It impedes forward progress, simple human development. For a nation, it affects security, and threatens political and economic stability.

If new money is printed to finance national debt (referred to as "monetizing debt"), it expands money supply. It may lead to hyperinflation, devaluing our dollar. Borrowing heavily may lead to higher interest rates, as we are now part of a global economy with competition for funding resources. High interest rates mean that our debt may replicate from the interest expense alone, leading to a larger portion of our tax dollars going to service debt. This takes away resources for productive deployment.

High interest rates increase our cost of funding as a nation, as individuals and businesses. It puts a squeeze on profits, and thereby our stock market, affecting our retirement accounts.

China finances a major chunk of our debt, but for how long will this continue if we cannot manage our fiscal affairs. Already other nations are pulling back from buying our debt. Investors too will chase returns in countries that show promising growth. Once the capital outflow out of a country starts, it's a different ballgame altogether. It leads to further job loss and revenue depletion in the face of ever burgeoning debt. One is at another's mercy as one loses self-reliance.

How is it that countries get into debt, you may ask?

It happens in any number of ways. It could be man-made, self-created through mismanagement and fiscal irresponsibility. It may be imposed by former colonial powers, as in the case of some Third World debt. There is the odious debt, where a despotic regime takes on national debt to serve its own purpose rather than the best interests of the nation.

How is it that countries come out of debt?

Slowly, like a family with enormous credit card balances, it takes time. Will we get out of debt as a nation, if debt is so large that it replicates itself from the interest expense alone?

At current interest rates, we add near half a trillion to our deficit annually, just to finance our national debt. With a deficit that has gone from $400 billion to near $1.6 trillion in 2009, where will money come from to shrink it, if we face such interest expense and revenue loss from a contracting economy in the face of the growing unemployed and aging baby boomer population?

Now imagine what happens to the deficit and debt if interest rates rise. At 10% rates, the annual interest expense on our $11.5 trillion national debt exceeds a trillion.

I am reminded of the Latin American Debt crisis (LDC), which started back in 1982. A number of countries, considered Third World, burdened with high interest rates and low commodity prices, were unable to service their indebtedness on commercial bank loans, heavily in debt compounded by fiscal irresponsibility and mismanagement.

For close to a decade these countries tried to restructure and reschedule their debt, with failed attempts. That period from 1982 to 1988 is sometimes referred to as one of those lost decades, a period of stagnation where countries were burdened under the weight of debt.

Eventually the debt was restructured with our saving guidance under the Brady Plan in 1989, and floated into the capital markets. The debt relief came with the caveat that economic reform, such as fiscal responsibility and control of inflation, would need to take place.

Going back further in history, there was the debt restructuring after World War II, whereby we allowed Britain to repay its debt at a lower rate in order to rebuild. German debt, on the other hand, was cancelled, so that they could reconstruct. We were a creditor nation then. We went from creditor nation to an ocean of debt.

How did we get there?

Here's one reflection.

𝄞

Once upon a time, there was a kingdom ruled by a King and Queen of strength and vision. They set the tone for the land to stay true to its ideals and objectives. It became an economic superpower, a creditor land in the 1950s. It's people worked hard and took care of each other. They saved, manufactured and produced.

The twinkly land of lights was peppered with

small businesses and opportunities, where people knew their business proprietor by first name. They trusted each other and sometimes a handshake was all it took to make a deal.

Businesses were mostly loyal to their workers, as they took care of them in their old age. The young felt full of hope as they looked into the future. They knew that if they worked hard they'd advance. Those at the top mentored and took care of them. Seeing the future with all its opportunities gave them tremendous motivation.

A new King and Queen came into power straying from ideals and objectives, intent on maintaining there power. Businesses saw that they could increasingly gain sway, to grow big in all sorts of ways. They grew obsessed with numbers.

Some took on increasing debt to grow as they steamrolled small businesses. Big companies rolled across the land as profit coffers bulged. Some came to disrespect the older, put the younger in the galleys.

They sought new ways to get bigger and plump profits, so they outsourced jobs to other kingdoms where labor was cheaper. Cost cutting and generating profit at any cost destroyed the work of so many a loyal subject.

The land began to change as workers discovered and built a new world. They began to create new and fast products that enabled them to create even newer services of all types. They even built businesses around handling inefficiencies of what they created. Trusting each other grew difficult, so much so that it took a legal treatise to just make a deal. They got a bit giddy with all this new stuff.

Businesses encouraged people to spend, tempting them with wares, even if unaffordable. They sold people debt to buy that which they could not afford. Some people began to change, to let go of financial inhibitions, to succumb to the allure of wares.

The land went from saving and producing, to consuming and spending, where the economy whittled towards being predominantly service-based. The land imported products, those its people once upon a time so beautifully spun, to take care of each other. Both the land and its people borrowed and consumed their way into debt where neither could pay their bills without taking on more debt.

Those predisposed towards finance, developed a world of their own, a world where they learned how to make money by off-loading and transferring risk with fancy instruments. They traded amongst themselves and with powerful computers to enormously please the King and Queen. They were allowed to run free. They lived in the highest grounds of the kingdom, frolicked in dollar bill-laden pastures, sequestered from the rest. The King and Queen turned a blind eye, even enabled the profligacy as they took on so much debt and risk.

One day, the King and Queen woke worried. The consumption of the land sent so many dollar bills to other lands. They looked at their monstrous debt and ephemeral asset creations, begotten of the highest grounds of the land. They came to be puzzled as to what to do. They just spent more, taxed and borrowed.

The world wants to live well too, as we cannot exist in isolation in lifestyle once we've taken the step to go global. Like water seeking its own level, so too here.

Today, we may pay lower prices for some products sold through big discount supermarkets, which outsource labor and suppliers overseas. If other countries rise, cheapness abroad may dissipate. Our corporate profits may go the other way, getting squeezed by increased regulation, increased labor costs resultant from a lack of cheap labor abroad and labor expense on our shores. This may result in a compression of wages here at home, changing our lifestyle and standard of living. It may continue to affect our stock market, as it is dependent upon corporate profitability.

Our lifestyle may change as funding resources become more competitive and expensive, as we may run out of money to keep things nice, under the weight of debt. We are already aware of what is taking place within our states and municipalities. The trickle-down shows up in rising taxes and curtailment of services.

If we operate in a global economy, our actions, very obviously, influence the rest of the world. We are the largest economy with the largest debt load.

Who will get us out of debt?

With trillions in debt already and trillions in looming entitlement obligations, we may not. The normal channels of debt reduction would include increased taxation and spending cuts. Productive innovation that creates jobs in the private sector is another component as it increases tax revenue. In the meantime, if we're spending much more than we take in, what are we doing?

How can we sustain spending of money we don't have, which continues to this day with little sign that the spending and increase in debt is abating?

It's deeply troublesome.

As we finance our ever-widening debt in the trillions, we may cause dislocations in other parts of the world. For example, those regions that may have managed their fiscal affairs prudently may no longer be insulated from our turmoil as they compete with us for investor money.

In chasing wealth and power, perhaps it is changing the seismic game for us. Wealth may shift globally from the West to the East as we find ourselves in debt lock-down, while other countries may rise. Some of those countries have surpluses, not deficits.

Debt and uncertainty are just two sides to the same coin, perhaps another trade.

In taking on such debt, did we create an uncertain future?

The markets submerged into deep freeze August 2007 in a way I had never seen in decades on Wall Street. This crisis tested investment managers, even those who thought themselves indomitable. It wiped out livelihoods and wealth, even destroyed whole markets that were operative for decades.

A news flash came across my computer screen on June 2, 2009 entitled, Next Crime Wave? FBI Targets TARP Fraud (By Reuters). I reached for my eyeglasses to make sure I was reading correctly.

Where are we going if yet another wave of fraud

and corruption rolls forward, put into motion by the multi-trillion bailout and stimulus package?

"Oh my goodness," my first thought; seems to me like this could be yet another *Pandora's Box*.

Plagues come in all forms, not just locusts and visible disease. They take the form of deception, "doublethink" and doubletalk. The slow creep within a system may go unnoticed as a festering infection, perhaps manifesting itself, now and then, on the weaker, the innocent, the trustworthy where it's impact is hidden, until one day it erupts on to the world stage.

𝄞

Mrs. Mayfield announces that it's quiet reading time. I walk over to the bookshelf and pick up Alice in Wonderland.

Alice meets the Cheshire Cat at a crossroad:

"Would you tell me, please, which way I ought to go from here?" asked Alice.

"That depends a good deal on where you want to get to," said the Cat.

"I don't much care where — " said Alice.

"Then it doesn't matter which way you go," said the Cat.

" — so long as I get somewhere," Alice added as an explanation.

"Oh, you're sure to do that," said the Cat, "if you only walk long enough."

I'm thinking this Cat is kind of a trickster. Alice shouldn't have said "I don't much care where." She should pick a direction. There may be a lot at stake if she doesn't.

What if I didn't know where I was going?

Chapter Five

The *Orwellian* World

f

Spinning Wheel

January 30, 2009

Spinning Wheel, I remember playing you on the piano in second grade. You were one of many pieces within the "Thompson Book of Piano Music."

I now hear you in my mind as if it was just yesterday. But why is it that, you, I recall? Was there something you meant to tell me?

I seem to remember a picture of a maiden at a spinning wheel, juxtaposed onto the music score, making something for someone else. She had a small business of her own. She spun her wheel for a purpose to create a sweater, a blanket, something of some use to someone else. And in return, I do believe, that someone gladly obliged with payment for her work beautifully spun, deeply valued, perhaps a family somewhere warm to make. This gave her reason to continue her work.

What were we spinning this last decade?

The Last Investment Bank, Second Decade 1998 to 2008

What is business really all about? What does it mean to you?

I believe it's about making profits, but in a way where goods and services are exchanged for mutual benefit, additive to our daily lives, and additive to the whole of humanity. Daily we are presented with opportunities to make each other's lives better.

My father used to say, "to those whom much is given, much is expected." It became a creed in my life. As I traveled the financial world, I tried to lift those around me, with me. I wanted them to succeed and feel valued along the way.

Have we lost ourselves in growth, complexity, spreadsheets and numbers when it comes to profit? Have we become like the businessman on the Fourth Planet of The Little Prince?

If I had a bullhorn, I'd describe the last decade like this.

Who turned up the amplifiers?

And now we're getting even bigger — big banks with big glaring neon signs in our neighborhoods to remind us that they're there, big government, big interests, big deficits, big national debt, big compensation, big talk, big markets, big money flows, and big anything else, yet unimagined.

We've grown big in the name of big growth and profits, made fast for few, creating failing financial institutions with balance sheets weighted with big dumpsters filled with big bad paper, to be financed by us all with big trillions, slowly for decades to come. We're fixing big debt with even bigger debt. What a big spin. It's out-of-control!

What are we doing?

Now picture an arch.

We start with 1998, at the beginning of that arch.

We just bailed out the hedge fund Long Term Capital Management. Glass-Steagall is repealed by our legislators in 1999. The financial system is transforming, mutating, the competition between big banks and Wall Street investment houses is intensifying. Banks are getting bigger. Profits from the traditional ways of doing business, buying and selling of securities, like stocks and bonds, are getting squeezed. Securitization and credit derivatives are driving profits. Hedge funds and private equity funds are increasingly gaining momentum with investors.

By the time we make it to the other side of the arch in 2007, we're in a financial crisis.

Of the major Wall Street investment houses, two fold into the big banks, two become bank holding companies and one goes bankrupt. The true intent of Glass-Steagall is turned upside down. Hedge fund assets hemorrhage. Private equity shops are overburdened with debt. We witness an outpouring of scandals and fraud across our land as if its everyday normal.

What happened as we went up that arch during this last decade?

We amplify, magnify. We grow big financial institutions, with complex products to make for complex markets. We over-reach, over-sell and take on too much debt. As we tinker with financial engineering to create all sorts of fancy complex investment products and markets, do we really understand what's at stake at this crossroad, and where we are going with all this?

Nonetheless profits are turbo charged, amplified, managements are incentivized by their boards to do so, as an interconnected labyrinthine financial world of new products, markets and financial players swells at such pace, such scale and such breath, and such complexity!

Who kept the lantern burning?

The regional brokerages and banks, that "stuck to their knitting" throughout the decades, under fierce competition from their bigger brethren and were managed well, had no need for bailouts.

𝄞

A lynx makes an astounding leap now and then. As I made the leap to Senior Managing Director, I found myself in what I perceived to be an *Orwellian* world.

What is an *Orwellian* world?

It derives from George Orwell's novel, 1984, a dystopia – opposite of utopia.

It is a world that creates its own reality and favors "uns" in word usage.

Inside an *Orwellian* world, one feels like "what is, is not and what it is not, it is." Doublethink and "doublespeak" live within such a world. Inconsistent concepts are put together to create a reality, to simply accept without dissension. Incongruent concepts are supposed to make sense.

For example, "bailouts" to such an extent within

a free market capitalist economy? It feels so crazy where one begins to say, "am I in the twilight zone?"

In an *Orwellian* world, language becomes a tool to successfully obfuscate or mask true meaning.

Have you experienced this?

For example, does renaming "toxic" assets, "legacy" assets (under PPIP) make any sense to you, like they may go away?

When I think of "legacy," I think of something memorable, enduring. It's almost like someone is giving you a gift. "Toxic" assets caused the financial crisis.

I've often wondered how we came up with the name for the Troubled Asset Relief Program (TARP). Who feels relief, as we've been relieved of our jobs and money while troubled assets remain?

Big banks are functional and solvent, so why is lending impaired?

Banks are profitable, but they've been plugged into a multi-trillion taxpayer-funded intravenous feed (IV) and, where have all the trillions in toxic assets and derivatives gone?

In an *Orwellian* world, what is known is *un*known. For example, we all know that some of the same folks, who got us into this *raucous mess,* are at the helm trying to solve it.

In an *Orwellian* world, what is complex may become *un*complex; when expedient, like for the purposes of pushing profits to make millions and billions. But then, the *un*complex becomes way too complex as a tool to hide behind for the purposes of accountability.

Knots knotted by word spin, doublethink and

"doublespeak" become so complex that it may mask reality and enormity of a problem, such that coming up with solutions remains elusive. It's like trying to grab hold of mercury.

What do we end up with?

We end up with truth being masked by *un*-knowability through complexity. We've manufactured complexity in instruments through layers of securitization that masked reality, so we could easily manufacture complexity in use of language to obfuscate reality. Call it verbal engineering.

How do we solve a problem if the scale of the problem eludes us and few, if any, take accountability? Or is the multi-trillion ashen cloud hovering above us just too dark to see through that it needs to be veiled through complexity as it would scare us all?

Getting at truth to ascertain true reality becomes problematic in a world of illusion.

Within the world I lived in, truth became *un*truth, one of relative nature. It was a difficult world to live in. Limits and boundaries were applied differently to different people. Those on the "in" lived by another standard. Boundaries shifted or rules were bent based on expediency as if normal and acceptable. The right way depended upon where one wanted to go.

At times I felt like I was swirling to an eerie dissonant waltz, more like the "Waltz" in Khachaturian's Masquerade Suite than a mellifluous Strauss waltz. Yet, I created a hamlet within my own office, where I played my own music just to maintain normality. I listened frequently to Khachaturian's "Nocturne" and "Romance" within that same Masquerade Suite.

Perhaps a belief by the powers at be in the relativity of truth, the Machiavellian "might is right," is exactly what turned our lives upside down. When we operated under that premise, we turned Glass-Steagall upside down to serve profit. In so doing, it was one of those dominoes that set the stage for our financial crisis.

So much goes back to sticking to simple basics, the little things and details, like common sense. You know, if we jam things into tight spots, it's difficult when the doors open.

Most of us have storage lockers and garages. They may be stuffed full with all sorts of things, in disorganized and crooked ways, one on top of the other. It accumulates over time. Sooner or later, there's no more room and things start to collapse as we open the door. The wider it opens, the bigger the mess we see!

What would you do?

One could easily keep stuffing those closets, jamming the door, keeping fingers crossed, hoping that it all stays shut until the next time. Or one could go in and excavate to get to the bottom of it all and fix the broken system, reorganize it, get some closet organizers that clean things up.

When those financial storage closets opened, was it like what the fish told Sally and her brother about the mess in Dr. Seuss' The Cat in the Hat?

I think the first step to redemption is to simply recognize the problem.

𝄞

We're having a classroom discussion about leaders.

Mrs. Mayfield asks, "What makes a good leader?"

Billie raises his hand and says, "They like to conquer and win battles. They collect riches along the way."

I'm thinking, "Boy, he needs some help."

He's sitting across from me.

In a hushed tone, rolling my little index finger, I lean over and say, "Hey Billie, come here."

I whisper, "My parents are good leaders."

"Why?" says Billie.

"They keep me in line. You know, I kind of get tired of hearing "do this" and "do that." But I have to do what they say as they mean it. You should see what happens to me when I misbehave — no allowance, no ice cream. I had to kneel in a corner once for an hour! I didn't respect my sister when I broke her arm trying to give her a piggyback ride. My sister's almost the same size as me. That was kind of dumb."

"Sure thing," Billie pipes in.

"My knees were so red after all that kneeling I could barely stand up!"

"You're kidding?" mutters Billie.

"No, Billie, I'm not. But I think my parents love me, even when they get tough. They say it's for my own good. So I believe in them and think that they're probably right. That's why I can't figure out why they go to Confession, as they don't need to."

"Maybe it's because they make you do all that stuff you complain about or maybe it was kneeling in that corner," whispers Billie.

"Nope, it's because they say that they want to instill character and values, so that when I grow up I have good habits," I respond.

Billie goes on to say, "do they let you watch TV?"

"Only on Saturday nights with the whole family. I like to cuddle up with them to watch *The Jackie Gleason Show.* My mom makes sure that the refrigerator is stocked way ahead of time; so that there's plenty of popcorn and strawberry tarts for everyone."

The *Andante*

My beloved music best describes the last decade of my professional life. I felt like the oboe in the *Andante con moto* movement of Franz Schubert's Symphony Number 9.

The *Andante* starts with a haunting, solitary solo oboe playing its beautiful melody, almost marchlike. Then come intermittent interjections from the orchestra, mostly strings. The oboe just keeps forging ahead, playing its own melody. The back and forth between the oboe and the orchestra continues.

About five minutes into the piece, a French horn is heard in the very background, followed by melancholy music. Then the orchestra asserts itself. The oboe goes quiet, but then comes back to play.

The French horn returns more noticeably, sounding a haunting premonition–like warning, followed by the oboe staying true to its melody, again marchlike. Melancholy music follows.

Now some ten minutes into the piece, come the interruptions, powerful eruptions from the orchestra and strings, growing ever more forceful and intense as if to drown the oboe out or make it go silent. A back and forth interchange takes place. The oboe continues to march along with its melody to assert its presence.

The orchestral strings overpower the oboe as it tries to interject, culminating with a suspension of play after an intense battle like interchange, where the oboe is nowhere to be heard. In music, the term "suspension" is a climax where the music may cease entirely, momentarily.

The oboe comes back, sadly and differently, together with melancholy music. The oboe melody is heard again. Not giving into the force of the strings and orchestral cacophony, the oboe perseveres, its melody returns. In the end, the oboe is heard.

𝄞

I reach the pinnacle of my career in the early 2000s. I am named Senior Managing Director. It's a seesaw between me and a few other teams, when it comes to being the number one producer within the Chicago retail division. Nationwide the division houses some 500 or so brokers, populated with a few of my gender.

I remain within that top echelon for years. I go from solo broker with an assistant to growing a group focused primarily on investments for corporations.

The firm I joined in 1988 had now grown from a somewhat obscure secondary shop of 5,000 to a top-notch investment bank of some 14,000. Here I go again, in the arms of another birthmother, one that creates the subprime mortgage-backed security in the mid-1990s. The firm becomes a formidable competitor in mortgage securitization, underwriting and trading.

The tenure of its management was unique to Wall Street. Some of the same folks who ran the company back in its private partnership days were still running it. The firm spent this last decade accumulating the best talent with stellar credentials. My academic qualifications now fit the place. In this respect, I felt at home. What was a somewhat sleepy old world brokerage firm was now transformed to a Wall Street powerhouse, across the range of underwriting and trading activities.

Now when I looked around, there were many to learn from. The brightest and hungriest investment bankers, traders and salespeople that money could buy populated the firm. This working group was the backbone that drove the firm's success. It was about output and production, no slacking off in this place.

The firm's offices came to now reflect its success and the earnings engine powering this titan. A headquarters erected in splendor graced the Manhattan skyline. Sleek and streamlined she was, all mirrored in glass. Her beauty was effortless in form and proportion. Inside, lobby ceilings soared to the sky. Dark wood paneling accented the marble floors. She had power, state of the art technology and money written all over her.

As I walked past the security entrance towards the elevator, the magnificence of the buzz was unmatched. She tantalized me, like the bank revolving doors of my childhood. I came to call her *The Appoggiatura.* In music, this is the embellishment to the primary theme.

So what was taking place in the financial world

at this time?

In the year 2000, the forces that brought us to this financial crisis were aswirl. We were digesting the excesses spawned by the Internet revolution. Internet companies sprouted in the late 1990s at an exponential rate. They came to market with initial public offerings (IPOs) opening multiples above their initial pricing, even for companies that had no earnings.

Turned out, the Internet bubble was no different than previous asset bubbles as investors go from one Maypole Dance to the next. Asset bubbles are pretty much the same throughout history in their insanity. Investors do the same thing over and over again expecting a different result. They drive up prices for assets thinking that each time, they're sustainable. Yet, with each bubble the stakes get higher with technological advancements, increased money flows and global interdependence.

So what happened in the aftermath of the technology and Internet bubble bust?

We lined up the dominoes for our current financial crisis. The collapse of the Nasdaq and September 11, 2001, ushered in a liquidity boom to stave off an economic downturn. The then Fed Chairman embarked on an interest rate-cutting mode all the way down to those 1%-type levels. This fueled the securitization boom and with it, came the unsustainable escalation in asset values.

Debt-driven liquidity put the runaway train in motion. Banks and Wall Street investment houses took on debt to keep the securitization machine pumping. Consumers bought homes for all sorts of reasons, some speculating, some converting their dwellings into piggybanks. Hedge funds bought securities with debt to enhance returns. Some private equity funds increasingly bought bigger companies with debt.

The debt siren purveyors were on just about every street corner, as perhaps truth was being marginalized as to what we could and could not afford. Were we as a society truthfully changing in changing the truth as buyers and sellers for expediency?

Consumption based on debt doesn't last.

Was there a letting go of financial inhibitions, a morphing of social mores and an accepting of risk as if risk took on a new meaning in this *Orwellian* world?

Were we as individuals, institutions and government looking at risk as if it was *un*risk, subconsciously thinking that if things go awry, we could simply walk away from our obligations, turn to bailouts or borrow more?

𝄞

Success.

We all like it. It feels good.

It's not just for the chosen few, but those chosen few might just have spoiled a thing or two that might now make many feel not so good.

How many of you have heard that success is about being at the right place at the right time?

It's true, but it's also about preparation and seeing opportunities when they present themselves. As I tell my children, "just try it, go for it, what have you got to lose, when an opportunity presents itself."

It's the early 2000s and the firm decides to build

out its municipal auction rate securities business. Steeped in the coverage of corporations at Salomon Brothers, I develop a business plan to complement my existing business with growth in this area. Corporations were buyers of auction rate securities.

What is an auction rate security?

It is a debt instrument issued by a corporation, student loan issuer or municipality with a long-term underlying maturity. Before the financial crisis hit, the auction rate securities market had grown to some $330 billion, becoming an important financing conduit for municipalities as well student loan issuers. It provided a competitive investment vehicle for investors. The auction rate securities market was in existence since my days at Salomon Brothers in the mid-1980s, albeit of smaller size.

Briefly, here's how an auction rate security works. The interest rate is typically reset every 7, 28 or 35 days through a competitive bidding process called a "Dutch Auction." In a Dutch Auction, buyers and sellers have the opportunity to buy, sell or hold their shares on those reset dates so long as there are sufficient bids to clear the auction. Bid rates are lined up from lowest to highest, with the "clearing rate" being the lowest bid rate at which the last share can be sold. All buyers then end up receiving the clearing rate for the upcoming period until the next reset.

Many firms at the time were already active in this market. Growing in the municipal auction rate market was a natural area of growth for our firm as we were already one of the top underwriters in the municipal market.

Timing was perfect. My children were getting older with wheels to drive themselves to activities. For many years, I felt I could skyrocket in my field, but didn't, as I made the choice to be a mom first. It created a pent-up demand within me, that given the time and opportunity, propelled me to excel. It all came together — timing, training, experience, and knowledge.

Mother was able to devote more time to her career. What many do with their careers in their twenties, I did in my forties. I threw myself into my work. My growth was exponential. Anyone that drives revenue within an investment bank carries weight.

Within the culture of this firm, rare was the woman in sales or production with my tenure. More often, women found their way into other departments, not necessarily on the frontline in production, buying and selling securities.

I was an anomaly. The Chicago office managers would come and go, but I was the resident female fixture in production within the Chicago office. I felt like a trophy, taken off the shelf on the rare occasion that one of my own might be passing by for an interview, with the ubiquitous question, "why are there so few women here?"

Why?

It was all over the Street that this division was not female friendly. The numbers told the story as the female to male ratio left much to be desired. Here's what it felt like living in this world — do as they say, play "nice in the sandbox," embrace mistruths with no dissent, but we'll take your production.

Max used to tell me, "You've found a way to operate in a man's world."

This one was tough. Within organizations, credibility is gained by proving oneself. Despite doing so and having become a Senior Managing Director, the top title, being second-guessed became a way of being after awhile. Proven competence was ignored for expedient agendas.

Max would kid me about being too innocent and trusting.

"It'll keep you in the game. You won't get discouraged," he'd opine.

How right he was!

I bought into the firm mantra, corporate propaganda. This "All For the Firm," no individual interest rules. Later to learn, but for those in the club, as rules were applied differently depending upon the agenda.

I hadn't much to do with New York, early on in my career. I flew under the radar. An occasional account dispute would arise, but it was more often than not handled at the regional office level. Referred to as the "reasonable professional woman" within their circle, I played into their hand when it came to account disputes. Not for the sake of politics, but out of respect for authority, upholding the values my parents ingrained in me.

Well, my growth trajectory did catch the attention of New York, like maybe there's something to the kind of business she's built.

Word came back, in discussions amongst them, "is this woman for real?"

Honestly, last time I looked I was.

I drew attention, but not the kind I wished for.

Like, "wow, you're doing a great job, what can we do in terms of resources to help you grow." Oh, no, no, no, not at all!

A new dynamic would soon emerge, a kind of plucking of accounts and prospects. Me losing the account or prospect dispute was always their end-game; subtly played out, as to leave hardly a foot-print. It wasn't always the, "you can't have this," more often a creation of a circumstance where I'd lose.

"Let's toss a coin," they'd flippantly say, with me in Chicago, them in New York on a conference call. How would you choose?

I felt they were amused at raising my hopes that I'd win. That I'd have a fair hearing only to have my hopes dashed each and every time.

"The heads or tails" scenario seemed to never end. If you pick this one, the next one won't be yours so be sure. To be sure about a prospect wasn't always easy. There was never a next one, when I gave one away.

Was it calloused behavior or was it the powerful exercising their power carelessly, disregarding what in their view was the weaker, as their self-interested agendas took precedence?

I played by the rules, towed the line and believed in them to come through. The account and prospect battles raged in the 2000s between New York and Chicago. That, in and of itself, is a novel. Stay tuned.

I believe we view others within the context of where we come from, within the framework of our up-bringing and experiences. I believed each time, that maybe some good would come out of one of those disputes. That just maybe, that "next" time would be "the" time, that there'd be a change of heart.

Why is it that for some enough is never enough?

The same tape played and played and played. You know, business is tough enough without having to battle the resistance from those who are supposed to take care of their own, one with big production numbers too. Imagine doing the legwork to develop an account relationship and before you know it, they're yanking it out from underneath you.

So how did I survive the constant pummel?

I marched to my own tune regardless, with the elegance, finesse and panache that the little girl was taught once upon a time. I executed my responsibilities to my clients and took care of my group to the best of my ability.

𝄞

It's 2005. I'm in my beautiful corner office, referred to as the "yoga studio." It's calm, a welcome embrace from the account conflict barrage.

Beautiful cherry double doors grace the entry into an L-shaped office. Serene, with four sleek sage colored Italian club chairs in the corner surrounding a round cherrywood coffee table. Our trading desks are custom fitted into the three bay windows making for an even sleeker décor. My CD player is right next to my trading screens on low volume during trading hours. I up the volume a bit for those moments during the day when I close my eyes to transport into a world of beauty, my beloved music.

I run my office in a way where everything has its order. It's our hamlet. Things are put away, organized and customer ready, always prepared just in case someone drops by. I set the tone for the office. When it comes to our customers and each other, it's about integrity, respect and loyalty.

Expectations are spelled out. Customer service is high on our radar. Prospecting targets are set and achieved. Our energies bear down on productive engagement whether it is trading, servicing accounts, prospecting or simply watching and studying the markets.

There's a calm in my office environment, but for the account and prospect conflict disruptions. We're operating on all engines, full steam ahead. Despite the disruptions, we build one of the largest cash management teams in the firm through sheer work.

Encouraging and protecting my group became a full time job in and of itself. Even I developed a mantra "we're not giving into them and we're standing our ground, as they deliberately chisel at our business. We'll just keep coming back, as they tighten the screws!"

One can hold out, but ultimately it takes its emotional and business toll.

How do you take over a fortress?

Cut off its supplies.

In our business, it's cutting off the prospect pipeline. A prospecting system houses prospects or leads that one registers as one's own. Prospecting and marketing, like any business, feeds its growth.

How do you cut off a prospect pipeline?

We're in our office having a group discussion.

"Can you believe they've been farming our registered prospects filtering them elsewhere, so in effect we've been working for someone else without even knowing it?"

It didn't matter whether we registered a prospect or not. It was a *fait accompli.* They back up their own. We lose.

I fear for the financial world.

"Tell the truth," said my mama and papa when I poked my sister's *Kissy* doll.

"Don't take the ice cream all for yourself, leave some for someone else," they'd say.

Is this how a "House of Cards" gets built?

Labyrinth or Spider Web

Spartacus comes to mind. I feel like him in this hubristic world, trying to persevere and take care of my group. Never thought that the gladiator training in the Salomon Brothers program would come in this handy. I am responsible for their well-being. They have lives, a need for a livelihood as others count on them.

Amidst the stormy account battles, what's going on in the financial world and how is it shaping up?

I'm watching a runaway train gaining momentum as financial institutions grow at an accelerated pace in complex products and markets.

Salomon Brothers — 1985 and the balcony overlooking the trading floor — seems so long ago. Yet, it went by in a flash!

It was a simple world back then, just buying stocks and bonds for a commission. Insurance companies stuck to their mainstream business. Securitization was just getting going. There were few hedge funds around. Banks were doing lending. Wall Street investment houses underwrote securities, traded with customers, and amongst themselves, but nothing like the counterparty world in the trillions that would come to be.

What's a counterparty?

It's who you're in a deal with, the other side of the trade. It could be anyone of our financial institutions – banks, Wall Street investment houses, hedge funds, insurance companies, pension funds, endowments or any other investor.

What was I thinking on the Salomon Brothers balcony, right after I gave birth to my little Gabriel?

Imagine if markets grow big, develop in complexity or people change and vigilance diminishes, with no force to bridle that which might unleash, could there someday be a big game played, the likes of which we've never seen, with far reaching consequences spilling brute disorder outside this room? Like sirens of *Ulysses*, voices beckon those ships only to cause them to be shipwrecked.

Big, complex, people change, vigilance diminishes...

What's a force?

I think about the two forces within a fairytale.

We learn from childrens' books.

So, what happened in Dr. Seuss' The Cat in The Hat when mom went away?

The Cat came in. If we were to write a story today, he'd come in with financial engineering and debt, instead of his helpers. While no one's watching, what a mess that free-for-all made.

Modern day weaponry — financial engineering and debt — used without a bridle, created a financial world with potential for systemic risk, the fancy words we hear in the news. Systemic risk means endangering the system, causing a spillover into the economy, if any one financial institution, considered systemically significant, were allowed to fail.

This is what too-big-to-fail means.

How on earth did we do something so unearthly?

Allow such systemic risk to develop, to create bailouts of staggering celestial proportion within a free market capitalist economy, removing the essential freedom-to-fail.

Mortals unbridled. They have an insatiable desire to conquer, for profit and power creating some big financial institutions laden with complex products. Their creations got too-big-to-succeed, through excessive debt usage and complex financial engineering, too-big-to-succeed, because it's too complex to understand or control.

So many strayed from their mainstream businesses, lured by the lucrative fees that the securitization engine drove alongside those credit derivatives. Some products, like toxic assets were built on false premises and even derivatives were written on the faulty. So, of course, it takes down those who play in the faulty from the get go.

There's a map on a stone wall, right near the Coliseum in Rome, showing how far the Roman Empire spread, before it collapsed. It got so big that it could no longer be contained. Empires throughout history have fallen apart as they try to rectify too many disparate groups.

Conquerors even use maps of past empires to give themselves a false pedigree, to give people a false sense of culture and continuity with the past, that their conquests are for the good of all, as they mask true intention, hiding who they really are.

Is the 21st century financial fairytale empire, one built on computer entries, for the good of all?

I think maybe not.

A labyrinth is a complex place with all sorts of interconnected paths, where one could easily get lost. You'd have a hard time finding your way out. It reminds me of a spider web; no straight path from one point to the next.

Did we build a financial labyrinth of financial institutions, some of which may be labyrinths on to themselves, coming together to create an interconnected world, where some created, others traded, in complex instruments amongst themselves, as counterparties, with exposures one to the other, of such scale and complexity, that if one were to go down, it puts the whole financial system and economy at risk?

Are you lost yet?

I'm thinking, something like this needed a centralized brain, where someone's watching, keeping track of it all. Otherwise, we lose our way.

If one visually sees this interconnected world as a spider web, one begins to understand what too-big-to-fail starts to mean. Think of the spider web as the financial system and the different points at which the web connects as our financial institutions acting as counterparties, with exposures one to the other, through all sorts of financially engineered products and markets.

Visualize a big spider web hanging from a ceiling. Then give it a poke, like the poke of subprime loan defaults. A chunk comes down, perhaps the whole web eventually, falling down on to the ground, our real world.

One credit market after the other froze starting right around August 2007 with the subprime market loan default poke. It took down our financial institutions as they got stuck holding those depreciating toxic assets with all the debt they took on. Bank credit froze. It hit the real ground, destroying our jobs and assets.

Up there, in the spider web, entries in a computer, is where the new investment world came to increasingly live. A new brand of financial capitalism emerged. Profit generation came increasingly so from the creation and trading of exotic financial instruments in an interconnected world.

As profits from the traditional ways of doing business eroded, financial institutions sought new innovative ways to grow and make money. If banks, brokerages and insurance companies had "stuck to their knitting," perhaps they wouldn't have come together to create such a complex world requiring staggering bailouts.

As a simple example, our major municipal bond insurers, known as monoline insurers, strayed from their "bread and butter" business of insuring municipal issuers to insuring toxic assets. In so doing, they jeopardized their mainstream business, the model upon which their business was built over decades.

Perhaps they misunderstood what they were getting themselves into, blinded by the pull of lucrative fees. They collapsed when the subprime market collapsed, as they insured toxic assets needing to make good on those commitments. In the process they endangered the municipal issuers, like our states and cities.

How?

Municipalities found their cost of funding skyrocketing, as a result, from the taint of being associated with these insurers who had exposures to tainted toxic paper. Those higher costs trickle right down on to us in the form of curtailment of services and higher taxes.

While the insurers gambled their mainstream business away, other financial institutions gambled on their downfall.

How?

By shorting their stock (selling borrowed shares with the anticipation that they could be repurchased at a lower price) or through use of derivatives, which we'll get to shortly.

Imagine, our largest insurer, AIG, could have taken us down if we had not bailed them out — meaning paid off the counterparties that they were insuring, who in turn were betting on the collapse of our housing market. And we, as taxpayer, even paid off some of our own banks, making them whole, as counterparties to AIG. Paying off those who are betting on our downfall, one way or another, in an unregulated world?

We created a global spider web.

Replicate this across many institutions within our financial system, and globally. One begins to understand the scale of the problem. If the real economy deteriorates, the spider web sags even more as some of those created instruments, continue to fall in value or are in need of an unwind.

Perhaps there is something to preserving the amorphous nature of life, instead of trying to impose such man-made creation on to it. By imposing this man-made creation on to ourselves, have we now created an amorphous situation?

We need look no further than Iceland's financial meltdown, born of banks taking on too much debt and engaging in financial engineering. A small fishing country of some 300,000 came to be enamored with financial engineering and Wall Street's ways in the last decade. Real estate values skyrocketed. Fancy cars were seen on the streets. Gambling by few created a foreign exchange and debt lock-down for a nation for years to come.

Dangerous tools become weapons in the hands of the unbridled. A spear thrown in battle does damage to a single life. Debt and financial engineering of scale and complexity affect not just a single life, but a nation, a world.

Debt creates artificial value in assets. When debt is issued with loose credit standards or outright deceptive practices, it compounds the problem. As asset values come down or even vaporize, debt remains. It needs to be paid by someone or written-off.

Debt begets more debt, as we're fixing too much debt with more debt. As our nation borrows, or if it monetizes debt, to stem what's lost, either is a debt.

Is this interconnected empire of an unprecedented scale, like the map on the stone wall outside the Roman Coliseum?

𝄞

I'm walking the streets of Buenos Aires at age fifty. I'm struck by a real estate offering of a magnificent condo, in a beautiful vintage building, for $150,000 US. Being the curious type, I turn to my husband.

"Let's go in and take a peek."

The realtor doesn't speak English, so I suggest that we communicate via the computer with the instant language translation.

I type, "Is this a mistake, perhaps another zero?"

"Oh no!" she types back.

"Why so low?" my response.

"There is no residential mortgage market. People pay what they can afford in cash," she types back.

We soon take our leave.

Let's be truthful, how many of us like to prove our points to our husbands?

I remark, "Been telling you that asset values are unsustainable, as they are backed up by debt, unearthly, that if there's a poke, we may face a collapse of Biblical proportion someday."

Once upon a time, Argentina printed money to meet the government's exploding spending and budgetary needs. It led to inflation of a magnitude where the whole financial system was eventually restructured.

Alternative Investments

What else defined this last decade?

Alternative Investments; the catchall investment category—hedge funds, private equity funds, structured notes, derivatives, fund-of-funds...

One of my mentors back in the early 1980s used to say, "just wait and see we're moving towards managed money."

We did.

"Am I the oddball?" my first thought, as I return to my trading desk from a fund-of-funds hedge fund meeting. I'm shocked that fund-of-funds managers hire private detectives to snoop, to follow investment managers.

A fund-of-funds is an investment fund comprised of other investment funds. It is similar to a "feeder fund" that conducts its investing through other investment funds or managers. Very simply, investor assets are directed to other investment funds or managers through these conduits. The investor pays a fee for due diligence for investment fund or manager selection.

When they mentioned the smoking dope part in Central Park during that meeting, were they kidding and is this why the need for private detectives?

So now we have a colorful twist to the traditional due diligence process of manager examination and verification.

I don't get it, what am I missing?

The world has changed. Decades ago, a handshake worked when one cut a deal with someone. Financial institutions managed monies for years; don't remember the private detectives. This highway's got too fast a lane for me. Nowadays, getting duped is an added concern in addition to the usual worry over investment returns. What a twist!

Is it true that I'm as dated as my children would like me to believe?

I bought a cell phone a mere decade ago, a laptop a year ago.

Would I invest in an asset class where private detectives are sniffing around?

What lurks beneath all this?

In the last decade, anyone could put up a shingle and be a hedge fund manager. This asset class bulged to some two trillion, largely unregulated.

How can an asset class in the trillions, with use of high debt and secretive proprietary trading strategies, be unregulated?

The hedge fund Long Term Capital Management shook the financial system with a mere few billion or so bailout, just ten years ago. Even though some financial institutions may spout that they were in no need of bailout, that's debatable. In a world of interconnectedness and exposures one to the other, no one exists in isolation.

We've moved beyond the relatively miniscule few billion to gargantuan unprecedented trillions in bailouts. If a few billion rocked the financial system, just ten years ago, imagine the impact of trillions. It stretches credibility to believe that a successful solution to a multi-trillion dollar financial crisis has been and even could be easily crafted. In the meantime, the mega-ton debt elephant sits in the room.

In the last decade, banks and the Wall Street investment houses jumped on the fund-of-funds mantra, as fund-of-funds managers were sprouting around the country. This fixation with packaging and repackaging has the financial world mesmerized. Hard to believe that some "feeder fund" managers collected fees as high as 20% of the annual investment return, but they did.

Some victims of the $65 billion Madoff Ponzi scheme became so, through the "feeder fund" conduit. In a Ponzi scheme, existing investors are paid with monies coming in from new investors. One has simply got to ask the question, what is going on here, if the basic tripod of due diligence — checking for reputable accountant, third party custodian and accuracy of trade confirms — was missed.

I believe any investment class has a place in a portfolio, when it sticks to it's original intent. It's in the amplification and distortion where the problems lie. Nowadays there's so much out there, with the crafty gaming the system, that it's difficult to decipher what's real or unreal, without the basic ingredient of trust. For example, is a "feeder fund" manager really doing due diligence or is the manager a grand scale marketer?

Do we do our homework before investing?

Or is it just *carte blanche* acceptance of an "accepted norm," pushed on to us. Or, do our wants for outsized performance cloud our judgment?

We get carried away with the "big," the "name," and the "connected" assuming that just because they are, that's safe. Investment missteps may create needs for just basic needs as the degree of untrustworthiness rises. If we rely on a referral, what strings the process together is trust. Trust is so basic. It's opposite, deception, creates scandal and destruction.

What truly is the root of this financial crisis?

Reflect upon how toxic assets were created; reflect upon the clamor at the bonus trough, even now, as financial stewards leave such deficits and debt for the citizenry to mop up; reflect upon the millions who have lost their jobs and homes; reflect upon how some Wall Street firms made fortunes pawning faulty securities to their customers while at the same time selling them short for their own trading account; reflect upon how bailouts and TARP are spawning fraud; reflect upon how pensions and 401Ks of those who worked a lifetime have been decimated; reflect upon the largest $65 billion Madoff Ponzi scheme in history; reflect upon how assets and livelihoods of loyal employees were destroyed by the managements and boards of the firms that self-destructed.

As investor, how is the trade being made for you? As citizen, how are "we the people" being represented?

There's a beautiful word in the English language. It's beautifully basic, vocation. It's a calling. It's about staying true to one's profession rather than true to the idolatry of profit and power.

Before executing a trade, I ask, "Would I buy this for myself?"

Would I give away 20% of my annual investment return to a highly leveraged investment vehicle, with secretive proprietary trading strategies, unregulated, with an ancient sounding name?

Decades have taught me to trust my gut, that trends can be broken, that there are few, if any, investment geniuses. "Too-good to-be-true" is plain old too good.

Vogue applies to fashion, not necessarily to investing.

𝄞

Hedge funds and private equity funds exploded in the last decade. Investors poured money in, looking for performance and diversification. Of course, the banks and Wall Street investment houses scurried to keep up with the rising hedge fund and private equity fund buccaneers.

It's such a lucrative fee-based business!

Banks and Wall Street firms developed their own hedge funds and private equity funds within their asset management divisions.

Hedge funds and private equity funds have been around for a long time, going back to the 1970s. Both are largely unregulated private investment vehicles for institutions and qualified individual investors, meaning "sophisticated investors." Both vehicles were perceived as somewhat risky investments decades ago, with not only the potential for big gains, but for loss of principal as well.

So what does a private equity fund do?

Private equity funds focus on buying companies

with the intent of restructuring them, making them better for a future sale, traditionally small to mid-sized companies. Investors pay a management fee and there's an investment participation upside component for the partners.

Some private equity fund barons, involved in buyouts, inhabit homes that even look like those belonging to Louis XV!

How do they do it?

They do it with lots of debt from a banker or two. Some private equity shops were carried away in the era of cheap credit and investor money gush. They bought big companies; the bigger the company, the bigger the fees.

Like real estate prices, company prices were bid up as the boom was nearing its apex in 2005-2007. So much so that it even caused distortions in the mainstream mergers and acquisitions market for those companies who were looking to do strategic acquisitions. Imagine, making money by straddling companies with enormous debt?

What wasn't distorted in this last decade of amplification?

I think of the Peggy Lee song *Fever.* Only it wasn't that kind of fever. It was money fever!

What does a hedge fund do, besides breed billionaires?

A hedge fund may buy or sell any financial instrument or asset. It doesn't necessarily need to hedge anything, as the name would imply, but it could if it wants to. A hedge fund could simply buy and hold stocks or employ any type of investment angle. The early innovative hedge funds dabbled in traditional markets, but with an esoteric twist; less liquid stocks, more concentrated positions and currency plays, for example.

The typical fee structure includes a 2% annual management fee and 20% participation by the manager annually, in the investment return.

Rather lofty fees!

They came about as a result of proprietary trading strategies, like paying up for scarcity value for perhaps outsized returns. Unlike other asset classes, where competition brings down fees, this did not happen as the hedge fund industry exploded in size to some two trillion, largely unregulated.

Why were hedge funds not required to register with the SEC as is the case for other investment entities?

Hedge funds were not marketed to retail investors, but rather to "sophisticated investors," those savvy enough to understand the inherent investment risks. They got around it. This asset class grew to such size and influence in the markets. Yet it remained outside the regulatory framework. When it came to regulation, perhaps a "look-see" or was there a bit of "look-away?"

Leading up to the Stock Market Crash of 1929, there were all sorts of investment vehicles that were not registered. The ensuing decade spawned regulations requiring registration of securities and investor disclosure through the prospectus process. With this crisis, discussions are underway to bring hedge funds, private equity funds and even venture capital firms under SEC registration and disclosure requirements.

Did it seem that so many aspired to be hedge fund managers over the last decade?

I believe we peaked at some 9,000 hedge funds or so.

What about barriers to entry?

Near non-existent as just about anyone could put up a shingle. With lofty fees and practically no regulation, little wonder this industry grew to near two trillion in assets.

The Land Run of 1889, for public lands, comes to mind when I think about the exponential growth of the hedge fund industry in the last decade. Picture thousands of people lined up on horseback, at high noon underneath the scorching sun, ready to ride and stake out a plot, only in this case they're after your money, for their money fever!

In that rush to put up a shingle, the industry attracted some hedge fund cowboys of notorious nature, some fraudsters, and then some youngsters who hit the jackpot for a few years, then rode off. I think it attracted the wannabe geniuses, those who amassed the most amount of assets behind them. If they're really big, they may even control the markets.

Lucky streaks can last for awhile. Spoils fill coffers amply, unleashing near unlimited resources to develop the most sophisticated proprietary trading programs.

When kids amass the largest arsenal of toys and friends behind them, they can bully and push other kids in the neighborhood out of the way, and be in control. They perform. Until something out of the ordinary of a more natural order rumbles. Miracles may happen, but for sure they are not man-made.

The early hedge funds in the 1980s exploited market inefficiencies, in a world where information was not yet instantaneous. They'd find an undiscovered news bite and pounce on it.

As decades progressed, hedge funds had to find new ways to get performance in a world of instantaneous information flow and increasing competition; a world in which a hedge fund was sprouting on just about every street corner. Hedge funds are all about making excess return above the overall market, fancily called "alpha." It means reward for extra risk.

In a world of instantaneity, hedge funds took to debt and proprietary trading programs telling them when to buy, when to sell. That proprietary trading trump card advantage diminished as the hedge fund space got crowded.

Hedge funds are highly leveraged.

What does that mean?

Hedge funds use debt to amplify returns. It's like buying stock on margin. Hypothetically, if you're big, say with $20 billion in customer money, you may borrow up to maybe $80 billion, maybe more. The difference or spread between what one earns on the securities bought with debt versus the cost of debt is the enhanced or amplified return.

What if the markets turn south?

Back in October 2008, when the markets swooned and fell precipitously it was in part due to hedge funds deleveraging — meaning they sold stock to pay off debt. Those fancy name hedge funds contributed to the nosedive in our 401Ks.

There's always the money angle on Wall Street. Banks and Wall Street investment houses created their own hedge funds. But, they also grew prime brokerage divisions. Prime brokerage divisions focus on clearing trades and lending money to hedge funds, another lucrative business. For some banks the prime brokerage business was a coveted asset. As some financial institutions fell, the vultures circled to pick up the most wanted assets of the fallen.

As the decade progressed, seems to me that our financial institutions increasingly became traders or speculators. Banks and Wall Street investment houses set up their own proprietary trading desks, trading for their own portfolios alongside the hedge funds and other institutional investors within an interconnected labyrinth.

One may argue that profits within the financial world increasingly came from casino-like activity. If you guess right, you win. For example, trading in opaque and unregulated credit derivatives, with little transparency — where pricing is not visible — was far more lucrative than some of the traditional businesses.

Did banks and Wall Street investment houses forget who they were?

I think they had an identity crisis. They came together with other financial institutions to create a financial *Jurassic Park* that jeopardized the flow of credit and capital from those who have it to those who need it in a way that protects the economy from shock.

Priorities, and staying true to objectives and standards — maybe it's as simple as that.

Even our largest insurer AIG, which we now own

not of our own will, strayed from its mainstream insurance writing business to play with credit derivatives.

Mortals, not harnessed, drift. The more from pure intention they stray the more they liken to rapacious wolves consumed with sight of their meat. What if many sloppily stray, from pure intention towards fatal flaw, from calm to torment, perverting that which they've been entrusted to protect, even underneath the Masonic all-seeing eye of our everyday dollar bill?

Policy makes a difference when we begin to play with a matchbook of uncommon risks and consequences. Like big bonuses clouding business decision-making, what is it that clouded political judgment?

Derivatives

So we have a spider web world. In it we have financial institutions — banks, hedge funds, insurance companies, pension funds, endowments, bond funds and other investors. They are active in the derivatives market. Like securitization, derivatives have been central to the modern day bank business model, driving profits.

What in the world is a derivative?

A derivative is exactly what the word implies. It is a derived or engineered financial instrument, whose value is based off of the value of an underlying financial instrument or asset. That underlying financial instrument or asset could be a loan, commodity, bond, stock, index and the like. Types of derivatives include options, futures, forwards, and swaps. Together, they make up a world in the hundreds of trillions.

Have you colored Easter eggs as a child or with your children?

Here's how it went in our home.

We start out with four cups of hot water, each containing a primary color — red, yellow, green and blue. By the time we're done the four cups have become murky.

Amidst the bright colored eggs, out come the oddities, the derivatives, derived off of the primary colors.

Derivatives have been around for decades. One of the simplest derivatives is a stock option, whose value rises and falls based on the underlying stock. The last decade witnessed the explosive growth in the size and complexity of the derivatives market, particularly financial derivatives like credit default swaps.

Why should we care about credit default swaps?

They are at the heart of the financial crisis and the cause of the problems at AIG, requiring our bailout monies. A handful of the big banks have enormous exposure to credit derivatives in general.

A derivative transaction is essentially a financial bet or contract, between two parties, called counterparties — could be any one of our financial institutions — to exchange payments at some point in the future based on the performance of an underlying financial instrument or asset. Think of it, as making a bet with a friend about the value of some object at some point in the future when you settle out.

Derivatives are used to transfer risk (it's like buying insurance) or for speculation. Speculation is like betting or gambling. Speculators, unlike investors, thrive on making quick profits. Derivatives simply shift risk to another party. Credit derivatives shift credit risk while credit default swap derivatives shift default risk.

What is a credit default swap?

Credit default swaps are derivatives designed to provide an investor with insurance or protection against debt default of any kind. Credit default swaps are also used by speculators to simply bet on the credit quality of a company or debt.

Suppose one buys a bond and is worried about a default – Counterparty A, a financial institution holding the bond, pays insurance premiums to counterparty B, another financial institution underwriting the credit default swap, and if the bond defaults, counterparty B has to make counterparty A whole on the amount of insurance bought. It's a little more complex, but is illustrative enough for our purposes.

These contracts can then be traded amongst financial institutions, as speculators, those who have no connection to the underlying financial instrument or asset, with little money down. It's kind of like betting in a casino.

Created in the late 1990s, credit default swaps were originally used to limit credit risk for bondholders. In the last decade, speculators increasingly used them to bet on the survival of a debt issuer.

What does unregulated mean?

It means that there is no regulated exchange and centralized clearing marketplace where these credit derivatives or contracts are traded. A regulated exchange makes pricing as well as who owns what visible. Futures and options, for example, trade on regulated exchanges where prices are visible. Debt or credit derivatives are traded over-the-counter (OTC), where private parties, like our financial institutions, negotiate contracts over the phone.

Pricing opaqueness and marginal capital requirements, to make good on the contracts, create sizeable opportunities to make money. Hence, speculators or betters could provide guarantees with little to no capital down, thereby assuming little risk, but making a lot of money in the process if they bet right.

With this crisis, regulatory discussions are underway, but lobbyists are already in the wings to thwart the process. The idea would be to move the OTC derivatives trading onto regulated exchanges and to have trades filter through clearing houses that guarantee they settle out.

Credit default swaps became an integral part of the modern day bank business model. They provided a lucrative source of income in the form of fees for financial institutions that sold them and big spreads for those who traded in them. During the boom times of the last decade, few worried about default risk, so the credit default market grew to near $60 trillion notional (notional means the underlying value of the security or asset).

Like any other investment, credit default swaps have a place in a portfolio, providing liquidity and risk management within the debt markets. It's in the application, the getting carried away and amplification, that the problems lie.

For example, writing insurance or credit default swaps on faulty securities and troubled issuers, without proper credit analysis and risk assessment is troublesome. Imagine what a complex mess, if contracts are then assigned or traded amongst speculators with little to no capital requirements where it's not altogether clear if the party holding the contract can make good on it.

The unwind started with the collapse of the subprime mortgage market which set off a chain reaction for the financial institutions who wrote credit default swaps on mortgage securities. The lack of risk controls and proper credit assessment showed up. If financial institutions were writing insurance on that which is faulty from the get go, how could this be anything, but a moneymaking fantasy?

For example, we created toxic assets — *Frankenstein One* — by off-loading risk through securitization. Then we found a way to transfer the risk of say an investment in a toxic asset, to someone else through the credit default swap market — *Frankenstein Two.*

What do we end up with when we "create" the faulty, write insurance on the faulty, mix in a lot of debt and markets stop going up forever?

Bailouts.

We bailed out AIG and its counterparties making them whole (some of the betters on the other side being our own banks) as they were betting on the fall of our economy in some form or another. How could the better on the other side not come out winning if the entity writing the insurance didn't do their homework?

Turns out that what was initially a transfer of risk amongst counterparties became a regurgitation of risk on to the American public. I think it's like handing us a mop for someone else's bad bets.

There are trillions of these credit default swaps. They may sour if the economy continues to deteriorate and defaults increase. Further to this point, the credit derivatives market is concentrated within just a handful of big banks.

Why?

The modern day bank business model is so dependent now on fat profits from the opacity in the OTC credit derivatives market that perhaps it keeps the lights on as bad loan losses mount. Just think of how much money one could make where few dominate the market and pricing is not visible.

I came to think of this credit default swap derivatives world as a virtual casino where betters skimmed off enormous profits as a result of its opacity and minimum capital requirements. Our financial institutions created their own moneymaking betting world, one that grew on an unprecedented scale, unregulated.

The conservative multi-century old Barings Bank of England collapsed in 1995 when a young trader involved in unauthorized derivatives trading made a wrong bet. In 1994, our own Orange County, California declared bankruptcy after suffering over a billion in derivatives related losses.

Time and again, the regulators seemed to back down.

Seems to me, that as some of our financial institutions wrote credit default swaps, and even created the debt instruments on which the credit default swaps were written, like subprime mortgage securities or questionable securitizations, they gave speculating wannabe geniuses, the ability to flourish. The all-too-visible foolishness of some, gave others the opportunity to prosper enormously.

For example, I recall reading about a hedge fund in existence for a year and then closed by its own choice. It returned north of 800% in one year during this crisis, going long credit default swaps on subprime mortgages. As subprime mortgages collapsed, the value of those credit default swaps increased. There are two sides to every trade and someone took the other side — Oops!

Was anyone really investing, flowing capital to real enterprises that create products, additive to our economy or was this a fantasy world of created securities and speculation that allowed some to, quite plainly, get lavishly rich?

This is, in part, how money was being made in this interconnected world where any one is too-big-to-fail; a world that reached into ours. While we just went about our daily lives trusting, who was protecting us from the wolves?

I reflect upon MBA School. I learned the basic principles of business and capitalism. If there is a major sector of the economy that is built on speculative growth, it crumbles eventually. When it's our financial system, the backbone of the economy, it's serious.

When two decide to bet or enter into a trade, one wins, one loses. When two individual traders or speculators trade in credit derivatives, the consequences of their actions are limited to them. When our financial institutions bet with one another in an unsound way, it's troubling. That's why Glass-Steagall mattered as it separated commercial banking (for lending) and investment banking (for speculation).

In the last decade, it appears that financial markets evolved and innovated around the notion of making money by off-loading risk or transferring risk to someone else. I wonder about underpinning standards or was the standard simply to generate volume and fees, for profits, for bonuses.

Did anyone at the financial and political helm say, "Hey, wait a second here, where are we taking our nation?"

The best political and economic systems are compromised when principles embedded in those systems are not upheld. If political and economic systems find themselves within an envelope of those who seek to advance their self-interested agendas with impunity, it's a deep problem for us all.

As the curtain rose, what fairytale did we see?

Unfolding before us in a democratic nation is the unprecedented massive transfer of wealth from the masses (now chained with debt as a result of the financial crisis) to the benefit of a segment of the population most responsible for this crisis. We privatized profits to few, and socialized debt and risk on to the hard-working masses, our children, for years to come.

I think about the Ionic columns of Continental Bank. Were they meant to convey stability or ruins? Underneath the mask, were our financial institutions betting our economy, and with it our livelihoods and lives for the sake of unbridled profit? Is turbo charged growth and profit, simply a masquerade for basic human greed?

We all know that innovators are ahead of the regulators, but now that regulators are taking a look once again at the credit derivatives market, we are leaving the door ajar, not to regulate "all" credit derivatives. How can our financial system take pride then in being safe, secure and transparent?

Liquidity within our markets comes from transparency and standardization.

An article in the *New York Times* lends further insight. It is entitled Even in Crisis, Big Banks Dig In for a Battle Against Tougher Regulation (By Gretchen Morgenson and Don Van Natta Jr., June 1, 2009).

Sound familiar?

The common French phrase, "Plus ça change plus c'est la meme chose," comes to mind.

Translation: The more things change the more they stay the same.

Why are our banks fighting against regulating the very products that led to this financial crisis?

Regulation would lead to transparency. Transparency means smaller profits. You see, fat derivative profits rely on complexity and secrecy, essentially non-regulation. Anything with complexity and secrecy in the financial world puts us at risk as this financial crisis has clearly shown.

I think regulation across the board for "all" types of credit derivatives should be a "slam-dunk," given the taxpayer bailout burden. There are two necessary prongs to that regulation; forcing "all" credit derivative trades onto public exchanges where pricing is visible and establishing a clearinghouse system which ensures completion of a transaction if a party to a trade defaults. So far, the latter prong is being addressed as well as the former, but for standardized derivatives only, not the customized ones. Banks are fighting regulation of customized derivatives.

If we allow what hasn't worked to continue, we begin to script the next chapter presaging a yet dark age to come within our Age of Modernity, maybe one with even more foreboding consequences.

Looks to me like another crossroad, like Long Term Capital Management a decade ago. Tell me this financial empire, this fairytale, with all sorts of man-made creations in it, a credit default swap market in the trillions, betting on failure by trading in default risk, is real. Initially meant to limit risk, this credit default swap market may create limitless risk, unintended consequences.

Policy broke down the barriers that kept banking, insurance and brokerage separate, paving the way for institutions to come together and create a complex world with such systemic risk.

Decades ago, financial institutions bought a bond and simply sold it if they worried about a company defaulting. No credit default swap market existed. It put the risk and responsibility with the investor, no escape hatch.

Imagine the trust that need exist in this counterparty world, amongst counterparties, for it to function if unregulated. That when a party says they are healthy, they indeed are. Otherwise, the whole web might just come down. Or will we, the taxpayer, now implicitly be the backstopping party for all the unregulated credit default swaps as the government can ill afford a too-big-to-fail entity to fail?

I don't think I want to be on the hook for potential bailouts forever or at least for as long as too-big-to-fail entities are allowed to exist.

Further, imagine if a large money speculator bets against a company with credit default swaps creating a feeding frenzy. It could tip a company into default. What if the bet was based on compromised premises?

A whole company and the livelihoods of those within it could disappear. These are dangerous weapons.

I'm perplexed. If so many are truly worried about default risk, what does this then say about trust and confidence in our companies straight up, those that underpin the stock market?

Financial engineering...which way are we going with it all?

I came across a September 5, 2009 article in *The New York Times* entitled, New Exotic Investments Are Emerging on Wall Street (By Jenny Anderson). Just like Wall Street securitized subprime and "liar" mortgages that eventually led to disaster, Wall Street plans to embark on capitalizing on securitizing or packaging life insurance policies purchased from those who are older with a high probability of death or those who are ill. The securities would then be resold to pension funds and other investors.

Wall Street would collect lucrative fees not only from the securitizations, but the subsequent reselling and trading of these securities. The value and how these securities trade, I suppose, would depend on how long someone lives. There is even such "matter-of-fact" discourse as to creating pools diversified across sundry diseases, just in case there is a cure say for any one, that would then render a securitized pool near worthless if concentrated too much in a single disease. Are we about to create the toxic assets of tomorrow?

Just think about this for a moment. The longer people live, the worse these pools would perform as their premise is based on "fast death" to avoid paying the insurance premiums over a long period. Imagine the implications. Embarking on this potential $26 trillion "life settlement" securitization market feels rather ghoulish to me. Where are the policy gatekeepers?

So now we are not only betting on the default of our companies, but potentially embarking to trade and bet on human life.

High finance or *Wizard of Oz?*

The Dissonant Waltz

When I stepped out of that meeting in New York, I felt like, "the only thing missing is a fanny slap; is this real and is this the year 2005?"

What's more, if this were another point in time, I felt like I'd be quartered!

So, I go to New York to take a stand for what's right, to fight for my team.

What court is a court where it's a *fait accompli* before one even walks in?

I dispute. I lose. They've got their own agenda. I'm living in an *Orwellian* world.

I am but a little lone angelfish swimming in a pool of misguided piranhas, as I flap my fins to swim straight to stay alive among them. They can do with me what they wish; yet I will not tilt their way as it is not the way!

I'm beginning to think that this *enchanted prince,* this place is not what it's all cracked up to be. But, you know, we want to believe that which we want to believe.

Right outside the office from which I depart people sit behind their desks working. They look up. I have a diaphanous moment. I feel like I'm in the scene from *Rosemary's Baby* where she comes out to see her baby with all the people smiling around her.

I need to depart, quickly. I feel something deeply ominous going on. I'm so unsettled that I can't even make the customary rounds to the trading desks to visit with the traders, as I often do upon visiting the New York headquarters. Those colleagues of mine; they're just doing their jobs, they're superlative at what they do. They trust. Oh my goodness, if only they knew what I felt!

What lies beneath those trading desks, a rumbling volcanic mass?

I need to find a place to sit down, to absorb all this. I make my way to the floor that houses the executive offices and dining rooms. I knew that there were a bunch of sitting rooms there and believe me I needed to sit down. As I park myself into one of the club chairs, I'm overwhelmed with emotion, knowing inside that something doesn't feel right about this place anymore.

I forgot I hadn't eaten anything that day, nor could, as was the case so many days before. I couldn't even feel exhaustion anymore as the level of stress throughout the last few years had now culminated to a point where I came to live with pain and little sleep. I had to remind myself that yes this was the year 2005.

My innocence about the place burst; things were never the same after that. I was overwhelmed with apprehension. Could it be that this place was not what it seemed?

I feel that something larger is looming on the horizon.

If this all came from the top on down filtering through the flock, could it be that sooner or later this would beget ruin of some sort? Could it be that the same was playing itself out elsewhere within the firm, another division? How would I possibly know? Who'd have the courage to stand up to them or did they simply all leave? I retreat within myself and start to think.

This was a grand floor, no other way to describe it. Beautifully paneled in medium-toned wood throughout with high ceilings. Spectacular oriental rugs graced the floors. One main railroaded hallway connected the lavish conference and opulent dining rooms on the one side with sitting areas on the other. Inlaid paneling adorned the sitting room where I sought to catch my breath. Ensconced in an oversized leather club chair, I was no longer ensconced in the dream of this place.

Instantly, the ambience of the place vanished, melting into the walls. The doors to the chambers of my heart were closing one by one. Once upon a time, I loved being a part of such a financial powerhouse, the pinnacle of capitalism laid out before the world encapsulated in a single place manifesting itself in its physical glory. This is not the kind of waltz I had in mind to be dancing.

Could it be that this is just a premonition of larger problems within our financial system, hidden from the rest of the world to see?

"They're in it for themselves!" I'm thinking.

I continue to reflect about where this whole financial world is drifting. I think about employees who work sincerely and investors who invest while trusting the system. We can all get taken down if it falls. So much wealth will vaporize.

I trusted, disruptions notwithstanding, just continued to hope and work. I made a lot of money for them, a consistent and top multi-million dollar producer for years. What now of my team? What am I to say to them?

I always took the blows to protect them and give them hope. They worked earnestly, with lives and others to take care of. My wings were clipped yet again, bound this time around. I feel the need to free myself from all this, no way to flap amongst them. I wasn't in that flock. I wasn't one of them, nor would now ever want to be.

How many years before things within the financial world unwind?

I'm deeply troubled with the most foreboding feeling. So powerful, unrelenting, it almost leads me to cancel my dinner this evening with a customer.

"Leave New York," my gut tells me.

Not unlike the gut feeling I had decades ago after finishing the Salomon Brothers training program. My soul is elsewhere. I want to go home. In that moment, I rejoice that I put my children and family first for all those years, that I protected my heart from all this. The way I felt then is captured in a song I heard Andrea Boccelli sing years later, *Go Where Love Goes.*

I disengage from the club chair, my favorite briefcase in hand. I leave that floor to take the sleek elevator down to the lobby, as I had so many times before, always with excitement, this time with sadness.

I see my reflection in one of the mirrors before entering the elevator. I'm beautifully attired; dressed in a sleek Italian, impeccably tailored, dark gray suit, form fitting. The jacket is ever so slightly pinched at the waist, just as I like it, with one of my white chic cotton tailored shirts; the tall Italian collar and dramatic cuffs, with my signature, ever-present pointy high heels.

But, the smile is missing.

I take the elevator all the way down to the lobby. As the elevator doors open, I turn left and there she is. I now stand in the underbelly of *The Appoggiatura.* She is now simply an embellishment without a primary theme. I am no longer in awe of her beauty. A lost soul this magnificent building has come to now have. A house is not a home without a soul. This is the primary theme.

If we disrespect the work of individual employees, undermine it to serve self-interested agendas, what then when it comes to customers and shareholders?

If this can go on at the individual level at a single financial entity, what then if this plays itself out in one form or another at other financial firms? Before you know it, the string of entities that make up the financial backbone of this country may be at risk, like an apple rotting from the inside out.

Could this firm be but a microcosm of larger problems brewing across our financial world and how is it that they will manifest themselves someday?

I reflect upon what I learned a long time ago. The family's heartbeat comes from its members and their concern for one another. We extend outward, like a fan, to form the basis of society, reflected in its institutions and government. I believe there is such a thing as character and values that lead us to behave in a moral and just way. It's that simple.

As I think about the financial world, I recall my Lithuanian lessons decades ago. Rasputin showed up one day to beguile the *Czarina*, to make her feel like he was working for her. She believed in his curative powers, his message, as she was desperate out of love for her hemophiliac son. The face to the *Czarina* was one of a monk who can cure, yet he was debauched underneath, beholden to ambidextrous ways.

With a heavy heart I leave New York the next morning, but with resolve to now preserve the business that we already have. I'd continue to take care of my clients in the best way possible and those who worked with me, to give them hope.

The torch of a brave heart is mine to pass on, as the women within my lineage are relying upon me. My maternal great grandmother loved my great grandfather so much that after his death, she'd visit the attic to lovingly spend time with his items. One night a kerosene lamp accidentally set fire to their home. She burned and suffered for weeks back in Lithuania, with little help for her wounds, until she departed. She was laid to rest right next to the love of her life to live forever with him.

My grandfather loved her so much that he rebuilt her home by hand, just as it was. Upon his early death, my grandmother loved him so much that she did her best to take care of their three children, one being my mother. She fled Lithuania, as a widow on her own with her three children, under the Communist invasion amidst gunfire, to come to this country for freedom. She kept her family together amidst life threatening chaos, with love and a heart, that which endures.

For all those in my lineage who loved so deeply, I remain strong as a new path or direction would be sculpted. I would know when to act. As my plane is taking off that morning, I think about something I once read some time ago. A dying person is asked, "How do you know that you are dying?"

The reply, "I see a flower for the first time."

Do we wait as we're passing through, like the thornbird impaled on a thorn of a flower right before its death, to sing the most beautiful melody?

I look at the majestic skyline of Manhattan as the plane is rising ever higher on a beautiful sunny morning; buildings with powerful people, indomitable, making millions, even billions, at the pinnacle of financial firms.

Yet, the pinnacle of all possibilities is not atop those firms. Black limos scurry from one place to the next. Urgency and intensity connect *passers by, with numbered years,* to cell phones. They fall deep into an abyss of power and money, drawn by insatiable need and want for more.

Private jets, at their call, whisk them where?

Inflections come when the unreal begins to look real. I conjecture as to what Rome's inflection point might have been like.

Debates in the Roman Senate grew increasingly self-interested and chaotic. They lost sight of what made them great as they grew too big, less vigilant. They thought themselves indomitable, as the centurions marched, legions of them, conquerors vast. They accumulated riches in the process, disregarding life. They decided who lives, who dies.

Political decay set in, infiltrated leadership ranks. Societal norms and families broke down. They took their "eye off the ball," grew less disciplined, even outsourced their army to the barbarian mercenaries, luring them with power and wealth. They took on too much debt. Their global conquests created a disenfranchisement of belonging as they lost their sense of identity.

One day, the Visigoths made the unreal real.

Were they the enemy?

What were Roman citizens thinking right before the Fall?

What discussions took place in Roman homes?

Did they have an inkling of what might befall them or did they deceive themselves into being complacent, thinking it goes on forever?

Empires crumble as civilizations rise and fall. They leave behind ruins. Love, music and the artistry of a single flower endure throughout the ages. The little cornflowers my mother embroidered on her mother's dress live forever in her heart.

Into what chamber should riches accumulate?

The chamber of the heart, as a storied floor of *The Appoggiatura* will someday soon and forever be clothed in cobwebs.

As my plane rose above clouds, a gentle Hand prodded me along. I didn't retreat to my music. Instead, I felt like Scarlett O'Hara in *Gone With The Wind* as she vowed to persevere.

Chapter Six

The Legacy of an Empire

"El Cid"

May 6, 2009

I pick up my "Financial Times" today. A headline story grabs my attention — "Subprime groups spent $370m to fight regulation" (By Edward Luce in Washington, May 6, 2009). The Center for Public Integrity, a journalistic investigative and non-profit organization, conducted an independent investigation into our current financial crisis. They concluded that political contributions and immense lobbying (by top US subprime mortgage originators and our largest banks) created the regulatory lapse and lack of oversight that led to this financial crisis. The investigation further unearthed that despite the signals, Congress, the White House and the Federal Reserve waffled as the subprime mess spread.

Government for the people or government in captivity?

I think about the stone wall outside the Coliseum in Rome…conquerors in the past have used maps to give people a false sense of pedigree and security.

Are we veiling…trillions in bad loans and tainted complex securities are swooshing around somewhere…and those credit default swap derivatives…are we OK with them even being around, let alone regulating them? Are all these financially engineered instruments our modern day Visigoths who eventually ransacked Rome and led to the collapse of an empire? I think betting on our companies defaulting is like betting against our own economy, our own good.

If we mask same behavior, what's to say that the next engineering marvel won't be our last?

Are we mired in unknowability of where we really are… are we at the start or the end of something larger than ourselves…beyond our control?

I'm wondering if we're simply buying time…perhaps we'll even go so far as to allow credit derivatives to remain unregulated, business as usual. Will lobbying to not regulate credit derivatives be like the lobbying for subprime mortgages….look what that led to.

The eventual destruction of the Roman Empire by the Visigoths took time. First came the infiltration, then the ransacking.

Trillions in bailouts, backstops, loan facilities and the like have been deployed to stem the financial crisis… it's not just that $700 billion TARP…yet bonuses are back…while the citizenry is left with ballooning deficits and over $11.5 trillion in national debt.

I am reminded of the "Hoarders and Wasters" in Dante Alighieri's "Inferno" (Circle 4, canto 7). Plutus, the wolf-like wealth demon guards the entry. Money is meant to be in circulation...if hoarded and waisted, well of course, things freeze.

Revolutions are born of extremes, disparity and economic imbalance brought on by errant policy, corruption, and spoils to few…they come about when the consequences of the former reach the daily lives of the masses where access to basic needs becomes impaired.

"Après moi, le deluge," said the King of France Louis XV (1710-1774) as he was being warned that his country could no longer sustain the burden of debt, right before the French Revolution.

Translation: After me, the deluge.

Centuries ago, there lived a man by the name of Rodrigo Diaz de Bivar. He was a Castilian knight and came to be known as "El Cid," meaning lord. He defended Spain against the Moors in the 11th century and became Spain's national hero.

Within the feudal system in the Middle Ages, the lords ruled with power and wealth. "El Cid" broke out of that mold, transcended beyond obsession with power and wealth, to stay true to ideals. Legend has it that he led with strength and humility, with courage, vision and integrity, with loyalty and a heart.

The Last Months

I am mesmerized by the exotic — but not exotic investments — ever since my parents took us, once, to the US Virgin Islands when I was 16 years old. I had seen the movie, *South Pacific,* being taken by not just the beauty of the backdrop, like the palm trees and sunsets, but by what the sounds of those days and nights must have been like.

The view from the sky enraptured my every sense. The speckled islands bathed in turquoise. When the small plane landed, I felt like I was in Paradise, with lush green vegetation, the palm trees swaying to their own music and rhythm.

Truly, I stepped into an uninhabited-feeling type of world that 1971, as we made our way towards a tiny wooden building, a version of an airport terminal. The naturalness of it all appealed to me; the vision never left me.

My eyes could barely contain themselves the next day, as I stepped onto Megan and Cowpet Bays. It was then, when walking the beach of Cowpet Bay, that I had a dreamy thought. If ever, an out of the world dream were to take place, I'd make such a place a home close to my heart.

And so, like the love affair with school and achievement, my love affair with the Caribbean began. I sometimes came to call myself a little bit of an island hippy. Not really one, but for that natural feeling that came as a welcome reprieve from the sophisticated rapid-fire investment world I lived in.

I introduced my children into this world, as we explored island after island together. Not only did we learn history, but mother came to study, and learn a bit about real estate in this part of the world.

One day, some 13 years ago, we fell upon a spot that we came to call home.

The Island – July 2008

I retreat to my favorite spot in the world.

This home is right on the doorstep of the ocean, undulating in shades of turquoise, as close to creation as one could be. It has our souls and hearts etched into its white stucco walls. We retreat here in quiet solitude, into silence, but for the waves that engage and release. The wet salt air is ever-present.

Many years ago, there wasn't much on that beach, but for us three. And that was the beauty of it all. Its shores became the repository of our memories. Together we built sandcastles out of white powdery sand, listened to the sound of the crystal clear aqua ocean and watched the orange bursting sky as the sun went to sleep.

We'd linger in our comfy surroundings, atop white slip covered cushy sofas, with interesting conversations, my eldest never without a book. In the evenings, we'd light a few candles and continue to just be together.

As my boys grew older, they'd outrun their mother, in distance and speed, on the white sand beach. Years before, I'd push them to do so. They couldn't outrun me then. Now they can, but in their loving kindness they slow down for me.

This was a place and point in time for us; way before the rest of the world came to discover how beautiful a place it was. I kept things the same throughout the years so that my children, and theirs someday, could see the memories locked in place.

I leave the mainland that July, for a purpose, to continue writing as I felt a pull to do so. I was broken up inside over what I had witnessed leading up to the fall and takeover of our firm. I felt punctured. Within the heart and soul of this home, I found the salve and fortitude to overcome some of those emotions, and to continue doing what I needed to do, simply write. I just wrote day-in-day-out all day, surrounded by nature and my beloved music.

We are all too familiar with emotional sorrow. It's not visible, yet it feels like an open wound to the chest that bleeds and oozes. One would simply not be human, to not experience sorrow when one witnesses a firm, where one spends twenty years of their life, suddenly die; a death that left a big question mark in my mind.

Deep down in my heart, I felt that this was just the beginning of something much larger. A human crisis would soon unfold and many would suffer. I didn't pay too much attention to news or those who wanted us to hear what they wanted us to hear.

I just knew inside that this was big, and bigger than anyone let on, simply because I lived in this *Orwellian* world and saw it unfold. Stretch a rubber band and it comes back snapping with a vengeance.

Inside this financial world, I came to wonder at times whether it was real or fantasy. Where chasing growth and ever-fleeting profit in homage of greed, "till death do us part," became life and the end-all for so many. Some were like hamsters on wheels of wealth seeking, where making millions and billions seemed so ordinary; a million was just a "buck," considered insufficient. It just wasn't enough.

And so, I got away from all those matters, that when we see our last sunset, our time here is snuffed out, matter only as only they should. I left my briefcase and Italian wardrobe behind. That country whose operas, fashion, history and home of my faith, I can hardly leave behind.

I flew with my music in hand, Puccini opera included, to remind me of Italy. My little device housed my library of music and memories associated with it. This was the only form of communication I welcomed and my newly acquired laptop for writing. I cleared the decks entirely. Into a form of 21st century seclusion I went for some 30 days. I would not leave the island until I finished the first draft of this book.

Like being with my grandmother, I existed in the moment.

Those childhood memories I lived again, this time unencumbered by constant information flow, the bombardment of phones and all forms of communication. Where everything is "breaking news" where if something really "breaking" were to happen, how would we know?

I reconnected with the life of my childhood. The blue sky, the clouds, the stars brought me back to lying on the grass with my sister. Surrounded by the sounds of nature at night, I watched the moon swell, play hide-and-go-seek with the clouds. I fell asleep to Prokofiev's haunting *Romeo and Juliet* ballet, that bridge connecting the memories of my life.

I washed my clothes by hand and let nature take care of the rest. I took the time to go to the grocery store, making sure I picked the melon and cucumber, just as my father had instructed the little girl with the big bow sundress to do. In the evening, whenever I sliced cucumbers, I relished the sound of the knife swooshing through, as it thumped on to the cutting board. I took the time to linger and slice slowly. My prayer book was with me, but this time I wasn't confused why everyone was sitting on clouds.

On that island, I rose with the sun and just watched what takes place when all the noise stops. On that beach every morning, every form of life participated in its own way for which it was created to make things beautiful as a whole for the eye, to just see.

The turquoise water, the white silky sand beach, the blue sky and green vegetation; all those vivid colors are so perfectly chosen to go together. Every type of bird and insect is just doing their job.

The sun went to sleep magnificently in a sea of orange red. And, after a tropical rainfall, the palm trees lulled it to sleep, dressed in silver tinsel from its rays. The radiant splendor of creation, in its full glory, is a gift for us just to notice.

The Raucous Mess

Underwear goes inside the pant or zippers jam!

That's what started it all. The most basic of basics was muffed, discarded, the ability to pay back a loan or mortgage. When we strayed, disregarded the most obvious, everything else went haywire.

This is the basis for any kind of business, two parties in a contract making good on their commitment, grounded in trust. It's the most basic of trades.

Let's be frank here.

Home ownership or real estate lending in general has an affordability component to it. Do we just throw credit at any asset to any borrower, like "spaghetti to a wall," and hope it sticks?

It isn't sticking.

Do we just extend credit by gouging out the verification of creditworthiness, based on the fantasy that asset prices rise forever?

Like any other asset bubble, they don't.

Would you give someone a loan willy-nilly without verifying the party's income or assets? Would you not ask for documentation? And, if you saw someone doing that, would you not take a stand warning the party that they may possibly lose their money?

This was done on a grand scale.

What kind of business is this when two parties enter into an agreement, where the creditor is extending credit to an uncreditworthy party, unable to make good on a commitment? Or, where the creditor doesn't fully disclose terms of the arrangement, feeding off of another for profit, knowing the wobbly nature of the engagement from the get go? Or, the borrower isn't truthful as to affordability of a home or misrepresents their income, enabled by a system that allowed this to happen?

I'm wondering if the financial world is simply running out of ways to make money such that we discard basic standards, even take to the faulty, for expedient profit, packaging it as innovation.

We can create fantasy in reality and make others believe it real. *Abracadabra*, create a triple-A rated mortgage security from unsound mortgages, ones that deny risk and basic business principles. The fantasy here is the belief that this fantasy can somehow live in reality.

As I roll the film in my mind starting with MBA school, I wonder if we progressed, or drifted into illusion within the financial world. An industry meant for wealth preservation, maintenance of orderly markets and credit flow, destroyed wealth and livelihoods to such extent, simply by not staying true to its objectives, enabled by policy and mortal flaw. Because of the enormity of the human toll, it shrouds the good aspects of the financial business, the good work of many.

Was this last decade simply a masquerade ball for self-enrichment for the elite? Is it reflective of societal changes where even in the pursuit of wealth and power some no longer want to assume personal responsibility and accountability?

"No, no," said my mama and papa, "things don't work that way in life."

Does not freedom without responsibility lead to anarchy?

Anarchy connotes lawlessness and disorder, which leads to waste. Waste is at the center of Shakespearean tragedy. Shakespeare's tragic heroes were the obsessive type. They too strayed by action or omission, bringing destruction upon themselves and others.

Capitalism gives us freedom, but with it comes responsibility. In a March 17, 2009 *Financial Times* article entitled, Let fairness triumph over corporate profit, the writer, Trevor Manuel, explores the need for the state to impose checks and balances within a capitalist system. For example, the political economists, Thomas Hobbes and Adam Smith, recognized that the powers at be need to keep an eye on greed and influence.

We actually did the exact opposite; nurtured greed and political influence. Who failed to restrain a financial system from developing in such a big, complex and disorderly way so as to create legalized lawlessness? As a matter of policy should our financial institutions be allowed to buy influence when it comes to financial policy-making when the financial system is the backbone of the economy?

It feels perilous, given the consequences.

The word raucous means boisterous and disorderly. It connotes entanglement or snarl. It is the opposite of restraint. There was nothing restrained about the individuals and institutions that gave this financial crisis life, as profits were turbo charged. Its entangled nature now has entangled us all via debt lock-down.

This is a human tragedy.

It is pulling those in, who had nothing to do with the making of this crisis. It is even penalizing those who behaved responsibly all along. This is diametrically opposed to free market capitalism, upon which our economic democracy rests.

The old-fashioned doesn't really go out of style. We begin to connect the dots that when we tear down boundaries, when a basic foundation like trust is missing, a house of cards goes up. It goes up in a disorderly entangled way and then creates a boisterous collapse in the process.

Through our choices and actions, either by commission or omission, will we eventually vote ourselves out of democracy?

Where's the analgesic?

I think of The Little Prince.

The Enablers

Who led us into this *raucous mess?*

Let's string it together. It almost reads like an Agatha Christie mystery novel, like "who done it!"

"Not now, later!"

Government policy – Democrats and Republicans both. The Community Reinvestment Act of 1977 (CRA) encouraged the private sector to make home ownership accessible to more people within their respective communities, including low and moderate-income borrowers. While good in concept, it eventually led to a degradation of the traditional principles of home lending in its implementation as financial institutions found a way to off-load loan risk.

Fannie Mae and Freddie Mac increasingly guaranteed too many risky loans, in part due to political pressure to increase their purchases of subprime mortgages. In the end, the government stepped in with a bailout and shareholders were wiped out.

The repeal of Glass-Steagall in 1999, which kept banks and Wall Street investment houses separate, had far-reaching consequences.

Overarching all this was the lack of a robust regulatory system, one that didn't keep up with the complexity and rapid changes in the markets. Strong lobbying efforts on the part of our financial institutions discouraged regulation and oversight.

Federal Reserve – kept interest rates low for a sustained period of time in the aftermath of September 11th. This made borrowing costs cheap, encouraging individuals and financial institutions to take on excessive debt, leading to excessive risk-taking.

SEC – granted an exemption in 2004 to the five major Wall Street investment banks, to leverage themselves 30 to 1 and even 40 to 1 from their original 12 to 1 capital ratio. This over-leveraging eventually led to the collapse of some major Wall Street investment houses as they took on ever increasing debt. They leveraged their balance sheets to play the spread between low rates and the higher rates on all those complex instruments.

"Give it to me, I want it!"

Managements – had incentives in the form of compensation, to turbo charge profits to the short-run. Some executives walked away with not just tens of millions, but hundreds of millions in compensation as they ran their companies into the ground.

Boards – were responsible for overseeing and approving the very compensation incentives that resulted in managements taking on excessive risk to generate short-term profits. They enjoyed perks in return.

"I don't care how I go down that slide"

Mortgage Originators — created all sorts of mortgage products enticing borrowers, including some who barely understood what they were getting themselves into. Basic common sense lending standards were discarded as loans were made. Some borrowers assumed too much debt. Since risk was off-loaded to someone else — through the securitization process — increasingly less attention was paid to the ability of the borrower to pay back the loan.

"I got the ball, it's mine, me first!"

"Monkey see, monkey do!"

Wall Street — packaged all sorts of mortgages into securities (originated by the mortgage brokers, banks and in some cases the brokerage firms themselves). Wall Street convinced the rating agencies that faulty mortgages packaged together were near riskless. Some firms bet a major portion of their business on securitization. Some took on excessive debt up to those high leverage ratios leading to their demise.

Banks — were major players in mortgage origination, securitization, writing credit default swaps and issuing home equity lines as homeowners took cash out of their homes.

"I don't want to do my homework!"

Insurers — insured all sorts of complex and exotic mortgage securities too few understood. They were active in the credit default swap market. The major municipal bond insurers strayed from their "bread and butter" business of insuring municipal credits to insuring even toxic assets, triggering turmoil in the municipal market.

Credit Rating Agencies – assigned ratings, even triple-A, to mortgage securities too few understood, as ratings standards were compromised. They strayed from their business model of true credit assessment. There was too much money to be made in the form of rating fees. Investors relied on those ratings in making their investment decisions, ratings that turned out not to reflect the true nature of risk.

The Unpeeling – August 2007 to February 2008

Like an onion, the contraption we built over decades began to unpeel.

Spring 2007, two hedge funds, highly leveraged and loaded with shaky mortgage securities, collapse. The problems begin to roll. The subprime credit market freezes late summer 2007 as underlying borrowers are defaulting on their mortgages. When markets freeze the normal brokerage process of buying and selling securities comes to a grinding halt. The swoon begins as our financial institutions and investors find themselves stuck and bulging with toxic assets on their books, precipitously falling in value.

I turn to my group and say:

"This is eerily reminiscent of the Savings and Loan crisis, a few rumbles initially and then the volcano erupts, only this one's going to be the motherload."

I'm connecting the dots. How disastrous would

fallout in a some $12 trillion residential mortgage market be; what if the $60 trillion credit default swap market starts to unwind as a result?

It could wipe out the capital of our banks and collapse the economy if uncontained. I don't even want to go there; too morbid a thought!

No surprise that the residential mortgage market swelled to over $12 trillion in the last decade — roughly $10 trillion of prime loans (those with good credit history); the rest a potpourri of subprime mortgages (those to less creditworthy borrowers), Alt-A mortgages (those with tainted credit), "liar" loans (those with little to no income verification and no documentation) and even "Ninja" loans (no income, no job, no assets).

The sheer volume of deal flow in the last few years was relentless, unsustainable, and it alone made me queasy.

To my husband I'd say, "How can anyone understand all these complex mortgage securities, some aren't even tradable; where are they all going and to whom, such volume and so many types. What happened to straight bonds?"

I worry. Hard to shed an upbringing where responsibility and consequences resonated in the walls of our home.

Experience taught me that an investment bank can fail and this one was up to its gills in mortgage paper and just coming off two hedge fund blow-ups.

Have you seen the movie *Jaws,* the first one?

Do you remember the scene in the boat at the end of the movie, the quiet right before the attack?

That's what it felt like inside the firm, that Fall 2007.

Things went so quiet from the top. I didn't like the quiet, nor the body language whenever a meeting took place.

I'd think, "Someone's not leveling with us."

I knew the culture and it didn't feel right.

"Could we see some financial *Enrons* out of all this before we're done?" such thoughts cluttered my mind.

One day, my 77 year-old mother called me at work, having read an article in a leading business journal about the activities of our CEO.

Her first words to me in her Eastern European accent were, "Vat (what) kind of company do you vork (work) for? Protect your money right avay (away). Iv (if) this can go on, imagine vats (what's) going on underneath all this!"

I've always believed my mother had laserlike insight into events or those about to take place.

𝄞

As we made our way into the Fall of 2007, banks and Wall Street investment houses were forced to take billions in toxic asset write-downs, which eroded their capital, restricting not only lending, but potentially threatening their ability to stay solvent. It obviously led to the need for capital raises.

We all saw those capital raising efforts in the news that Fall of 2007, through the sovereign wealth funds (investment portfolios of governments worldwide) and other private investors. Unfortunately, they got bitten as bank stocks continued to plummet. The ability to shore up bank capital from private investors eventually dried up.

So what happened?

In steps the government to keep the financial system afloat, like an intravenous feed (IV) that hospitals plug into you. This IV came to be in the trillions, providing liquidity and funding to our financial institutions, just to keep them alive through all sorts of backstops, bailouts (TARP included) and other programs.

The $700 billion TARP became amorphous as problems grew. It's like if the ceiling is leaking from so many directions, and you've but one bucket, you're running from one place to the next. To me, that was TARP.

No surprise that the subprime market freeze, created a domino effect, freezing every credit market by the Spring of 2008. And then, actual credit froze where banks were reluctant to lend to you and even each other. When credit doesn't flow, that's when it hits the real economy, consumers and businesses both.

Why did all these markets freeze?

The vital element of trust, for markets to function normally, evaporated.

Trust, very simply, is based on honesty and accurate disclosure, honest business dealing, not uncertainty and falsehood.

At first, few banks and Wall Street investment houses seemed to fess up as to the extent of their asset problems, or at least it wasn't apparent to the general public. The weakest of the financial institutions fell first, those with the most amount of debt and concentration in mortgage assets. It makes sense, doesn't it, that those, most concentrated in that part of the market, would be shown up first?

Others, perhaps hoped, that the financial malaise would not spread long enough to pull them in, as they relied on more diversified business revenue sources to sustain them. I felt like the big banks — perhaps the strongest of the weakest, yet themselves impaired — came to be the command centers to take on the rest of the financial casualties. It felt like financial institutions were folded, one into the other with such rapidity, like a quick sweep.

Major mortgage originators and many others went bankrupt; few were folded into the banks. Some of the major Wall Street investment houses were bailed out, others not, through government-engineered deals, selectively, in a free market capitalist economy. The major independent Wall Street investment houses would disappear within months of each other — two folded into the big banks, one went bankrupt and the other two were converted into bank holding companies.

So, what am I doing within my office as this crisis unfolded?

I kick my office into high vigilance gear. We always were, but this time, ever more so as news, market developments, were fluid and rapidly changing.

Over my decades on the Street, I witnessed market dislocations, typically confined to say a specific market, where everything gets painted with the same brush for awhile until some time passes and buyers return. Other markets provide a counterbalance.

What was different this time, was that the contagion of the subprime market spread to every credit market from mortgages, to bonds, to agencies and lastly to the municipal market, taking down the stock market, freezing credit and eventually slamming the real economy. This time around, the buyers did not return. They remained eerily absent.

Being in the midst of it all was like being in a raging forest fire, no other way to describe it; it was no longer business as usual.

I'm thinking, "When's it going to abate?"

We're just taking it day-by-day, just trying to do our best to fulfill our responsibilities to our clients.

February 2008, the $330 billion auction-rate securities market falls victim to the crisis, one of the last to fall. We're seeing a classic run on this market triggered by the liquidity fears now plaguing every credit market. Our financial institutions, being themselves capital constrained, aren't stepping in to support the auctions, allowing these auctions to fail. A failed auction means that investors essentially get stuck holding the bonds as there are no buyers.

Our financial institutions are unable to take in inventory as they're already swooning with other inventory and needing to preserve their own capital. One after the other those auctions are failing, some resetting to maximum rates as high as 12% tax-exempt. Imagine what this does to municipal borrowing costs jumping from what may have just been at a 3% or so level to 12%.

The failure of these auctions literally freezes access to funds for investors, like corporations and individuals. Inability to access cash for day-to-day needs triggered yet another liquidity crisis within this already larger rolling credit crisis. Corporate balance sheets, in some cases, are now frozen with what came to be known as impaired securities.

With the onset of a run on the $330 billion auction-rate securities market, every credit market had just about frozen. Whole markets that worked for decades would be wiped off the map.

What happened to what was a functioning market — the auction rate securities market — providing needed funding to municipalities while at the same time competitive yields to investors would now become one tombstone of many to come before this crisis is over. As whole markets disappeared, so too livelihoods of those within the industry.

What was going on in the credit markets, was now taking its toll in creating a climate on the Street and within the firm like none I had ever experienced; one of disorder. Fear and panic seized up the markets. Relationships seemed to be disintegrating. Customers were upset with financial institutions for not bidding. They couldn't, as there were no buyers on the other side. Taking anything into inventory wasn't an option either as firms looked to preserve capital, as those toxic asset write-downs were eroding capital.

I kept thinking back to my days at Salomon Brothers decades ago when the interchange within the firm was so orderly and fluid; trader-to-trader, trader-to-salesperson, and salesperson-to-customer. If you needed help within another department, people were, well, simply helpful. We trusted each other. I had never in decades witnessed anything like this. The glue of trust, that holds everything together in any system, was missing.

Putting all the pieces of the puzzle together to wade through these turbulent times tested everyone's mettle. I kept my team calm, not letting on that underneath I was worried about where this whole credit crisis was going, the impact it would have once it slams the real economy. Dealing with unchartered waters, I continued to do what I always did best, take care of my corporate clients the best way I knew how, walking them through this jagged terrain.

As we made our way into March 2008, the credit markets had now been frozen for an unprecedented eight months. The normal brokerage process was still not functioning. The natural flow of business whereby bids and offers to buy and sell securities by customers, with financial institutions taking in inventory, continued to be severely impaired. Capital across financial firms was constrained from the massive never-ending multibillion-dollar asset write-downs. Business had reached a grinding halt.

I'd reflect over the decades. Banks got bigger, in part to have capital to compete on a global basis. And now there was no capital to commit to just doing the basics — lending plus facilitating the normal flow of buying and selling securities. I began to wonder if decades of bank profit would be wiped out by the capital write-downs to come. And, if bailouts were to follow, they're going to be in the trillions. By the time we're done, I wondered about the ultimate cost of this financial crisis.

What exactly was the point of all this?

And, what exactly was the point of some financial institutions paying their employees with illiquid stock amidst such mismanagement?

It was not uncommon practice on Wall Street to pay employees in illiquid stock as part of their compensation called "skin in the game." I believe this "skin in the game" is a debatable issue when one does not have input over risk-taking and other management decisions as an employee. It presupposes a level of moral ethics and trust, where managements and boards act in a prudent and disciplined way in the pursuit of profit, in the best interests of shareholders. Seems to me that the events of the financial crisis have proven otherwise.

December 2007, the deferred compensation monies of the Senior Managing Directors — those monies that were taken off the top of one's already earned compensation for that year — were placed by management into company stock, at some $89 a share at the time; not a voluntary contribution. Two and a half months later the stock collapsed to a mere couple of "bucks." Assets of loyal employees were near wiped out in the end.

Were the board and management not aware of the precarious condition of a firm, so concentrated in mortgage assets and so heavily in debt, in the midst of a credit market meltdown when the earned monies of trusting employees were so deployed?

Can the problems within our financial system be fixed by regulation and more debt or are we facing a much deeper enemy?

How did the word "liar," as in "liar" loans become an "accepted norm" for lending?

The Fall – March 2008

Dreams, what do they tell us?

March 10, 2008; it's Monday before the start of Holy Week. Easter Sunday is just around the corner and we'd soon be coloring Easter eggs. I awaken, startled, uneasy, in the middle of the night.

I begin to just write, on a yellow paper pad. I don't own a computer, nor planned to ever buy one. I much prefer to live in the world around me. My computer trading systems are all set up at work and that's the extent of my virtual life.

I watch the sunrise, quickly shower, and then slink into one of my Italian suits. Off I go!

On my way to the office, the feeling of that dream lingers, like a premonition of sorts. It just doesn't leave me that day. As I tried to push it back, it came up, like a buoy in water. I felt like something big was about to happen.

The daily pounding of bad news is incessant and continues that week of March 10, 2008. "Normal" headlines are now replete with mortgage companies and hedge funds imploding, scandals *galore*.

I keep hearing Max's words, "Your word is your bond in this business and act that way."

Isn't truth our internal sun?

Just like nature, everything has its place to make the whole work, or it doesn't. The sun doesn't rise at odd times nor forgets to set. The sun is the sun. It does what it needs to do. No one tells the sun what to do nor regulates it into submission. It regulates our days.

I woke to the sun that day.

Monday and Tuesday; rumors circulate regarding liquidity issues, stemming from secured lenders pulling back from financing the firm. Investment banks rely on short-term commercial paper borrowings as well as secured lending repurchase activity to finance inventory and ongoing operations. Any pullback by one lender may cause a cascading effect for others to withdraw.

Liquidity is like oxygen to an investment bank. It can disappear within days as investors, creditors and customers withdraw funds because of worries about a bank's solvency.

The rumors begin to swirl and start to take a life of their own. News spreads of now a major investment bank refusing to step in and back up our firm's counterparty risk. Other investment banks refuse to insure the firm's debt via credit default swaps. That Wednesday, despite explicit and public assurances by management that the rumors are false, I am overcome with a foreboding feeling.

The option activity in the stock had already been telling the story. The selling accelerated with volume spiking through the roof. All of a sudden activity in the 35 put options spiked and then the ghastly 5 puts appeared. This meant that speculators and investors were buying the right to sell the stock at 35 and then 5, signaling the stock would nosedive. Speculators appeared with such ferocity.

The stock had just been trading around $80 or so. By Friday, what seemed like a potential classic run on the bank was already afoot as hedge funds and other clients were now withdrawing their funds. The ship was sinking.

The place felt rudderless. Instinctively that Friday, I called all my clients to review with them "the safety of assets" procedures, walking them through what might happen in the event of a dealer failure. I had already lived through milder panic two decades ago while still a rookie at Salomon Brothers.

I know what fear and panic can do. I ruled out no option at this point. Taking care of my clients was priority number one. I went home that Friday, remembering sitting in that club chair of the New York offices several years earlier.

Sunday night, Palm Sunday and the start of Holy Week, my home phone rings off the hook with messages from friends shocked that the firm was being sold for a mere couple of "bucks." They wondered if perhaps this was a "typo."

It took one week to take down what was once a venerable Wall Street investment bank, that had been around for close to a century. Those who foolishly overleveraged and fell, allowed some to reap enormous gains, perhaps the speculators even exacerbated the fall. All sorts of rumors circulated about foul play.

What of the lives that would be transformed forever?

Nothing prepared me for what was yet to come. I read about takeovers in newspapers many times before. They are mentioned casually in the media. Until one lives through one, one cannot possibly understand the devastating impact on lives.

What does work, done with a heart, mean to you?

As a little girl, my father used to tell me that work is "food for the soul." For me, it's daily prayer — done with sacrifice, devotion and discipline.

Is this not what has made our country great?

People working with a heart, with sacrifice and devotion for a purpose, beholden to our founding principles; this haven, this one spot in the world where people come to make a life for themselves and their families. My family came here that way, with so much hope that their children could live in a free way.

My parents used to say, "Freedom is not a given. It is something to cherish, preserve and fight for."

I find myself in the midst of a forced takeover of a firm, within a free country and free market capitalist economy. It felt like a giant steamroller came in to flatten the place. It was surreal. A firm in existence for 85 years, melting away so quickly.

I had no say as to what would happen to the lives of those within my group, as I had been given a take it or leave it proposition. We were a very close group. What would you do?

I stay; those within my group may need to go. I leave; they may have a shot at staying to sustain themselves with whatever residual business was left. With the takeover, there was no certainty given as to whether we could even cover our existing accounts. They were largely institutional accounts already covered by the acquiring company. We are unable to sleep as we worry about what will become of our livelihoods. I watch those within my group come into work, exhausted and sick.

There's nowhere else we could go as a group to do

our business as our accounts were covered by other groups within other firms. A meeting took place that April 2008 with the power at be from the acquiring company presiding. Upon repeatedly voicing concerns about my inability to sustain our business under the acquiring company's new structure, that it was a job redundancy issue, and expressing concern about what would happen to those who worked with me, it was pretty much disregarded, with no response as to what would happen to those within my group.

At that very moment, I joined the sisterhood and brotherhood of all those around the world who cry to be heard, whose voices are silenced. I felt their pain and frustration. I vowed to speak for them. Truth is a stranger in a world of deception.

No negotiation.

No severance.

Twenty years of devotion to my firm as a multimillion dollar producer having reached the top Senior Managing Director level; some thirty years as an ordinary tax-paying citizen for my country, many of them as a hard-working single mother.

𝄞

I leave that meeting and begin to worry about the kind of work environment that awaits our children.

What is a dehumanized work environment like?

It's one of facelessness, one lacking personhood and civility. It's where human relationships and interaction are reduced to cost-effective transactions, motivated by self-interested agendas. It's where one feels like one cannot disagree for fear of reprisal. It's where what used to be a family feel within corporate culture has broken down.

It's where we are so institutionalized, that the human face disappears; where anonymity and uniformity rather than individuality is prized. It's an environment missing a soul. It's when an acquisition takes place, it dispenses of lives in a machine-like fashion based on cost-effectiveness.

In growing big and analyzing numbers, have we analyzed ourselves out of happy and productive engagement? Have we allowed bureaucracy to replace true free market capitalism?

The movie *Brazil* comes to mind. It represents a dystopia, opposite of utopia. It portrays how unbridled growth and bureaucracy together with misapplied technology bottleneck anything from getting done, dehumanizing the individual. It is a world where one can't easily get a straight answer from anyone as one is routed through a turgid system where the institution's protocol dominates. The inefficiency is oppressive within such a world. The obsession with layers of process, paperwork and protocol overrule the human. One spins like a top out of frustration.

We need only call the outsourced circuitous "800" Human Benefits numbers at one of the mountainous institutions to understand how frustrating it is just to get an answer to a question, and that's after having been delivered an almost dictionary-like packet of paper describing the process of how to access or communicate with such a department.

I have an MBA and have trouble navigating. The length of time it takes just to get through to a human being on one of those lines is an exercise in tenacity and patience. The phone labyrinth of "push this or that button," with "this or that ID," is enough to send one into a straightjacket or on to a couch. And, if one pushes the wrong button, one needs to start all over again.

What used to take a few minutes years ago, may take an hour as the burden gets thrust on to the user, as our services are increasingly delivered through layers of inefficiency. Those at the apex see cost-cuts in outsourcing such a function, missing the point entirely as to what a Human "Benefits" department is supposed to be all about.

How many of you feel the same?

Brazil comes back and a particular scene in an alley. It portrays men walking home from work; all dressed the same, dark gray hats and topcoats, just walking past each other, creating a uniformity and facelessness.

How do things become that way?

Slowly, but they do, as we devalue the human.

Do we want our children to feel faceless within the big pyramids of the empire builders as millions of dollars get suctioned to the top?

It may not even matter if they work hard as a constant crop of the newly earnest may replace them, eventually giving birth to armies of the disillusioned. Will we as a people reclaim the freedom within our work environments, unshackle ourselves from the masquerade of the shacklers? Will we reclaim our small businesses and entrepreneurship together with the feeling of belonging, true free market capitalism, one that rewards initiative across the board, rather than it being concentrated amongst the few?

When I started my career, being able to see a bright future and knowing that one is rewarded for hard work and effort was a tremendous motivator. It is the built-in motivator, that freedom-to-succeed, within our free market capitalist system that keeps our economy humming. And it is, without condition, not just for the few. There used to be enough to go around for everybody.

The desire to be valued and appreciated, while at the same time having the opportunity to be financially rewarded is at the heart of human desire. It's what's made our economic system and our country successful. What future do we give our young people when the big institution and bureaucracy rule?

The top big banks control over half our lending when there are 8000 other banks, some with strong balance sheets able to lend. Near half of our land's deposits may come to be concentrated in the hands of some few big banks. They may come to control our borrowing costs. Already a handful of big banks dominate equity underwriting.

And yet, who thrust the spears to create such wounds and heartache within a nation, throbbing ever more so, day-by-day, as they find no rest?

Deep thick storm clouds don't deceive; they bring thunder, lightening and rain. Debt storm clouds form on our horizon vast, deep and dark, thick, as debt compounds, backed up by looming entitlement system liabilities in the tens of trillions!

Kokia Vaidyba!

Lithuanian for: What a performance!

Will the legacy of the empire be the legacy of debt?

Chapter Seven

The Masquerade

Human Masks

March 16, 2009

A masquerade gives people license to be unbridled in pursuing self-indulgent activities. A mask protects, but it calls upon one to be creative, to engineer a way to mask reality.

What lies beneath human masks?

Calm souls or ones tormented by greed, power and hubris? What fears stoke torment to have it all here and now as if to secure immortality? Yet, underneath the distractions, lay simple truth.

Death comes and true fairytales come true.

What happens at the very moment the body dies, the soul lives and presents itself as it has in life...do we fly through dark valleys...reach beautiful peaks or do we brave dark valleys here to reach beautiful peaks?

Whose fears have chained us?

Into the chains of heavy debt...

It's always this way throughout history, isn't it?

Few hurt many.

Perhaps this financial crisis is a culminating summative reflection, a mirror, of the collapse of values that take us beyond here and now. As a contraption was built over decades...as it accelerated in the last...did we devalue the important along the way, even the human face of another?

The heart puts a human face before us in every engagement we undertake. If we don't stay true to this most simple of truths, we drift. Any sort of creation, distortion and consequence is then possible.

Our man-made fabricated creations now devalue themselves. They mask reality — toxic assets…ratings and pricing models…house values…financial asset prices. Fabricated asset value melts…it is illusory if not based on truth…it disappears yet debt from the fabrication lingers.

Falsehood and debt have no intrinsic value; so would it not be logical that we cannot build something of true sustainable value with that which has none…yet we throw debt as a nation to bailout, prop up, that which has been falsely created with debt?

Like the crossroad where Alice meets the Cheshire cat, do we truly understand what is at stake at this crossroad?

I am reminded of a short story by Edgar Allen Poe, first published in 1842, entitled, "The Masque of the Red Death." In Poe's haunting story, a Prince Prospero and a thousand of his fellow wealthy nobility sequester themselves in a walled abbey as they seek to escape the Red Death, a plague afflicting the land. Their intent is to await the end of the plague in their lavish surroundings, unmoved by the plight of the population at large.

One evening, Prince Prospero hosts a masquerade ball for

all his guests in seven rooms of different colors, one of which is black. In the midst of merriment, a figure wearing a skull-like mask, representing a victim of the plague, makes its way among them. Prince Prospero demands to know its true identity beneath the mask. A chase ensues throughout the seven rooms until the figure is cornered inside the black room. As death reveals itself, Prince Prospero falls dead.

"Quo Vadis"…

Which way are we going?

The Masquerade Ball

Once upon a time, there was a Cinderella,
who slipped into a Masquerade Ball,
as an unexpected guest.
She was bedecked with curvaceous billowing gown,
of yellow satin taffeta,
clasping itself tight around her knees,
fanning out,
gracefully forming a lingering gathered trail.

A strapless lace corset, of yellow color,
pinched itself at the waist to sculpt her feminine silhouette.
Her blonde hair parted to the side, rolling itself,
into a high French twist.
Crimson red revealed plumpness of her lips.
Two South Sea lustrous pearls dangled from a distance,
as she gracefully walked towards her destination,
through iron gates flanked by walls of stone.

A Masquerade Ball,
for the plutocrats it was.
Financiers from every sphere,
politicians, officials, all together.
No lavishness it spared.
No limits, no boundaries,
in creating fantasy for their jollity,
indifferent to the travails of most.

Set on lush grounds green, of acreage vast,
a stony manor stood sumptuously still,
against the dusk of the evening.
Passers by, with numbered years, arrived in human-like masks,
in chauffeured shiny black limousines,
one by one.
Decked in tuxedos, some caped, few felines among them.
Laughter echoed as they entry made.

Cinderella stood afar, detached,
to peruse this grand parade until the last of them took ingress.
In the dusk, up wide gravel road,
hugged by arms outstretched of lawns primped and meadows far,
she walked in solitary way.
In slow motion,
as if to float towards entry of this fantasy chateau.
A "Nocturne" melody played inside her heart till entry neared.

Before advancing steps of three,
she placed half mask of lynx,
upon complexion velvet.
With grace,
through double doors she stepped,
into a vestibule, circular.
Shiny white marble caped
the floor, ceilings, walls.

In the middle stood
a fluid black sculpture of seven feet,
chiseled to form one piece of upwards flowing marble,
curving to the right into a semi circle at the top.
Four concentric circles of black marble surrounded its base.
Full view she made inside this tomblike structure,
turning in circular motion only to return.
Her trance disturbed, by inner chatter.

Beyond, a ballroom washed in sage,
seductively beautiful and amplified in space.
Intricately carved, white swirling moldings framed its walls,
shouldering beveled ceilings twelve feet high.
As she made her way into a crowd dreamlike,
the unreal, frozen smiles unfroze and froze.
The music played, not of her kind.
Dissonant, out of synch with Nature.

Coquetish in demeanor, she caught the eye of one.
A prince of facial feature, would swoon a woman make.
Her heart thumped once and skipped a beat,
as near his presence made.
As he walked forth, all eyes fell locked,
on tall and handsome creature.
Enchanted prince, of most beguiling kind,
he magnetized her glance.

His arm stretched out to beg the dance,
she readily succumbed.
As two embraced, meltingly entwined,
a solo violin played her "Nocturne" melody,
to rouse her inner chatter.
The "Waltz" began and swirl took hold.
She closed her eyes seduced.
To dream that he might be the one, to capture heart and reason.

He swept her past French doors ajar,
a shiver took such hold.
She felt the touch,
of ice cold hand,
and wakened from her trance.
Before her eyes,
befell a face,
of flesh-like waxen feature.

A moment passed,
a smile beguiled to lure her in its favor,
yet cracks she saw around the lips.
His eyes froze cold, as if to lock with world of the undead.
Mere beauty cape his looks became.
Quick way she made to disengage,
escape and swirl through crowd alone.
Then music stopped, the "Waltz" to end.

She looked around and saw no heart,
no life,
no ball as if it would be done.
Only floor to ceiling mullioned windows,
few French doors ajar, hissing voices,
and flapping windblown dollar bills.
They engulfed the walls,
the ceilings, floors.

A chandelier hung from up above,
diamond crystals trembled in the absence of light.
The hollow room itself took on indigo and eerie dusk.
Her "Romance" melody played within her heart.
The moon half-cloaked in ashen clouds,
cast few dim rays of light,
with particles of dust,
on to the shiny marble floor.

She walked outside,
through doors ajar,
and stood to take full view.
Beyond vast lawn,
horizon distant,
she saw her land emerge,
with twinkly lights.
A sight at once so grand.

Upon her eyes befell the movement of foreboding ashen clouds.
They grew above her beloved land to form a creature,
tentacles vast with reach into nestled homes.
The sight became a monstrous cloud.
She shuddered at its view.
Was this the real or unreal, she gasped at once with fright.
Funnels swirled with debris of toxic nature,
spray of dollar bills to make.

In the distance, muffled sounds of voice,
emerged amidst flapping doors.
She made her way down corridor.
The festive noise picked up.
Light cast out from domed chambers,
where great merriment once took place.
They grouped in rooms, yet connected, through interlocking doors.
Shadows cast complicit movement, from one room to the next.

Masks hung outside the rooms, grafted on to hooks.
Once jollity in each chamber now became subdued to tone,
of ominous nature.
"What do we next, and even can we?"
They quick made way to banquet posh.
A feast for them was in the making.
They ordered up, with help of each,
menu item best suited for their taste.

Cinderella took flight,
to warn the chef,
not serve their fowl with any coriander,
nor poultry with paprika,
nor soup with any dill or bay leaves.
To marinate,
and douse instead the meats with all sorts of salts,
a touch of rosemary and thyme.

They all convened to cavort in room of grandiose grandeur.
Gold-leafed walls met faded frescoes,
veiled by time,
some yet discernible human souls,
from calm to torment went.
Twelve foot high ceilings curved,
to embrace glittering mosaic,
of semi-precious stones.

Black shiny marble floors,
took on,
rectangular mirrored table,
set in welcome,
of its several hundred guests.
Finest china,
crystal, silverware,
designed for the occasion.

Black porcelain candelabras,
with crystals of no tremble,
gold candles lit,
a line on mirrored table made.
Red silk velvet sofas lounged,
around perimeter of rectangular room.
Three sets of twelve foot mullioned doors,
some light into that room tried make.

They convened and as they leaned,
upon the mirrored table,
a gruesome sight befell her eyes.
Rusted chains entwined around their necks.
What form this prison will it take,
as crime committed measure cannot make,
against such bountiful a land,
trusting souls to scorch.

They began with somber tone,
as few gents began laments.
Their firms gave birth to toxic loans,
they then fed to their mates.
Their mates succumbed to debt,
to buy those toxic loans to pool.
They grew and grew and grew they did,
fees dollar bills became.

Now they decried,
their firms took on,
too much debt to take.
No top talent now they be,
mere mortal souls,
locked in chains of dollar bills,
who came to spin,
toxic loans to fantasy, then debris.

In step few gents, with gift for twist, to fix things with a swirl,
as conquerors vast they did enlist,
to make it look acquisitive,
to calm the masses with one swipe.
Yet markets swooned and credit froze,
as no fool they proved to be.
No solvent system now is this, as one gent, after the next,
revealed themselves so sick.

Pipes in a harried gent, to plug an intravenous feed,
liquidity of such massive quantity.
Was this beguilement of the land, profits siphoned off of fantasy,
yet help they seek to bail them out,
protect their pants from any wrath.
Their coffers filled, they need secure,
from anguished souls,
they seared.

Dilemma came upon some gents and felines in that bunch.
Merriment in domed chambers,
interlocked for all to see,
no place to hide,
as entrails, trillions, on nearby forest floor,
no longer be contained.
The game they played no longer lived,
yet no atonement, no remorse.

Oh hand of law,
what justice here be done,
as you allowed thievery and falsehood to play within your rule.
Is this the rule of law,
to chain a land with debt,
as dangers lurked beneath.
Yet pots of gold, came to lure, even you from true intent,
when debt and toxic pools combined to make our land to bleed.

Domed chambers now have come to spin,
bailouts,
spending sprees,
without accountability,
with sprouting shoots of some foul play.
Thrust sludge of debt into our lap,
and tell us we own stock,
in that of not our will.

Stress test the master tricksters,
those cloistered,
where deception be an art,
where financial alchemy made stocks to float.
Back on to clay-like soil they'll stick,
as a graveyard will be shown to be.
No spin can mask the all too real,
inside this financialgate.

Such fools you think us be,
our shores to pound with grievous debt,
engulf our homes with cries,
such human sorrow hence to come,
for decades long, our children now to bear.
Our world will change and change for us it will,
as we come to wheel dollar bills,
a trip to mart to make.

Posturing you'll do,
the populace to calm.
Yet no fool we'll come to be,
as no calm to land will come,
until justice will be done.
As truth reveals itself,
only then and only then,
to cloak the land with balm.

French doors then flapped into that room,
gusts of wind,
swirled across rectangular table,
to disturb the diaphanous veil,
the apparition.
Eerie haunted souls pulled back faces,
to reveal fuzzy wolf-like ears, gray snouts beneath.
Only to return to human form.

Winds took to howls,
gaining force and wrath.
It made them hold their breath,
to shiver,
as stealthy toxic vapor rolled with creep into the room.
Few passers by shut the doors,
themselves and friends,
from elements to protect.

Then feast began as chef prepared,
their meats with salts of sorts.
The clock struck twelve.
Echoing bongs,
a menacing prelude made.
Cinderella gasped,
to flee the Ball with might,
to tell the story of that night.

Chapter Eight

The Heart of A Lioness

Mass on the Island

March 10, 2009

Dark brown slatted open shutters run up and down the sides of a low one story A-frame building as I walk in. The cross breeze breathes a gentle welcome to this most serene of places.

It's a red wood structure on the outside, painted light yellow inside, made bright by the sunlight. Around the upper perimeter of the walls, wooden triptychs of the Stations of the Cross. A large Crucifix hangs above the simple wood Altar, draped with a white lace cotton cloth, like the lace curtains in my grandmother's home.

Beige metal fold up chairs, neatly line up on the left and right, rows of five to make for some twenty five on each side. The floor is simply white tile. The candle flickers in a red glass casing, suspended like a swing in the right corner.

I kneel down.

Some time ago, I read about a lioness in the wild that found a lost calf. Instead of looking at that calf as food, this lioness rose above her nature and became a mother to this calf. Conditions were such that food was scarce for the two of them. Even as the two began to starve, this lioness did not stray from being a mother to this calf.

From Cinderella's Diary

April 23, 2008

I stay past five o'clock in my office, to mourn. I am at a crossroad. Dark and sad moment, I feel pain, inside this disturbing financial world. What tundra of frozen hearts forms gangrene of mistrust and deception?

My memory flies to childhood…I stand in a room of mirrors in a circus. I turn away from the distortions. I find an image before which I stand still.

For decades, a little girl stood still to see but one reflection. The world she lived never lived inside her and never came to change her as she set her own stage, her performance to make.

Oh Fairytale, how much pain will you now inflict, how many dragons will need be slain, as you work to awaken, your truth to protect?

Oh inner voice, why do you not let me be? Why do you speak, make me struggle over these past weeks? How can I pen emotions that have no words to express them?

My eyes swell, no longer tears to hold, as one by one they fall, onto my trading sheets, buys and sells, scratched in red marker, now splotched.

For every worker who
has been let go,

For every worker
afraid to speak up and speak out as
injustice takes place,

For every worker
betrayed by the management and
board they trusted,

For every worker whose work and life
were disrupted by corporate takeover,

For every worker devalued within
their work environment,

For every individual and family,
suffering and worrying through
sleepless nights,

For all those across our heartland
whose savings, born of sacrifice, have
been destroyed,

For all those victimized by mistrust
and deception,

For any other act towards the
innocent where human dignity is
trampled,

Cinderella gives voice to
your pain.

A voice that will not allow the cinders of millions of scorched and seared hearts across our land and around the world to be swept away.

Oh grand acquirer, conqueror vast, hurry before the crumble. King of the derivatives world, mountainous temple, built on mountains of paper and computer entries. Who is in need of a bailout?

To stitch or disembowel? To impose will and take resources? Lives discard?

So many now wonder what will become of their lives.

What spreadsheet, what perfected science of cost-effective acquisition, will dictate who stays, who leaves? What is the object of disposal? Assets or lives?

Dedicated and loyal producers, decades of service, livelihoods gone. Fear, worry, and suffering swirl.

Great companies create value over the long run. No?

With products, people, managements, and boards. How powerful a combination if done right, how lethal, if done wrong.

What is the performance like within the financial theater? Products melting as the lights go on…in the trillions? People…disposable and replaceable props? Managements…collecting the cash for one-way tickets to a theater of the absurd? Boards…in costume in the background, yet disappearing in the final act? Bailout safety nets someday for the falling flying trapeze?

My second grade, my upbringing comes back. I hear the voices of my mother and father, "do the right thing, be true to yourself, stand up, don't be afraid."

I think about my piano, the calm of the studio landscape, the integrity necessary to the process to get the piece right. I see my ballet teacher and become one with him. How he must have been hurt when he lost his life's work through no fault of his own.

Best friend, you stay with me. You play Bach's "Opening Aria" to the "Goldberg Variations," as if to comfort. Trance-like piano solo of longing...you settle into my heart. Peace amidst pain. How could they co-exist?

I hear every note...the pianist's intonation, like it was the first time, like the first kiss.

I listen. I look upon my desk, and its treasures, with the most intense feeling of love. Pictures of my children captured in moments of joy and experience of travel together. My daily coffee mug from my eldest son "Row Hard, No Excuses." The haunting photograph of the standing cross at Ground Zero taken by my youngest son when I took him to New York while on a business trip. Strewn across the right hand of the cross is an old piece of newspaper, windblown...at the foot of the cross the strength, the summit of all possibilities.

I think about my parents telling me that courage is

something one should never lack, and so as a little girl I practiced bravery when I spoke Lithuanian outside the home. My office and those within, this hamlet, brave and true to the fairytale that never ages.

A forced takeover of a firm…within a free country and free market capitalist economy?

Government intervention to such an extent to prevent a fallout from a systemic risk developed under the watch of our leadership, in the process disrupting so many innocent lives?

It's like ripping and uprooting people from the villages within which they quietly work…some 14,000 lives instantly change?

What dangerous precedent are we setting…what constraint upon freedom by the self-interested and uncontrolled upon us is this?

Thousands will go away…the disruption, the displacement…it's rippling through other lives…those working to take care of their children, some disabled, some in colleges…the stresses placed on marriages…those with obligations to older parents…these human stories behind all the noise…their silent movies playing for none to see...will the reels someday roll for all to see within the ethereal theater? Not news worthy?

Human faces or cost-effectiveness?

Oh truth, you respect life. You do not befriend deception

or appearances. You do not allow man to transform you to serve his needs.

How many have lost security and trust in the workplace, feel like they're doing the job of three in the name of cost cuts, see the hope for advancement fading for a job well done and just find a general sense of well being and happiness missing amidst all the stress? How many feel faceless within organizations too big to be noticed or appreciated? How many parents now worry about their children someday finding a spot to live happy and productive lives where they are valued as their future unfolds?

What world awaits us...an institutionalized world where big government, big interests, big corporate and financial giants lost in profit and power, the spoils enjoyed by few, beholden to each other, will someday rule a land of plague and crime infested ghost towns? Will this dance someday make an inferno the likes of which we've never seen?

An exodus is unfolding upon our shores...talented, overworked and experienced people across the spectrum of their chosen professions are leaving...they no longer contribute taxes and spending into the economy...the demise of the middle class working backbone, and small business, sandwiched between the two financially polarized extremes, is increasingly taken out by a system consumed with profit for few, drowning in paperwork and burdened with ever increasing layers of inefficiency. Oh big bureaucracy, you claim your victims only to victimize yourself as you stifle those capable, as you someday suffocate yourself.

As the day progresses, the office empties out except for the eerie feeling swirling around the place. I return to those familiar feelings of always loving the end of a productive day, the feeling of closing the door to my office at the end of each day in thanksgiving for being able to do what I so loved to do for so many years.

Always a serene moment beautifully amplified as the seasons changed from year to year, as the glow of the room would change. Sometimes it was already dark outside, other times the sun was just setting. I depended upon this place to take care of my children for all these years. I placed trust in those above to watch over us as we did our best to do our jobs. A business and a life was built in this place over twenty years.

Before closing the door each evening, I would pause and take in the feeling of the office with the hope that I would be there the next day. And sometimes, when I closed the door I would open it up again for a split moment and feel the silence, grateful for Someone's Hand in all this. That Someone found me a spot, a place and point in time, that both gave me the time and means to raise my two children. And I thanked Him for the not so good times, as I knew there was a purpose to all this.

Today is different. I have a heavy heart of sorrow as I

turn off my music with only the sounds of the city buzz and horns remaining. Before turning off my computer, the window comes up "Are you sure you want to exit the system?"

I pause for a long while, then click the everyday "Yes." My computer shuts down. It is time to go. I close the door to my office and choose not to go through my usual routine. The place and point in time are extinguished forever, but I walk away with my glass slipper.

May 1, 2008

Once upon a time, there was a heart in this place with a story to tell. Into what chamber should riches accumulate?

I'm back home, a little girl, sitting up in my bed reading, with the comfy pillow behind my back. It's late. My sister's already asleep. My eyelids are droopy. I rub my eyes.

I kiss my prayer book and place it on my nightstand. Before shutting the light, I kneel down before the Maestro, who conducts the piano concerto of life. I begin.

Our Father, who art in heaven,
Hallowed be thy Name.
Thy kingdom come,
Thy will be done,
On earth as it is in heaven.
Give us this day our daily bread.
And forgive us our trespasses,
as we forgive those who trespass against us.
And lead us not into temptation;
but deliver us from evil.
Amen.

I shut the light and jump into my bed. I look up, as I peacefully fall asleep beneath His Crown.

Bibliography

Bob Greifeld. Exchanges should unite to end flash orders, *Financial Times*, 6 August, 2009.

Charles Duhigg. Traders Profit With Computers Set at High Speed, *The New York Times*, 24 July, 2009.

Edward Luce. Subprime groups spent 370m to fight regulation, *Financial Times*, 6 May, 2009.

Eric Dash and Julie Creswell. Citigroup Pays for a Rush to Risk, *The New York Times*, 23 November, 2008.

Gretchen Morgenson and Don Van Natta Jr. Even in Crisis, Big Banks Dig In for a Battles Against Tougher Regulation, *The New York Times*, 1 June, 2009.

Henny Sender and Francesco Guerrera. BlackRock chief attacks Wall St. banks' 'luxurious' trading profits, *Financial Times*, 22 July, 2009.

Henny Sender. Wall St profits from Fed role, *Financial Times*, 3 August, 2009.

Ian Katz. FASB 'Close' on Off-Balance-Sheet Change, Herz Says (Update 1), *Bloomberg*, 30 April, 2009.

Javier Blas. Rogue oil broker triggered price spike, *Financial Times*, 3 July, 2009.

Jenny Anderson, New Exotic Investments Are Emerging on Wall Street, *The New York Times*, 5 September, 2009.

John Cassidy. Subprime Suspect. *The New Yorker*, 31 March, 2008.

John Kay. Lessons from the Rise and Fall of a carmaker, *Financial Times,* 3 June, 2009.

John Plender. How fading political will has let banks off the hook, *Financial Times,* 27 june, 2009.

Krishna Guha. Toxic Assets 'bridge too far,' *Financial Times,* 2 June, 2009.

Lina Saigol. Seeds of another pay furore, *Financial Times,* 1 June, 2009.

Lewis Carroll. Alice In Wonderland. First published 1865.

Louise Story. Wall St. Profits Were A Mirage, But Huge Bonuses Were Real, *The New York Times,* 18 December, 2008.

Michael MacKenzie and Jeremy Grant. The dash to flash, *Financial Times,* 6 August, 2009.

Michael Mackenzie. SEC runs eye over high-speed trading, *Financial Times,* 29 July, 2009.

Reuters. Next Crime Wave? FBI Targets TARP Fraud, 2 June, 2009.

Shaila Dewan. Alabama Area Reeling in Face of Fiscal Crisis, *The New York Times,* 1 August, 2009.

Susanne Craig and Deborah Solomon. Bank Bonus Tab: $33 billion, *The Wall Street Journal,* 31 July, 2009.

Trevor Manuel. Let fairness triumph over corporate profit, *Financial Times,* 17 March, 2009.